The fish course

This book accompanies the BBC television series
The Fish Course first broadcast from October 1987.
The series was produced by Ron Bloomfield and
Anne O'Dwyer.

Published to accompany a series prepared in
consultation with the Educational Broadcasting
Council.

Photography and styling: Tony Robins
Home economist: Angela Drake
Illustrations: pp. 18–35 Jim Hanson
pp. 276–295 Cliff Messiter, reproduced courtesy
of the Sea Fish Industry Authority
Microwave instructions: Janet Smith

BBC Books would like to thank the following for:
the loan of equipment – Elizabeth David, Habitat
and Office Landscaping

the provision of fish – The London Fish Merchants'
Association (Billingsgate) Ltd and the Sea Fish
Industry Authority

the provision of locations for photography – Rick and
Jill Stein of The Seafood Restaurant, Padstow;
Martin and Bunny Minter-Kemp; David and
Fred Lewzey; and David Jolly at Billingsgate

Published by BBC Books,
a division of BBC Enterprises Ltd
Woodlands, 80 Wood Lane, London, W12 0TT

ISBN 0 563 21251 9 (paperback)
0 563 21363 9 (hardback)

This book is typeset in 10/12 Baskerville by
Phoenix Photosetting, Chatham

Printed in England by Mackays of Chatham Ltd

Colour printed by Chorley and Pickersgill, Leeds

The
fish
course

Susan Hicks

BBC Books

Acknowledgements

I would like to thank the following people for their expert help and encouragement: Carolyn Cavele, The London Fish Merchants Association (Billingsgate), Amanda Courtney of the British Trout Association, The Scottish Salmon Growers, Phillip Diamond for advice on fish preparation, Kit Legg (fisherman) of St Agnes, Isles of Scilly, for supplying fish and shellfish, and Natalie Legg for recipe ideas and enthusiasm. Also at Billingsgate Market, very special thanks to Robin Bruce and Jack Shiells of C. J. Newnes and Partners for advice and help with the glossary, Lou Hart for advice on shellfish and Peter Bennett for advice on smoked fish. At Newlyn Fish Docks, Cornwall, thanks are due to Nick Howells for information and for supplying superb fish for our photographers on location.

Finally, I would like to express thanks to Jenny Rogers for her expertise, guidance and support, and Jennie Allen for her skill and cheerful dedication in editing this book.

Susan Hicks
July 1987

Contents

Cooking Times

Although I have given cooking times in the recipes themselves you may also find this chart, issued by the Sea Fish Industry Authority, useful. The information is based on a 12oz (350g) mackerel, an 8oz (250g) boned herring or cod steak, and 7oz (200g) of coley, haddock, lemon sole, plaice or whiting fillets.

	Poaching	Steaming	Braising	Baking	Shallow-frying	Deep-frying	Grilling
Cod steak	6–8	15	18–20	15	8–10	—	10–12
Coley fillet	6–8	15	18–20	15	10–12	4–6	10–12
Haddock fillet	6–8	15	18–20	15	8–10	4–6	8–10
Herring	8–10	—	18–20	15	8–10	—	6–8
Lemon sole fillet	4–5	8–10	10–12	10–12	4–5	3–4	4–5
Mackerel	8–10	—	18–20	15–20	10	—	6–8
Plaice fillet	4–5	8–10	10–12	10–12	4–5	3–4	4–6
Whiting fillet	6–8	15	18–20	15	8–10	4–6	8–10

Microwave Cooking

Throughout this book instructions have been provided, where appropriate, for using a microwave oven to cook the recipes. Please note that the times given are for a 650 watt oven. If you have a 600 watt oven add about 10–15 seconds per minute specified and 15–20 seconds per minute for a 500 watt oven. You should also refer to the information given on page 50 and your oven instruction booklet. Please also note that a double sheet of greaseproof paper or a cover suitable for microwave use should be substituted whenever aluminium foil is called for in the main recipe.

Introduction

I have always loved fish. I was fortunate to be born near the sea and brought up in a home where we regularly ate fresh fish of all kinds. By 'fresh fish', I mean *really* fresh. Literally hours from the catch being landed and sorted, my father would march in with a box of whatever had caught his eye – mussels, skate wings, cod, herring, plaice, mackerel and so on. Using an ancient but extremely sharp knife, he would fillet and prepare the fish in a matter of minutes. Cooking was simple and homely. Fish was never overcooked, and was always followed with plenty of vegetables. Now that I have my own family it has slowly dawned on me how lucky I was not to be subjected to a diet of frozen convenience foods.

Leaving home, I soon decided that the richly sauced restaurant approach to fish was not for me. Worse still, the restaurant or hotel 'fish course' was often a miserable, indefinable, fried or boiled object, apologetically squeezed in between the starter and meat course. But in fish cookery the different and subtle flavours of fresh fish and shellfish should speak for themselves and take pride of place on the table. The most critical judges of all – my children – agree.

I also discovered that fish was often far from fresh, usually overcooked and generally cloaked in rich, heavy sauces. I was astonished how many of my new friends didn't know the head of a mullet from the tail of a plaice, much less how to prepare, fillet and cook them. I could find only a handful of struggling fresh fish shops and these tended to have a disappointing range of fish: cod, plaice and haddock with the occasional tray of tired shellfish, and a freezer stocked with fish fingers.

My first holiday abroad was a revelation. Along the coast of the Mediterranean (relatively unpolluted in those days) I sampled my first bowl of bouillabaisse – home-made, cheap and exotic. There followed many more delightful discoveries during a six-week journey along the coast – astonishing platters of seafood, velvety soups, lobsters split and grilled, barbecued squid and roasted monkfish.

This was quite a culture shock for a provincial English girl. It was not so much that the British didn't know how to cook fish in their own traditional way, I thought, but that they needed *reminding*. For that matter, I needed reminding.

So when I moved to the Isles of Scilly twenty years ago, I was very soon rolling up my sleeves and dealing with lobster, crab, the occasional octopus and all kinds of sea fish. I taught myself how to gut and fillet by watching the fishermen. I asked them to save for me the spider crabs that were thrown back into the sea, along with conger eels and other fish for which, sadly, there was no demand. My father reminded me of curious delicacies like cod cheeks and skate nobs, and I introduced him to the delights of seafood salads with wild sea beet and samphire. From the reaction of visiting friends, I realised that, in fish cookery, a well-made fish stock was worth its weight in gold, providing the best possible basis for sauces, soups and stews.

During this time there was a gradual renaissance in the food world and fish was suddenly – and quite rightly – singled out as one of the healthiest natural foods.

My parents' generation knew that fish was nourishing healthy food, but not exactly why. They would probably have been surprised to learn that the Eskimos of western Greenland are among the healthiest people on earth, with far less cholesterol in their blood and far less heart disease than most races. In fact, research shows that the polyunsaturated fats in oils from fish like herring and mackerel are effective in preventing arterial disease. Fish is also one of the richest sources of protein and minerals, and contains very few calories.

So fish is being celebrated and rediscovered as a natural positively healthy food. New fresh fish shops are opening, and many supermarkets are cautiously testing the market with chilled displays of fresh fish. Occasionally they even have proper wet fish counters with trained fishmongers on hand. Many of these shops show daring and enterprise by selecting many dozens of species from among the fish we have in our rivers and around our coasts, and from among those of other countries.

I know from demonstrating fish cookery and from writing about fish that there is an enormous interest and curiosity about it – but still a little fear. This is why, in *The Fish Course*, I set out to write clear and simple explanations on cooking and preparation techniques. The recipes, too, are simple and unpretentious, so that the taste and texture of the fish is strongly emphasised in the final dish.

If fish is new to you, and you have been longing to try your hand at cooking it, the best thing to do is go straight to the section about shopping for fresh fish. Having read it, you will see that fish is easy to cook, versatile and interchangeable in recipes and methods of cooking.

It is not always possible to buy a precise amount of fish. A 'medium-sized' mackerel, for instance, can be one that is not too large or too small for one person. And yet you might prefer a larger size for a hungry adult, or a smaller one for a child. It is, therefore, a matter of common sense to adjust the amount of accompanying sauce, seasoning or stuffing. You may find an appealing recipe but decide that you don't like the flavour of garlic, or that there is too much onion to your liking. If so, adjust the recipe – the most important thing is to cook the fish perfectly and in a way that suits you. The best fish dishes are often the simplest. There are plenty of recipes of this type in this book, but I have not neglected terrines, fish soups and other more complicated dishes for more ambitious cooks. All in all, there should be enough recipes here for many years of cooking a 'fish course' which is always a delight both to look at and to eat.

The British Fishing Industry

Sometimes, when my sons have caught a few fish around our island, we sit and cook them over a beach fire in probably exactly the same way as Bronze Age people did thousands of years ago here. Not far from where I write, there is a Bronze Age fish trap – the remains of low stone walls built right out in the shallows so that, when the tide flooded and brought in shoals of fish, they became trapped. Whalebones were used to spear the fish – silvery grey mullets, wrasse, gobies, plaice, and shellfish such as limpets, mussels and razor clams were gathered and eaten with perhaps a mouthful of wild samphire or sea beet. But it was not until between the twelfth and fifteenth centuries that a real fishing industry began to develop in Britain. During that period fishing boats and trading ships began making long voyages – hunting for cod in the North Sea, or importing salted herring from Holland and wind-dried cod and saithe from Iceland. It was on a particularly ambitious fishing trip in the fifteenth century that John Cabot discovered North America, and announced that 'this kingdom would have no further use of Iceland' because the North American waters were 'swarming with fish'.

Right up until the 1960s fish were plentiful and therefore cheap in Britain – a nutritious, everyday food that could easily be obtained in every high street. But the 'Cod War' with Iceland in the early 1970s changed the situation almost overnight. When Iceland finally secured a 200-mile fishing limit, the deep sea trawling industry in this country went into decline, imports of fish rose dramatically, the price of fish increased and wet fish shops faded away throughout the country. Good fresh fish became difficult to obtain and by the end of the decade many children must have thought that fish only came in the shape of fish fingers or cod balls.

More problems were caused when fishing laws laid down by the EEC effectively reduced our share of fish in what used to be British waters. And although the member countries of the EEC have agreed on the fishing rules, it is clear that many of them fish illegally inside our meagre 12-mile limit. Even within the law some questionable fishing practices exist. In recent years, mackerel have been scarce around the islands where I live. This is hardly surprising when not so long ago we could see our own deep sea trawlers catching huge shoals of mackerel and transferring them to enormous Eastern bloc factory ships just outside our fishing zone. Over-fishing is a serious problem, so it is no wonder that the hunt is on again. These same deep sea trawlers are now travelling thousands of miles to fish in the Southern Atlantic around the Falkland Isles.

Sophisticated modern fishing methods have greatly reduced the element of chance where catching fish is concerned nowadays. Shoaling fish are easily detected by acoustic techniques (although the challenge of unpredictable weather and oceanographic conditions remains). Now huge factory ships suck up vast shoals of fish, miles of monofilament drift nets stretch around our shores and huge tackle turns over the sea bed, destroying valuable breeding grounds. The effect of technical advances in the industry has been to make one fish swim where two swam before.

However, technical progress in methods of farming fish, with the emphasis on careful husbandry and additive-free feed, has made a considerable impact on the situation. Although fish-lovers may argue that fish produced in this way lacks the appeal – and taste – of wild fish, the success of farmed salmon and trout are obvious examples of how alternative supplies could prevent the wholesale depletion of natural fish stocks. Rainbow trout, which is now available all year round, is cheaper than ten years ago, and farmed salmon of consistent quality is also not subject to season. Farmed cod from Norway, still in the early days of production, is showing great promise.

Cultural interchange and travel is being reflected in a slightly more adventurous approach to fish cookery in the 1980s and fish farmers are taking advantage of this. Sea bass from Turkey, carp from Israel, and cultivated mussels and oysters are just a few examples of their produce.

Fish merchants too are beginning to respond to our new international outlook and hundreds of species of fish and shellfish are now jetted all over the world. Look in on any bustling trading day at Billingsgate Market in London at the magnificent display of fish from many countries: our own gleaming mackerel and herring are offered alongside tuna, anchovy, sea breams, grouper and wrasse from Europe. A handsome pike and a crate of sea urchins may share a stall with exotic parrot fish from the Seychelles. Perhaps the next decade will see new and exciting patterns in the development of the fishing industry. I'm looking forward to them.

A bustling start to trading at Billingsgate, the oldest wholesale market in Britain.

Shopping for fish

There is a refreshing element of unpredictability in shopping for fish. The availability and price of sea fish fluctuates – there are seasons, weather conditions and overfishing to contend with. There should always be a steady supply at a stable price of farmed fish like trout and salmon, but the supply, demand and price of sea fish seems heavily influenced by fashion. For instance, oysters and salmon were once regarded as the common food of the poor, whereas now only the affluent can afford them.

Good fishmongers set up their displays of fresh fish early every morning. From the elaborate tableaux of fish in some shops to the simpler presentation on market stalls, all the fish should be 'stiff alive' with bright eyes and firm flesh. Any live shellfish should have some fight in them, and there should be a fresh, pleasing sea aroma. These are the fishmongers to befriend and patronise. They will advise on cooking methods, and be happy to fillet or bone out fish. If you are planning ahead, they will order especially for you.

'You get what you pay for' is never more true than when buying fresh food. Unless you are lucky enough to be able to shop at the fish docks, I strongly recommend paying a few pence more to a good fishmonger who knows his profession.

Unfortunately, there are poor fishmongers whose slabs display only languid, sunken-eyed fish. These fishmongers often employ inexperienced assistants with no grasp or knowledge of their trade. Many of the·best supermarkets have excellent wet fish counters but the chilled, packaged fresh fish on *some* store shelves is certainly past its best. In some areas, fish shops and supermarkets alike show a disappointing lack of enterprise in their selection. There are places where only two kinds of fish are sold: white fillets and smoked fillets!

If you query this policy, you will probably be told that there is no demand for lesser-known species, or that they cannot be obtained. Both these excuses reflect the sheep-like attitudes of customers and the blinkered approach of over-cautious buyers. The short-sightedness is, inevitably, counter-productive, as the most available and popular species are periodically fished out, thus becoming more expensive and harder to obtain.

In fact, today's sophisticated methods of transport and distribution make it possible to buy from a huge range of fish. I frequently hear fishmonger friends complain that the 'housewife' is too conservative and refuses to try lesser-known varieties. On the other hand, I am often besieged by the 'housewife' who longs to find different fish but complains that her fish shop – if she is lucky enough to have one – won't stock them! Look at pages 275–296, which give a comprehensive guide to the many types of fish available in the UK, and try ordering something different next time you visit your fishmonger.

Buying fresh sea fish

Appearance and smell: these are the two key pointers. A fresh fish should have bright eyes, the gills should be a healthy reddish-pink and the scales, if present, should be glossy and firmly attached. Press your finger into the flesh of the fish; if it is fresh it will not leave an imprint but will spring back into shape. Fish should have a pleasant, mild smell of the sea. If it has an unpleasantly strong odour it is past its best. The skins of some fish have a natural slime, which should not be rinsed off until you are about to cook.

When buying cutlets and fillets, it is harder to determine freshness – but the flesh should be firm and not discoloured. Older cutlets and fillets will have a dried, curled-up appearance, or look flabby and yellowish.

Obviously, the fresher the fish, the better. Among the few exceptions are Dover sole which improves in flavour two or three days after being caught, and grey mullet and John Dory which some connoisseurs prefer older. All other fish should ideally be eaten on the day of purchase. Fish should be stored in the refrigerator until needed – whole fish should be gutted first.

Buying fresh freshwater fish

The same guidelines apply, but there is a steadier supply and price. Some farmed fish will be very fresh indeed as they are often on sale only a few hours after they have left the farm.

Buying frozen fish

Frozen fish is a good option when supplies of fresh fish are low or of poor quality. Reputable brand names offer cutlets, fillets or whole fish that are frozen very fresh. When thawed correctly (see page 38), these fish will give good results in most recipes. The texture will not be the same as that of fresh fish, but the taste of quality frozen fish should be good. Avoid frozen products such as cheap, inferior fish fingers, fish cakes or crab sticks, which use minced or reconstituted fish (this should be indicated on the packaging).

Frozen fish should have undamaged packaging and should feel solid. Do not buy soft, mushy packages: these have started to thaw and may not be safe to eat. There should be no dull white patches on the fish which indicate freezer burn caused by prolonged or incorrect storage. There should be no small white ice crystals which suggest that the fish has started to thaw and been re-frozen. There should be little 'drip' when thawing. Once thawed, the fish should be firm.

Buying smoked fish

Smoking is a traditional way of preserving fish, but modern thinking on diet and health suggests that we should not be eating it in too great a quantity. The special grounds for concern are:

Additives
Azo dyes are often used to colour fish yellow or brown. These dyes are entirely cosmetic and have been associated with a range of allergic reactions.

Salt
Smoked fish is salty, but the saltiness can be reduced by careful pre-soaking and cooking.

Tar
Tarry deposits from smouldering wood are thought to be possible carcinogens.

Bearing these points in mind, always shop for good-quality smoked fish from reliable sources. The fish should have a pleasant smoky smell, a glossy surface and be firm to the touch. Poor-quality smoked fish will look dry and wrinkled with shrunken flesh.

Jim Collins of F. and D. Lewzey. The East End smokehouses produce some of the finest smoked salmon in the world.

Smoked fish may be bought whole or in fillets; fresh, frozen, and often vacuum-packed. To identify the types of smoked fish available, see pages 295–296. There is a wide variation in colour from golden yellow and pale brown to dark brown. There will always be regional differences in the colours, as many smokeries are small family firms with their own recipes and techniques. Look for undyed fish and support the fishmonger who sells it.

Buying shellfish

Live shellfish
If you have the opportunity of buying live shellfish or crustaceans from a reliable source, preferably as the catch is landed at a fishing port, or else from a good fishmonger, you will find the taste noticeably superior to that of ready-cooked or frozen shellfish.

When buying live lobster or crab check that:
● Both the main claws are present.
● They are packed and sold in moist cool conditions.
● They have plenty of fight in them. Avoid drowsy, listless specimens which will have been out of the water for too long. Lift them up: they should feel agreeably heavy in relation to their size. Lobster tails should spring back into place when uncurled.

Lobsters and crawfish:
Identifying hens and cocks
In both lobsters and crawfish, the tail of the hen is broader than that of the cock. The hen has slightly more shell around the tail piece, which protects her eggs (coral or berries). It is not prohibited to sell berried lobster. Some people say that all hen lobsters are left-handed and all cocks are right-handed (one of the pair of main claws is always larger than the other). This is probably folklore, so do not depend on it as a method of identification.

There is no difference in the taste of male or female lobsters and crawfish – and I think that the best weight, live, is around 1½ to 2lb (750g to 1kg) for the tenderest, sweetest flesh. Much larger lobsters should be cheaper per lb or kg as the flesh will be slightly tougher. This size is more suitable for cooking special recipes, such as Homard à l'Américaine (see page 209). In my view, smaller lobsters should be eaten as plainly as possible.

Crabs:
Identifying hens and cocks
When choosing a crab, remember that the cock crab has bigger main claws

than the hen and will yield much more white claw meat. The hen crab has smaller claws, but the brown meat (cream) contained in the body will often be found in greater quantity and quality than in the male crab. Another way to differentiate between cock and hen crabs is by looking at the underside of the body: the shape of the tail flap (apron) is round on the hen and pointed on the cock.

Most of our spider crabs are exported to France.

Handling live crabs and lobsters

Take care of yourself – and crabs or lobsters – when handling them as the claws can take a fierce hold of your fingers. Pick up a crab either by spreading your hand across its back to lift it, so that the main claws cannot reach you, or by holding one of its back legs. The swimming crab, however, is more agile (one of my sons calls it 'the crab with red evil eyes') and can flip its claws right back at you.

Lobsters or crawfish should be carefully picked up across the middle section of the back where the tail meets the head. This way neither the claws nor flapping tail can possibly touch your hand.

Try to treat these live shellfish as humanely as possible before cooking them. Keep them cool and moist (in a shady place and covered with wet seaweed or damp sacking) and avoiding rough handling.

The same general guidelines apply to Dublin Bay prawns, freshwater crayfish and spider crabs.

Buying molluscs

It is particularly important to check the source of supply of oysters, scallops, queens, mussels and clams. Ask your fishmonger if they have come from 'clean' water, or purification tanks, and make sure that they are as fresh as possible. Bivalves like mussels, scallops and clams should literally 'clam up' – that is, remain tightly closed when tapped. Any that remain open, or are cracked, should be discarded. See pages 32 to 37 for how to prepare and cook live shellfish, and always remember the golden rule that any bivalve which does not open after cooking should be thrown away.

Cooked shellfish

If you cannot bear the thought of dealing with live shellfish – especially large lively ones – make sure that you buy cooked shellfish from a reliable fishmonger or good food store. In the case of lobster and crab, your fishmonger should be happy to order them live and cook them for you.

The shells of cooked shellfish should be intact: if they are cracked, the flavour and texture of the meat may have been damaged by water during cooking. With experience you should be able to make a reliable choice of a good heavy specimen. Cooked shellfish which feel light for their size, or which have soft shells, may have 'moulted' recently and will be in poor condition. Poor-quality lobster or crab will contain liquid if the shells are cracked before cooking – test by shaking them gently. Chilled, shelled, freshly cooked prawns and shrimp should be firm to the touch.

Frozen shellfish

As with other kinds of fish, frozen shellfish are a satisfactory option for convenience when good fresh varieties are not available. An increasingly broad range of imported shellfish is now on the market. The familiar frozen prawns and shrimps, scallops and queens have been joined by frozen shucked oysters from Japan, soft-shelled and spider crabs, lobsters, and Dublin Bay prawns from Canada and the USA, mussels from Holland and many other species – farmed or wild – from all over the world. I personally steer clear of reconstituted 'shellfish', i.e. cheap, cunningly packaged, mainly imported 'prawns', 'scampi' and 'crab' sticks, which taste nothing like the real thing.

Buy the best-quality frozen shellfish you can find from a supplier you trust. That way you are less likely to find yourself paying extra for 'glazing' or the artificial 'plumpness' induced by the injection of water into large shellfish.

Fish preparation

Most fishmongers will clean and prepare fish to your liking, or it can be bought ready-filleted, either fresh or frozen, in supermarkets. However, it is useful to know about the various boning and filleting techniques.

First, remember that there are many advantages in buying a whole fish. It is easier to judge the freshness of a whole fish than the freshness of fillets or cutlets; and with a whole fish there is no waste – the skin, bones and head can be used to make stock which will give body to all manner of soups, sauces and other recipes. If you have a fisherman or fisherwoman in the family, or if you are on holiday by the sea, it is quite likely that some strange fish or mollusc will be proudly presented to you and you will be expected to cook it.

It is important to have the right tools for the job (see the section on equipment, page 53). Very sharp knives are essential; blunt ones will produce torn jagged flesh when filleting, and it will be almost impossible to skin a fillet. Use small sharp nail scissors for snipping out the innards of small fish like sardines. Ordinary kitchen scissors are useful for cutting off the fins and spines of larger fish, and garden secateurs or game shears are invaluable when removing the spines of fish like John Dory or large bream.

The step-by-step instructions in this section will give you a good general idea of how to tackle all fish commonly found. However, individual fish sometimes need different techniques and these are fully explained where necessary in the recipe section.

Finally, when discarding unwanted fish trimmings, do remember to wrap them up before putting them in the dustbin – for the sake of your neighbours and the refuse collectors!

Scaling fish

Some fish are easy to scale. Sardines, for example, need only the lightest touch, and grey mullet is firm and easy to hold. Other fish, like mirror carp, have larger and more stubborn scales. It is better to scale a fish before removing its innards: that way the fish still has a firm shapely body. If the fish has sharp spines, cut them off before you do anything else as they may prick or cut your hands. Some spines are poisonous.

Scaling is a messy job. Do it near, or in, the kitchen sink, or out in the garden, and spread the working surface with newspaper to catch the scales as they fly off in all directions. In the washroom at Billingsgate Market I noticed fish scales still clinging to a freshly laundered towel roll!

Lay the fish on a sheet of newspaper and hold it firmly as you draw the blunt side of a stout knife, a fish scaler or the sharp serrated edge of a scallop shell from the tail end to the head – that is, against the flow of the scales. Continue scraping until all the scales are removed. Wash the fish thoroughly under running cold water, using a colander to catch stray scales.

Cleaning fish

Following these steps for cleaning any round fish. The roes of some fish, such as herring, mullet and salmon (red caviare), can be saved and eaten. Carp roe is very good too, and do not be surprised if you find the carp's swim bladder, which is rather like a double balloon inflated with gas! The liver of some fish (for instance, red mullet) is a delicacy and should be left in place.

Using sharp scissors, cut off all the fins, or they can be left on if you prefer. If removing the head, cut it off with a strong knife just behind the gills and underneath the pectoral fins.

1   2   3

PICTURE 1 Using a small sharp knife or scissors, and starting at the vent, make a cut along the belly as far as the head. Take care not to puncture the innards as you do this as their contents may taint the flesh.

PICTURE 2 Using your fingers or a knife, remove the innards, wrap in newspaper and discard. If the fish head has not been removed, you may have to use small scissors to snip away membranes at the head end.

Wash the inside of the fish under running cold water, using your thumb to scratch away any dried blood from the backbone, and pat dry with kitchen paper.

PICTURE 3 Remove the gills if cooking a whole fish as they often have an unpleasant taste.

Cleaning fish through the gills

PICTURE 1   Prise back the gill, snap it out with your finger and thumb and use your little finger to hook out the innards in one go. This method is good for whole fish like trout: tricky but worth practising until you have the knack.

PICTURE 2   Use a teaspoon to scrape out anything you have left behind and wash the fish thoroughly under cold running water.

Tweezers can be used for cleaning sardines through the gills.

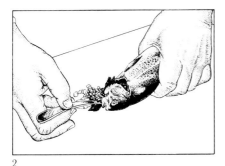

Skinning fish

Whether or not you skin a fish before cooking is a matter of personal preference. I think there are many advantages in leaving the skin on – it helps to keep the shape of fillets, adds to the flavour and offers some protection to the flesh. It is also much easier to remove the skin after cooking – but in any case the skin of some fish looks attractive and tastes good. All round whole fish should be skinned after cooking (for instance, poached salmon in preparation for dressing). All fillets are easy to skin.

Most flat fish are easy to skin whole. With some species, however (for example, plaice), the skin adheres to the flesh. When skinned, the flesh can tear easily, which gives it a jagged appearance. This seems to happen only with extremely fresh plaice. I do not recommend skinning or filleting small flat fish – it is tricky and fiddly and the results are disappointing.

A sharp knife is essential for skinning, whatever the fish. Dipping your fingers in salt, or using a piece of kitchen paper, will help you get a grip on wet fish.

Two methods of skinning whole flat fish

There are two schools of thought on skinning whole flat fish (for instance, Dover sole). Some people prefer the whole fish entirely skinned; others like to retain the white (blind side) skin which makes a tender and crusty surface when grilled or shallow-fried.

METHOD I

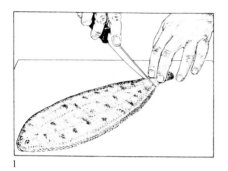

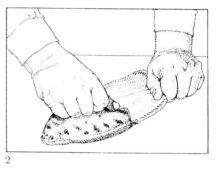

PICTURE 1   Lay the fish, dark skin up, on a chopping board or work surface. Using a sharp knife, cut a nick in the skin at the extreme tail end, making a flap of skin that you can firmly grasp.

PICTURE 2   Take a firm grip and rip the skin towards the head of the fish in one smooth movement.

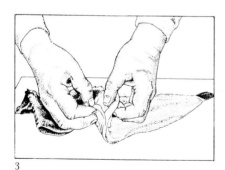

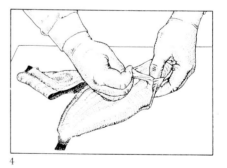

PICTURE 3   You have reached the jaws of the fish, so turn it over and use your thumbs to ease the skin over the head.

PICTURE 4   Hold the head and pull off the rest of the skin in the same swift motion towards the tail end. The whole skin can be saved for the stock pot.

METHOD II

Proceed as for Method I until you have pulled back the dark skin in one piece. Then cut off the head diagonally, close to the gills.
Using scissors, cut off the fins.
Scale the white side, wash and pat dry with kitchen paper.

Skinning fillets of flat or round fish

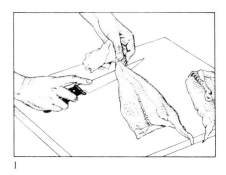

1

PICTURE 1   Place the fillet, skin side down, on a chopping board or work surface. Make a ½in (1cm) snip into the flesh at the tail end, then insert a sharp knife. Holding the skin in one hand, work the knife in a sawing action, slicing the flesh away from the skin. Hold the knife at an acute angle – almost parallel – to the fish to avoid cutting the skin.

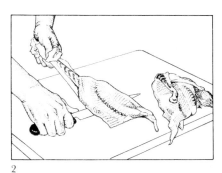

2

PICTURE 2   Keep the skin taut as you slice – on each sawing motion, pull slightly on the skin. You can stop occasionally and fold back the fillet to see how you are doing. If you are planning to make stock, save the skin for the pot.

Filleting Fish

Even though most fishmongers will be happy to fillet fish to your liking, many people will enjoy having a go at the various techniques described here. Some sophisticated recipes demand quite complicated filleting techniques, but here I have described simple basic methods which are easy to master. Work with a sharp knife in a way that is comfortable to you – if necessary, use a cloth or a piece of kitchen paper or dip your fingers in a little salt to help you keep a firm grip on the fish.

Filleting round fish

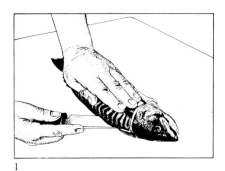

PICTURE 1 Lay the cleaned fish on a chopping board with its tail towards you. Hold the fish steady with one hand and make a semi-circular cut around the head (follow the bone structure and keep close to the head area). Now slice along the backbone from the head to the tail. You should be able to feel the backbone as you keep the knife on top of it while slicing.

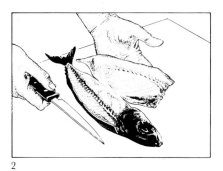

PICTURE 2 Lift the flesh gently and cut the fillet away from the body, taking care to avoid the rib bones.

Remove the other fillet by turning the fish over and repeating the process. You will now have two fillets – trim them ready for cooking and use the head, tail, bones, and so on, for stock.

The champion fish filleter of Great Britain takes three quick strokes to fillet a cod; I take at least twelve and I think I am fairly good – so persevere!

Filleting flat fish

It is not worth filleting small flat fish – you will get only thin little fillets which are hardly worth the effort. You can successfully fillet medium to large flat fish, however, and skin them afterwards if you wish.

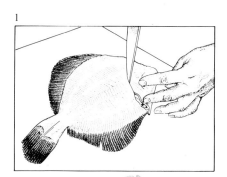

PICTURE 1 Place the fish on a chopping board with the head pointing towards you. To cut the head off, follow the 'shape' of the head with your knife. Save the bony head for the stockpot.

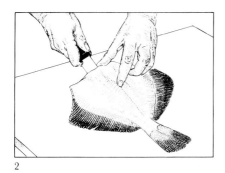

2

3

4

PICTURE 2   You should be able to feel and see the line of the backbone on the white side of the fish, down the centre. For two whole fillets (one from each side), insert your filleting knife into the flesh and feel the tip resting against the side of the backbone and on top of the rib bones. Using a damp cloth to keep hold of the fish with one hand, slide the knife right down the backbone, keeping on top of the side of the rib bones.

PICTURE 3   Work with long, slicing motions across one set of ribs to the outer edge of the fish.

PICTURE 4   Cut the fillet away from the outer edge fins and fold it back to reveal the backbone. Carefully release the flesh from the backbone and repeat the slicing motion to the opposite outer edge of the fish. Cut the fillet away from the outer edge fins. Lift off the whole fillet.

Turn the fish over and remove the other fillet in the same way. You now have two whole fillets. The head, bones and trimmings can be used for stock.

Cutting two whole fillets may take some practice and you may find it easier to start off by cutting four fillets. To do this, after cutting off the head, cut down the backbone of the fish, insert the knife between the flesh and the bone on each side, and remove each fillet separately.

The fillets may curl up or lose their shape when they are cooked so, after washing and patting them dry, score them lightly two or three times on the side formerly covered by skin. If the fillets are to be folded in half for poaching or baking, the scored side should be on the inside.

When rolling a fillet (*paupiette*), it is important that the side formerly covered by skin is on the inside of the roll. The roll will then keep its shape during cooking. If you roll a fillet skin side out, it will open during cooking.

If you wish, you can cook the whole flat fish on the bone (for instance, a baked sole) and then remove two fillets for serving. Transfer the baked fish to a warm plate and, with a sharp knife, push off the bony fins from each side (although, in the case of sole, these can be crunchy and good to nibble on).

Using a sliding motion with your knife, raise the whole top fillet from the bone, slide a spatula or large palette knife under the fillet, lift the fillet and arrange it on warmed plate or serving dish. Now remove the backbone and ribs in one go. They will lift off easily.

If you wish, you can place the second fillet on top of the first so that it can be served as a whole boned fish, garnished with fresh herbs and surrounded by, for instance, mushrooms, asparagus tips, steamed baby carrots or tiny new potatoes, and with the baking juices poured over.

Boning out a whole round fish for stuffing

Many people hate fiddling with bones at the supper table. Boning the fish out solves the problem. There are two methods: through the belly and through the back. Some fish are easier to bone than others – trout and herring, for instance, are very easy – while the bones of certain white sea fish, such as grey mullet, are more stubborn.

Boning through the belly

Gut the fish and remove the gills (see page 18). Trim away all the fins and, using a sharp knife, lengthen the opening from the vent right down to the tail end. The head can be removed if you prefer.

1

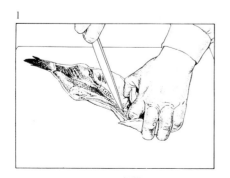

PICTURE I   From inside the cavity, work down the backbone of the fish, freeing each rib with the aid of a strong knife or kitchen scissors and your fingers – each rib should be snapped off the backbone. Now run a sharp knife down each side of the backbone to ensure that each rib is free without piercing the skin.

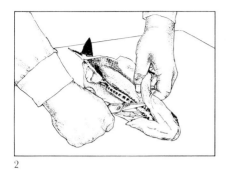

2

PICTURE 2   Use strong scissors to cut through the backbone at the head. Pull out the backbone, working towards the tail where you can cut it free. Remove the ribs using a knife, or tweezers if the fish is a small one.

An optional step when stuffing a whole fish – for instance, with prawns and vegetables and fresh ginger, or breadcrumbs and herbs – is to use a trussing needle to sew it up, but wooden cocktail sticks or toothpicks may also be used to secure the stuffing.

To produce butterfly fillets

This method is suitable for mackerel, herring, trout, sardines, pilchards and so on. If you cut off the head and tail before pressing out the bones you will get one flat 'butterfly' fillet. If you leave on the head and tail you will have a whole boned-out fish which can be stuffed.

Trim off the fins, slit the fish from head to tail along the belly and clean thoroughly.

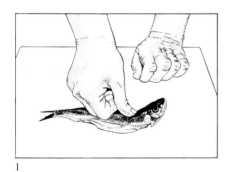

1

PICTURE 1   Open the fish out and place it skin side up. On a small fish use your thumbs; on larger fish use the heel of your hand to press firmly along the centre back. This will nearly release the bones from the flesh.

Now turn the fish over. Use scissors to snip through the backbone at the head and tail end. Pull away the backbone, working towards the tail end. Remove any stray wispy bones with your fingers or with tweezers. Wash the fish again and pat dry with kitchen paper.

Boning through the back

This is easier than it sounds. It is the proper way to bone out a trout for stuffing. You can clean the fish through the gills first if you like (see page 19), or remove the innards with your fingers after boning.

  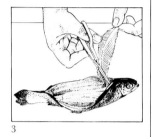

1   2   3

PICTURE 1   Trim off the fins, place the fish on its belly and, using a sharp knife or scissors, cut along the backbone.

PICTURE 2   With the knife almost vertical, cut the flesh away from the ribs on one side following the shape of the rib cage. Repeat on the other side.

PICTURE 3   Using strong scissors, cut the backbone at the tail end and pull away towards the head. Now cut and release the whole bone.

Place the fish, belly side down, in a lightly greased baking dish and fill the cavity with the stuffing of your choice – push the stuffing right up to the head and down to the tail. Dot with a few scraps of butter or margarine (or cover with greased greaseproof paper or aluminium foil), pour a little wine or stock around the fish and bake in the usual way.

'Pocketing' a flat fish for stuffing

This is an interesting way of cooking a whole flat fish, skinned or unskinned. The technique leaves you with a whole boned flat fish and a commodious pocket exposed to receive any number of stuffings – from a simple combination of queens, prawns or oysters with herbs and spring onions, for instance, to a refined mousseline if you are in the mood for a special-effort dinner party.

Outstanding flat fish like Dover sole should not be 'messed about' in this fashion, but other so-called soles, or large plaice, are suitable. When the filleting is completed, wash the fish thoroughly and pat dry with kitchen paper. Sprinkle the flesh with a little lemon or lime juice before stuffing. When the fish is cooked, garnish with fresh herbs or chopped spring onions, and serve with steamed vegetables and new potatoes.

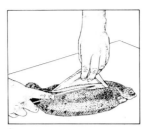

1   2   3

PICTURE 1   Place the skinned or unskinned fish dark side up on a chopping board. Cut down and expose the backbone from the head to the tail.

PICTURE 2   Cut one fillet away *almost* to the edge of the fish, then turn the fish round and repeat on the other side of the backbone.

Pick up the fish and bend it backwards in several places to snap the backbone. It will now be easy to pull away the sections of backbone and ribs using tweezers or scissors.

PICTURE 3   Wash out the fish, pat it dry with kitchen paper and check that no bones remain. It will look rather like an unbuttoned overcoat and can now be stuffed.

Preparing shellfish

It is well worth buying shellfish live where possible and cooking and extracting the meat yourself. The superb flavour is far superior to that of ready-cooked, frozen or canned shellfish – and the expensive species of shellfish will then more than justify their price.

Live shellfish should be treated in a humane way. For instance, some recipes demand that freshwater crayfish (*écrevisse*) should have their intestines removed while they are alive: I find this difficult and distasteful. Other recipes call for a live lobster to have its spinal cord severed before slicing the fish in half for grilling, barbecueing or steaming. In practice (and cookery instructions usually fail to point this out), if you do this the lobster will flap wildly around for many minutes like a headless chicken. This is unnerving for the cook and very cruel to the fish. The most humane way to kill a lobster before you begin to cook its flesh in a recipe requiring raw lobster is to drop it into a large pan of rapidly boiling water and boil for 1½ minutes – no longer. The following pages give a general guide to preparing the most common shellfish, and the recipe section gives instructions on dealing with some less common species.

Cooking lobster or crawfish and extracting the meat

Lobster and crawfish have similar bodies. The difference is that the lobster has tender succulent flesh in its two main claws, but the crawfish does not have these claws; instead it has two long spines which do not contain meat.

Kill live lobsters or crawfish as described on page 27, then boil for a further 8–10 minutes per pound to cook the flesh. While still warm twist off the main claws, and extract the white meat as for crab (see page 29). Twist or cut off the little legs – these can be used for stock. To extract the flesh from the main body, there are many methods. If you do not need to use the split lobster shell as a container for the finished dish, simply cut through the segments from side to side from the underside of the tail so that you have 3 or 4 sections. It is now easy to push the meat out with your thumbs. Remove the black intestinal cord before serving. When the intact shell is needed, I recommend the two easy methods below.

METHOD I

1

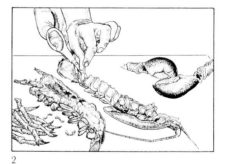

2

PICTURE 1 Snap off the claws and legs. Extend the tail, shell-side down, on a chopping board. Using a sharp knife, slice down the lobster from the head to the end of the tail – you may need to give your strong knife a sharp thwack with a mallet or rolling pin to help you cut through the shell.

Discard the sac between the eyes. This contains gravel and is a sort of stomach. Remove the 'dead men's (or devil's) fingers' – feathery gills, all of which are inedible. Reserve the coral

(roe), which are like tiny pink berries, and the liver (tomalley) which is a soft grey-green colour.

PICTURE 2 Using small scissors or a small knife, detach and peel away the translucent, thin, bony covering that protects the underside of the flesh. Remove the tail meat from the shell. You can save the shell for stock, or scrub it well in hot water before oiling it to use for serving the lobster.

Now, using a small knife or teaspoon, scrape out the intestine, a small black thread running along the centre of the tail. The tail meat can be sliced into pieces ready to serve cold with mayonnaise or other dressings. Alternatively, it can be gently reheated for hot dishes.

METHOD II

Another way of removing the tail meat is to place the tail, shell side down on a chopping board. Using small scissors or a small knife, cut down each side of the translucent thin bony covering of the flesh.

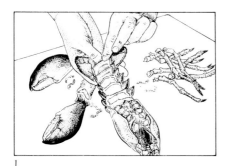

1

PICTURE I   Now peel off the covering in one piece. The tail meat can be extracted, also in one piece, and the (well scrubbed) shell used as a container for the finished recipe. Remember, too, that the pounded shell, claws and legs make very good stock.

Cooking a crab and extracting the meat

Drop the live crab into a large pan of rapidly boiling water and boil for 10–15 minutes, depending on size. While still warm, twist off the main claws and eight little legs – they will come away easily. If the crab is large, it is worth using a skewer to extract the meat from the cracked legs – otherwise pound them and use them for stock.

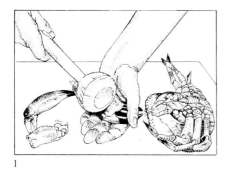

1

PICTURE I   Use a wooden mallet or rolling pin to crack the main claws. Hold a claw in your hand and let your hand 'give' slightly as you bring the mallet down. This will produce a clean crack. If you use a hammer or sharp instrument on a hard surface, you will shatter the claw and have the tedious job of picking splinters of shell out of the flesh.

2

PICTURE 2   Now, using your fingers, remove the white claw meat. You will find a flat bone (which feels and looks rather like a miniature plastic spatula) and you should discard this.

3

PICTURE 3   Crack the leg joints and remove the white meat with a skewer or the handle of a teaspoon.

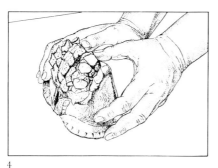

4

PICTURE 4   Now put the body of the crab on a chopping board with the head facing away from you. Twist off the legs using your thumbs, push the 'undercarriage' away from you and prise away this underpart of the body in one go.

5

PICTURE 5   Discard the feathery gills (dead men's or devil's fingers) as these are inedible. Scoop out any brown cream with a teaspoon, and pick out the white meat.

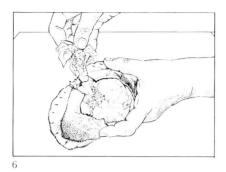

6

PICTURE 6   Remove the head from the shell and discard.

7

PICTURE 7   Sometimes the flesh in the main shell is watery, and occasionally it may look greenish. In both cases, although not poisonous, it should be discarded. Brown or pink firm creamy flesh, however, should be scooped out with a teaspoon and combined with the white claw meat.

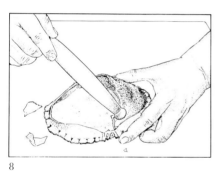

8

PICTURE 8   If you wish to use the shell as a container for the crab meat – for either baked or dressed crab – first tap out the thin shell inside the groove. Use the handle of a wooden spoon or the tip of a rolling pin. Then scrub it out with boiling water, dry it well and oil it lightly before use.

Preparing swimming crab and spider crab

The claws and main body of the swimming crab can be treated in the same way as those of the common edible crab. Spider crabs are time-consuming to deal with. They are best served with the legs cracked (the meat is particularly good) and the main body sliced in half. If the crabs are served in a mixed seafood platter, the meat can be picked out at table. Provide individual dishes of mayonnaise and wedges of lemon when serving. Finger bowls and napkins, or warm damp flannels should also be on hand.

Preparing oysters

This is the method for opening any species of oyster – the American term is 'shucking'. It is not easy for the beginner, and you must use a special oyster knife (an inexpensive item – see page 53). One invaluable tip is that if the whole oyster is frozen in your deep freeze, you will be able to open it with ease.

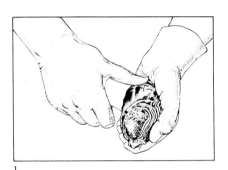

1

2

PICTURE 1   Wear a glove or oven mitt, or wrap a teatowel round one hand to help you grip the oyster and protect your hand from the knife. Take a firm grasp on the oyster, making sure it lies, flat-side up, in the palm of your protected hand. Insert the blade of the oyster knife – or a short, stout kitchen knife – into the hinge of the oyster, about ½in (1cm) deep, and prise it open. You may have to twist and wiggle the knife slightly as you do this. Take care not to lose any of the liquor from the rounded cup of the shell.

PICTURE 2   When you have prised open the shell, slide in a small sharp knife to cut away the 'moorings' from the top and bottom halves.

Now pull off the top part of the shell and, with the tip of your knife, flick out any flakes of shell that may have fallen on top of the oyster. The oyster is now ready to serve with its liquor – or to use in a recipe. Prop each shell up in a bed of crushed ice for serving *au naturel* with lemon wedges and pepper or tabasco sauce.

A whole steamed fish makes a dramatic centrepiece. This is Bass with ginger and spring onions (page 86).

(Overleaf) A selection of summery dishes using versatile cod: Cod steaks with lemon and parsley sauce (page 94); A warm summer salad with piquant cod (page 92); Cod kebabs with basil sauce (page 98); Grilled cod fillets with fresh tomato and basil sauce (page 99).

Preparing scallops and queens

You can buy scallops and queens prepared on the shell, or frozen without their shells – but when buying them intact make sure they are very fresh (see Shopping for fish, page 11). The shells can be difficult to separate. One solution is to place them, flat side down, on the top of a hot cooker, under the grill or in the oven for a few moments. This will make them gape slightly, and you can then use a stout stubby knife to prise them open.

1

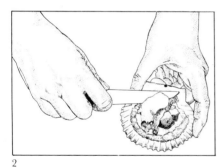

2

PICTURE 1   Run the blade of a sharp knife along the inside of the upper (rounded) shell and lower (flat) shell to release the membrane of the scallop from the shells.

PICTURE 2   Now rinse the scallop under cold running water, and use your fingers or a small knife to remove the membrane from the white lobe and pink coral and free them from the shell. Discard the greyish fringy skirt if you wish – this is edible and good for the stock pan but not usually used in the British Isles.

Trim away any other unwanted matter from the flesh on a chopping board. The rounded shell can be scrubbed in boiling water and used either as a container for a cold dish or lightly oiled to hold a baked or grilled dish.

Preparing clams

Clams can be steamed or poached open, like mussels, but if you wish to eat them raw, they can be opened with an ordinary stout vegetable knife. Take care to reserve the liquor. Razor shells can be steamed open and the contents eaten in their entirety.

Preparing squid

You can often buy squid ready-prepared, fresh or frozen. However, it is useful to know how to deal with the entire fish.

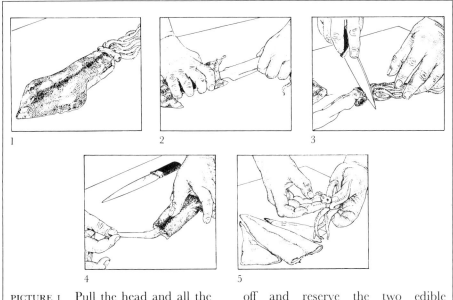

PICTURE 1   Pull the head and all the squid's innards out of the body sac.

PICTURE 2   Cut the tentacles off the head. Throw away the head and innards. Wash the sac under cold running water.

PICTURE 3   Remove the transparent fin (quill) and, with a knife, scrape off the membrane that covers the sac; cut off and reserve the two edible triangular fins.

PICTURE 4   Remove the squid's sharp beak or mouth from the centre of the tentacles.

Wash the squid thoroughly under cold running water and pat it dry with kitchen paper. It can now be sliced into ¾in (2cm) slices or left intact for stuffing.

Preparing mussels

Mussels should be tightly closed before cooking and open up when they are cooked. If they are gaping slightly as you scrub them, give them a tap – they should clam up immediately; otherwise discard them. You should also throw away any that do not open up when cooked or are damaged.

Mussels can be soaked overnight in salted water to clean them of grit or sand, although it is now possible to buy kilo bags of very clean mussels.

PICTURE 1 Scrub each mussel thoroughly and pull away the beard – a stubborn tuft with which the mussel clings to rocks. Scrape away any barnacles etc. The mussels are now ready to be steamed open in the recipe of your choice.

How to freeze fresh fish and shellfish

Home freezing makes good sense if you live near the coast and can take advantage of bargains when the catch is landed. Sometimes fishmongers have supplies which exceed demand, or there may be an enthusiastic fisherman or fisherwoman in your family. Home freezing is also invaluable for made-up fish dishes.

Freezing fresh fish is simple. Obviously, when storing bought frozen fish, you must put it in the freezer as soon as possible before the thawing process beings. *Never re-freeze fish.*

The fish must be as fresh as possible, ideally no more than 24 hours old. Rinse it under cold running water (or wipe it with a damp cloth). Pat it dry with kitchen paper. A good tip is to use a solution of water and fresh lemon juice when washing or wiping the fish – this will help to keep the original colour of the skin and flesh. Some fish may be frozen with their guts intact, and remember, too, to leave in the liver of red mullet and other species where this organ is considered a delicacy.

If, however, you are going to gut the fish before freezing, try stuffing the belly cavity with aluminium foil to help keep the shape of the body. I prefer to scale fish (if necessary) before freezing, and gills should be removed too. You can also fillet the fish, or make cutlets for freezing individually, and here the thawing time will be greatly reduced – although small fillets and cutlets may be cooked from frozen.

Glazing is not absolutely necessary for most fish but it is worth doing for really fine whole fish like prime salmon. It will keep the fish in perfect shape and condition, and give a slightly longer storage time. Having gutted, washed and dried the fish, open-freeze on a baking tray until solid – about 2 hours. Use the fast-freeze facility for best results. Have a bowl of iced water ready and dip the frozen fish in this until a thin coating of ice forms over it. Place the fish on a wire tray over the baking tray and return to the freezer. When the glaze is quite solid (after about 30 minutes) repeat the dipping and freezing process several times until a glaze about ¼in (0.5cm) thick has formed. Then wrap the fish in freezer foil or polythene and store in the normal way. Always wrap fish and shellfish with care to avoid odours and cross-contamination.

Do not be tempted to thaw fish in water as it will be soggy, difficult to cook and unappetising. Microwave ovens are extremely useful for de-frosting, but this needs to be done with care to avoid partly cooking the fish.

For conventional thawing, allow just enough time for the fish to de-frost completely before you are ready to cook. Place it in a cool area or in the refrigerator, and as soon as it has thawed treat it as fresh wet fish.

Freezing is also a useful way of dealing with left-overs which can be transformed into soups, fish cakes, quiches, fish pies, sauces for pasta, and so on. Many recipes of this type can be re-heated direct from the freezer.

Shellfish must be extremely fresh for freezing; certainly they must be cooked within a day of being caught. Freeze them on 'fast freeze' first as soon as possible after cooking the shellfish and cooling them. I always freeze the last lobster or two of the season to bring out for Christmas – I freeze them whole in their shells and they taste remarkably good.

Cooked prawns may be frozen 'shell on' or 'shell off'. Mussels can be steamed open, then frozen in their liquor, as can clams and other bivalves. The white lobes and pink corals of scallops can be extracted from the shell and frozen raw. Oysters can be extracted and frozen raw with their juices – they can also be frozen raw in the shell which, incidentally, makes them very much easier to open when de-frosted. Cooked lobster, crawfish, crayfish and Dublin Bay prawns may also be frozen in the shell, or you can extract the meat first. Crab meat can be extracted and packed into tubs for freezing. You can freeze whole dressed crab. I think it unwise to freeze a whole cooked crab in the shell in case the contents are watery or light, but this does not apply to spider crabs, lobster or crawfish.

Ideal storage times depend on the size of the fish and your type of freezer, but here is a general guide to maximum storage times (remember that it is vital to date-label the fish):

White fish	4 months
Oily fish	3 months
Cooked fish dishes	2 months
Smoked fish	3 months
Small shellfish	1–2 months
Large shellfish	3 months

Cooking times

The 'Canadian Cooking Theory' is a good rule of thumb. This is based on the principle that fish should be cooked as quickly as possible – and never overcooked. The fish is laid on a flat surface and measured at its thickest point. For each 1in (2.5cm) of depth, allow 10 minutes' cooking time. The rule does not, of course, apply to small pieces of fish to be used in soups and stews: these cook within 2 or 3 minutes. For frozen cutlets of fish to be cooked direct from the freezer simply double the cooking time. For extra guidance I have included a chart issued by the Sea Fish Industry Authority on page 6.

To test that fish is cooked, carefully poke a skewer or tip of a knife into the flesh. It should be opaque and ease away from the bone. Do not use a fork or jab at the fish – you will lose the juices. Remember that fish continues to cook in a baking dish removed from the oven, and while being kept warm.

Cooking methods

The joy of cooking fish is in its simplicity and speed. There need be no fear or mystery once you realise that, unlike meat, the flesh of fish is naturally tender and should never be overcooked.

Boiling is a fate worse than death for the poor fish, especially if, once having been boiled mercilessly, it is laid to rest under a blanket of thick floury sauce. Other fatal and regrettable cooking methods include imprisoning fish in gungy batter and deep-frying it in any-old-lard, or dousing already-rich and oily fish like kippers or mackerel with huge amounts of butter.

The delicate flavours and textures of fish need a light and sensitive touch. In general terms, the aim is to cook it in a way that suits its character and retains its natural juices. My own favourite cooking methods are barbecueing and grilling – most especially for oily varieties like sardines, mackerel and herring. Poaching, steaming and baking are methods I love too. With a little attention to detail and the subtle enhancements of herbs, spices and wine or stock, these methods produce exquisite results.

I also have a weakness for really good fish and chips! . . . and goujons, and *fritto misto di mare*. The good news here is that, by frying in good clean polyunsaturated oil and using a light tempura batter (see page 83), you can achieve undreamed-of crisp perfection.

The microwave oven has revolutionised many people's kitchens and, where appropriate, microwave instructions are given in the recipe section. Microwaving does not necessarily save time in fish cookery, but cooking smells are greatly reduced and the texture and flavour of the fish are fully retained.

Poaching

Poaching is much misunderstood. In the past it was too often associated with bland invalid food or nursery cooking. In fact it is a delicate skill, and highly suited to most varieties of fresh and smoked fish.

Bearing in mind that fish must never be overcooked, the most important rule for poaching is that the liquid should *never boil*. Boiling will break up and toughen the tender flesh of fish – the poaching liquid should be just under simmering point so that the fish is cosseted in liquid that scarcely shudders.

Poaching techniques

1 Choose a pan that is suitable for the size of fish you are going to poach. A fish kettle is purpose-built for poaching large whole fish, and its rack ensures that the cooked fish does not break up when lifted out. Otherwise, you could improvise by using a deep roasting tin. To help lift out the whole fish unbroken:
- Poach it wrapped in muslin or a boiled teatowel.
- Use a grill rack or cake cooling tray as a trivot on which to lay the fish.
- Make two or three 'strap handles' out of double-thickness lengths of foil. Place these lengths across the bottom of the pan, making sure that the ends are long enough to hang over the sides, and lay the fish on the foil cradle. When the fish is cooked, it can be carefully hoisted with the foil handles.

2 Fillets, steaks and cutlets should fit snugly into the pan so that the minimum amount of flavour escapes into the poaching liquid. Whether poaching whole fish, fillets or cutlets, the pan should be covered with a loose-fitting lid or sheet of aluminium foil.

3 The poaching liquid: in theory you could use plain water for poaching, but I think that all fish benefits from being cooked in a flavoured liquid such as a good court bouillon, fish stock, wine with added lemon and herbs, or milk and water with added lemon and herbs (see pages 69–70).

An instant method of poaching is to use a mixture of wine and water – or just wine – with a bouquet of fresh herbs, a slice or two of lemon and a few crushed black or white peppercorns: and here you could add fish trimmings for extra flavour. After the fish is poached, the liquid can be reduced and used as the basis for a sauce, or saved for a soup, or used in making aspic.

A simple court bouillon or fish stock needs preparing beforehand but is well worth the extra effort. Poaching fish in fish stock produces liquid which will transform a good fish dish into a superb one. Please remember to go easy on the salt. Most fish naturally contains salt and adding more also tends to draw out its natural moisture. Salt should not be added when poaching already salty smoked fish.

4 *Poaching a whole fish.* A whole fish should always be started in cold or warm liquid. Lowering it into hot simmering liquid will make the skin shrink and split. Use the stock with wine vinegar (see page 69) for trout, perch and other freshwater fish; use a milk-and-lemon-based stock for smoked fish (see page 70). Otherwise any variation on basic court bouillon or fish stock (see page 69) can be used according to availability of fresh herbs, the character of the fish and the nature of the recipe.

Nothing could be simpler than poaching a whole fish which is to be served cold (see, for example, page 228). Lower the fish into the cold or warm poaching liquid, bring it slowly up to just under simmering and let the liquid bubble once or twice, then remove the pan from the heat and set aside until it is completely cold. However, a large fish of, say, 6–7lb (3–3.5kg) or over should be poached for 6–12 minutes, then allowed to cool in the liquid. The fish will be perfectly cooked. Lift it from the pan and proceed with the recipe.

For hot poached fish you should calculate the cooking time according to the excellent Canadian Cooking Theory which is based on the thickness of the fish (see page 39), or use the simple rule of thumb of poaching for approximately 5 minutes to the lb (500g). Whichever method you choose, keep a watchful eye on the fish and do not let it overcook.

5 *Poaching steaks, cutlets or fillets.* The same principles as for poaching whole fish apply here, but steaks or cutlets to be served cold are particularly easy. Salmon steaks are a good example. Place them in the pan of stock, let the liquid bubble once, remove the pan from the heat and, with tongs or spatulas, carefully turn them over in the liquid and leave them until they are completely cold. They will be cooked to perfection.

Grilling

The three most important things to remember when grilling are:
- Always pre-heat the grill.
- Always oil the grill rack to prevent the fish from sticking.
- Always have tongs at hand to turn the fish.

All varieties of fish can be grilled, whole or in fillets, steaks, cutlets or kebabs; they can also be stuffed, parcelled in aluminium foil or vine leaves. In fact grilling is the simplest, quickest and most efficient way to cook fish.

Oily fish respond wonderfully to grilling. Large whole fish like herring and mackerel should be slashed three or four times down each side of the back and belly to allow the heat to penetrate. Smaller whole fish like sardines and sprats can be cooked swiftly without basting – their skins turn crisp and brown, making a lovely contrast to the oiliness of their flesh. White fish and shellfish need more care as they do not have this natural protection against intense heat. Well-flavoured white fish should be basted with a little oil and seasoning. Blander fish should be marinated in a blend of oil, citrus juice, spices and herbs – then basted with this mixture as they cook.

Grilling techniques

1   Oil the grill rack or kebab skewers to prevent the fish sticking.

2   Always pre-heat the grill.

3   Always plan to grill the fish just before you are ready to eat. Have salads, sauces and dressings ready so that the hot fish is served at its best.

4   Generally, grilled fish will take 4 to 12 minutes to cook, depending on its size and thickness and the distance of the grill rack from the heat. Juices which collect in the bottom of the grill pan should be poured over the fish when you serve it – or incorporated into a sauce or dressing.

5   Another kind of grilling popular on the continent uses a heavy cast-iron or cast-aluminium grill or griddle pan. Here the intense searing heat comes from below. This method is excellent for sardines, herring, anchovies and mackerel. The pan is not moved around on the stove; instead, you use tongs to turn the fish as you would over a barbecue or under a grill. The surface of these pans is sometimes corrugated but more often flat and smooth and should be lightly oiled and pre-heated before you start to cook.

6   Yet another way of grilling is to take out the grill rack, place the fish on the base of the grill pan and pour a little wine or stock around it. Continue to grill in the normal way. This is a method often used in restaurants. If you line the pan with foil first it is easy to remove the fish whole when cooked.

Steaming

The artistry of Japanese and Chinese cuisine is based on the skill of steaming, a most appealing and gentle way of cooking fish. The natural juices, flavour and shape of the fish are all retained – and the fish is usually served with an elegant garnish, some side dishes and sauces. In Britain, steaming seems to have cast aside its bland and frugal-image, and is once again popular with all who love the fresh clean taste of good food.

In the section on cooking equipment you will see that there are many excellent steamers available. However, one of the easiest and most effective ways of steaming a whole small fish, fillets, steaks or cutlets is to place the fish (with your choice of flavouring – herbs, spices and/or vegetables) between two heatproof plates over a pan of boiling water. Depending on the size and thickness of the fish, it will be exquisitely cooked in a matter of minutes.

Even so, when steaming – as with all other cooking methods – you must take care not to overcook the fish. Oversteamed fish tastes soggy and nothing much can be done to remedy the ruined texture of the flesh.

Steaming techniques

1   All white fish is suitable for steaming: fillets, steaks, cutlets and small to medium whole fish. Shellfish may also be steamed. In general, oily fish does not respond well to this method of cooking.

2   Consider the fish you are going to steam. If it is fine-flavoured, such as John Dory, bass or turbot, it will need very little in the way of seasoning – perhaps a dash of fresh lemon juice, or wine, with pepper and a sprig or two of fresh herbs. Blander, humbler fish will need a dash of wit and enthusiasm. Flavour and colour can be added with vigour: for instance, spring onion, garlic, ground spices, peppers, or fresh chilli peppers.

3   Calculate the cooking time according to the size and thickness of the fish (see page 39). Usually, 2–3in (5–7.5cm) of boiling water is adequate. If you need to top it up, make sure that you use more boiling water: adding cold water will halt the cooking process and spoil the fish.

4   Whichever type of steamer you use, the water should never come into contact with the fish.

5   If you wish, you can parcel the fish for steaming – together with extra seasonings or vegetables – in aluminium foil, paper, lettuce, spinach or cabbage leaves. The cooking juices will provide a moist dressing and should be added to the accompanying sauce.

Frying

This section covers deep-frying, stir-frying, shallow-frying, dry-frying and sautéeing. The two most important keys to the secret of success with each of these methods are:

● Use a good-quality clean oil (see page 56).
● Ensure that you heat the oil to the correct temperature.

If your frying is skilfully done, the results should be light and crisp with a minimum amount of residual oiliness. Most fish needs a protective coating before frying, particularly white fish which does not have a naturally oily skin. Try to steer clear of thick floury batters which form a soggy inner crust – look, for instance, at the apple or beer batters for deep-frying, or a swiftly made tempura batter (page 83). Alternatively, simply use milk, egg and fresh breadcrumbs, sesame seeds or oatmeal. Avoid lard, and use good-quality clean oil (see page 56) or a mixture of oil and butter, or clarified butter (see page 56). After cooking, oil can be strained and stored to use again a few more times, but discard it when it becomes cloudy or brown.

Finally, remember that all frying is potentially dangerous. Do not leave the pan unattended while you are cooking. When deep-frying, never over-fill the pan with oil. If the pan should catch fire, douse the flames with a damp teatowel. *Do not attempt to move the pan.*

Frying techniques

STIR-FRYING

1 Even distribution of heat is important for stir-frying which should, ideally, be done in a wok. A large shallow frying pan is a reasonable alternative if you are sure it makes a good contact with the source of heat.

2 Stir-frying is suitable only for small pieces of fish or shellfish. Prepare all the ingredients and assemble warmed plates and serving dishes before you begin to cook. Vegetables should be finely chopped. Side dishes, sauces or dips should be ready beforehand as the stir-fry will take no more than 2 minutes and should be served immediately.

3 About ½in (1cm) depth of oil in the wok or frying pan should be sufficient. Heat it up to the point where you can detect a slight haze – to test, drop in a small cube of bread, which should float and turn golden immediately. If you have a thermometer, use this to test the temperature which should be 350–380°F (180–195°C). Never leave a pan of hot oil unattended.

4 Always stir-fry small batches of fish at a time – stir and lift with a curved spatula, making sure that all the ingredients get their fair share of the searing heat of the pan. Keep the cooked fish warm on the rack attached to the wok, or on a plate lined with kitchen paper in a warm oven. Remember to re-heat the oil between each batch of stir-frying. If frying in batches, use a skimmer or slotted spoon to remove scraps between each frying session.

5 Beware of overcooking – most fish will be cooked in 30 seconds to 1½ minutes, depending on the size and thickness of the pieces and whether the flesh is soft or firm. One of the very few exceptions to this rule is squid, which should be treated like meat: either cook it quickly or braise/casserole it – in between, the results are rubbery.

SHALLOW-FRYING

Nearly all fish that is traditionally deep-fried can be shallow-fried – a safer, cleaner and more economical method. All types and cuts are suitable: oily and white, small and medium, whole fish, fillets, steaks and cutlets, strips (goujons) or cubes. White fish will generally need a protective coating.

1 For whole fish, fillets and steaks, calculate the cooking time (page 6) and decide on the batter, but do not dip the fish until just before you fry it.

2 Wash the fish and pat it dry before it is coated. Damp fish will produce a layer of steam which will prevent efficient searing and sealing.

3 Heat up a little oil in a sturdy frying pan until you detect a slight haze. It is important to sear and seal the fish on both sides before turning down the heat slightly and continuing to cook.

4 Do not crowd the pan with several pieces of fish – this will prevent air circulation, and you will end up unintentionally steaming the fish. Fry batches at a time if necessary, draining the cooked fish well on kitchen paper and keeping it warm on a serving dish in a low oven.

5 Always serve the fish straight away – prepare accompanying sauces or vegetables beforehand and time them accordingly. Sharp sauces or dressings, or a simple squeeze of fresh lemon or lime juice helps to offset the richness of some fried fish. Rich heavy sauces should be avoided.

DEEP-FRYING

All white fish can be deep-fried but the only oily fish that is suitable is whitebait.

1 The pan for deep-frying should be heavy and sturdy with deep straight sides. You can use a frying basket, or lift out the fish with a wire skimmer. The skimmer is also useful for removing crumbs and morsels that come away from the fish so that they do not burn, giving a bitter taste to the oil.

2 Deep-frying can also be done in a wok, but extra care must be taken as the oil will heat up very quickly, and you should not overfill the pan with oil or fish. A suitable depth of oil for deep-frying small batches of fish is one third of the way up the pan.

3 Watch the pan carefully as you *slowly* bring the oil up to temperature. As with all frying, make sure that the fish is patted dry before cooking as dampness will cause spitting and spluttering.

4 When you can detect a shimmering haze over the pan, test the temperature by dropping in a small cube of bread. If it immediately surfaces and browns, you are ready to fry. If you have a thermometer, use this to test the temperature which should be 350–390°F (180–198°C).

5 A thick batter is not essential. An alternative to batter is to brush with milk and then roll the fish in flour seasoned with a touch of finely chopped parsley, lemon rind or other flavourings. If you are using a batter, don't use the frying basket – the batter may cling to the basket, thereby exposing parts of the raw fish to the hot oil, which would then penetrate the flesh.

Baking

Gentle baking is a kind method of cooking whole fish, fillets or cutlets – and it greatly reduces cooking smells. Another advantage is that with added herbs, seasoning, stuffing, wine or stock the fish will remain moist and cook beautifully in its own juices. Fish can be first brushed with a little oil, a mixture of garlic paste and oil, melted butter, or natural yoghurt and spices. Whole fish or fillets can be baked on top of a bed of finely chopped vegetables and herbs, lightly moistened with wine, stock, or cider and so on.

Baking techniques

1 Always pre-heat the oven.

2 Calculate the cooking time according to the size and thickness of the fish (see page 39).

3 Whole fish baked uncovered is best stuffed to help retain its moistness.

4 All fish baked uncovered should be basted during cooking.

5 If you wish to cover the fish when baking, use lightly oiled greaseproof paper or a double thickness of aluminium foil.

6 Do not overcook the fish (test that it is ready by following the guidelines on page 39) – and remember that it will continue to cook in its hot dish even when you have removed it from the oven.

7 Do not throw away the cooking juices. They can be incorporated in a sauce, or saved for later use in fish soups or made-up dishes of left-overs like fish pies and risottos.

Braising

Braising is similar to oven baking. The difference is that more additional ingredients in the way of vegetables and liquid are used. There is a mingling exchange of flavours as the braise gently produces an all-in-one fish dish.

Braising presents a good opportunity to use a combination of economical fish. Adding smoked fish – for instance, smoked haddock or cod – will give an agreeable lift to the dish.

Because fish needs a comparatively short cooking time, the vegetables should be half-cooked before you add the fish. The braising pan should be covered with a lid or close-fitting layer of foil – and the braise can be gently cooked on the top of the stove or in the oven. Left-overs from a braise can be whizzed in a liquidiser or food processor to serve as a soup or use as a sauce for pasta.

Braising techniques

1 If using the oven, always pre-heat it.

2 Soften the prepared vegetables in a little oil before adding stock, wine or a mixture of wine and water. Heat until just under simmering point and braise until the vegetables are approximately two-thirds cooked. Now you add the fish: skinned fillets or cutlets, or large cubes.

3 Cover the braising pan or dish with a tight-fitting lid or a double thickness of aluminium foil and continue to cook gently on top of the stove or in a moderate oven.

4 Take care that the fish does not overcook, and remember that it will continue to cook in its dish after it has been removed from the heat.

Stewing

Stewing is really a kind of braise – or vice versa. Furthermore, some kinds of stew are really a type of soup! When cooking a stew of mixed fish, always add larger pieces or whole fish first, and the smaller pieces for the final minute or two. Most fish stews can be partially prepared and cooked in advance. Cook the vegetables and herbs in the liquid, then allow to cool and refrigerate. When ready to eat, re-heat, add the fish and cook for the specified time.

I once went to a wonderful party in Cornwall. It centred around a cauldron of fish stew. Fresh garden vegetables and herbs had been gently cooked in wine and stock with freshly picked tomatoes and slices of new potatoes. When they were nearly cooked through, a selection of fresh local fish was added – small whole ones and skinned and filleted pieces of larger ones. The stew was ready to serve in a matter of minutes. More than thirty people were given shallow bowls of this fabulous dish, strewn with more fresh herbs – and with garlic mayonnaise if they wanted it. It struck me that this must be the best method of cheap mass feeding since chilli con carne!

Home smoking

Fish can be hot-smoked or cold-smoked. In cold-smoking, the fish is cured by smoking at an air temperature not higher than 92°F (33°C) to avoid 'cooking' the flesh. All cold-smoked fish, with the exception of salmon, should be cooked before they are eaten. In hot-smoking, the temperature is higher in order to cook the flesh of the fish as it smokes – it does not then need further cooking. Before fish is smoked, it needs brining in a basic solution of salt and water, the strength of which can vary according to the nature of the fish and the flavour you require. Additional flavourings can be introduced in the way of molasses, honey or alcohol. Fuller instructions will be found in the booklets which accompany most home-smoking kits.

Smoking fish is a traditional way of preserving, now exclusively used for the flavour it imparts. This will be largely determined by the wood used to smoke it. Use only hardwood dust, as freshly sawn as possible, and preferably an unseasoned greenwood as the sap contains sugar. In the case of oak wood, for example, you can actually smell the sweetness – fruit woods such as apple and cherry have very distinctive flavours too. Dutch eel smokers use beech which gives a pleasant nutty flavour, and some Scandinavian smokers use very fine birch twigs to make the fire and then sprinkle on a small amount of juniper for extra tang.

However, most of us do not have access to a forest of trees and have to buy a pack of sawdust for home-smoking. Small, compact smoking kits can be bought at specialist kitchen or fishing tackle shops. They are fine to use in the kitchen – though it is better to set them up in the garden or back yard or even on a balcony in good weather when there is little wind, because the smell of indoor smoking does tend to permeate the home. My home smoker takes four medium-sized whole fish or up to eight fillets. In common with other smokers, one or two metal containers are provided for methylated spirits: filled, lighted and positioned under the smoking box, these provide the source of heat. From my experience, this is a haphazard and inefficient method of producing heat, as they constantly blow out or are stifled through lack of circulating air. If you have gas rings it is far easier to stand the smoking box over one or two of them for good results.

It is quite easy to construct your own large home smoker from a beer barrel or galvanised dustbin. The top and bottom should be removed and the barrel or bin supported on bricks to keep it off the ground. Make a fire using dry hardwood shavings or barbecue charcoal beneath the barrel. *Never* use firelighters or anything that might taint the fish.

When the fire is going well, cover it with damped-down sawdust to form a smouldering heap which creates cool smoke. Suspend the prepared fish on rods across the top of the barrel which should be covered with a heavy damp cloth to retain as much smoke as possible. Take care to keep the fire low: a temperature of 80°F (30°C) is sufficient. If you want hot-smoked fish, complete the smoking process and then increase the heat of the fire in order to cook the fish. Alternatively, finish in a domestic oven.

I have found home-smoking rewarding. A meal of fillets of grey mullet smoked over sawdust with a handful of pine needles and served warm with new potatoes and field mushrooms stands out in my memory. I have also enjoyed fresh warm smoked mackerel which is noticeably more succulent than the commercially smoked variety.

Barbecueing

Barbecueing is one of the oldest and most creative ways of cooking fish. On the seashore, in the garden . . . even propping up a hibachi on the (secure) window ledge of a small flat will evoke all the delightful sensations of alfresco eating. Barbecueing is always a social event, a marvellous ice-breaker and a great opportunity for everyone to offer expert advice.

Most of the rules for grilling need to be observed, but in the outdoors the scent of aromatic herbs and spices with sizzling fish seem to inspire greater spontaneity. Do especially remember to oil the grill rack, fish-shaped grids or kebab skewers.

Some advance planning is necessary. Most obviously, you must make sure that you have enough fuel – charcoal lumps or briquettes, or good dry hardwood. Put the barbecue in a sheltered area and seat the guests upwind of it.

Before I begin cooking, I always load up a tray with tongs, spatulas, oven gloves, teatowels, basting brush and herbed oils so that I don't have to fly back through the garden to the kitchen at a critical moment.

I light the charcoal or wood fire about half an hour or so before I begin to cook. Burning charcoal needs to turn from a red glow to grey, which is the right time to start cooking. Wood is more temperamental: get a good flame going, build up the fire and let it roar away until it dies down to glowing embers. A good thick bed of embers will produce plenty of cooking heat for at least an hour. If you like, half-cooked potatoes in their jackets, and foil parcels of vegetables can be pushed into the embers half an hour before you cook the fish. Otherwise, when the barbecue is lit and behaving itself, bring out bowls of salads, cold or hot herbed rice, hot potatoes and hunks of crusty bread. All manner of side dishes, dips and dressings can be prepared well in advance.

As fish needs only a little cooking time, you can cook quantities in batches for large numbers of people. Otherwise include mixed seafood kebabs which take very little space on the grill and look beautiful, or small oily fish barbecued just as they are. White fish should be marinated or at least basted while it cooks. Alternatively, try parcelling mixed morsels of seafood in aluminium foil with a little finely chopped fresh ginger, spring onion and garlic. Cubes of lobster can be alternated with king prawns on skewers for very special meals – a little of this superbly flavoured seafood will go a long way. Finally, do not forget to put out the fire safely.

Microwave cooking

The results of cooking fish and shellfish in a microwave oven can be compared to steaming, although the microwave technique is neither 'dry' nor 'moist' but electro-magnetic. It is certainly a healthy way to cook fish, as there is little or no contact with water and the vitamin, mineral and protein content is fully retained.

The air in the oven is unheated. Instead, very high frequency radio waves cause the water molecules in food to vibrate. Thus the *water* in the food is heated up and in turn the food itself is heated. This process takes a very short time, but then usually the food must 'stand' for a while after the microwave oven has been switched off. This is because the water molecules are agitated faster than they can transfer their energy to the other molecules – and during the standing time the cooking temperature in the food rises until the cooking is complete. Bearing this in mind, it is important to cook fish for the minimum recommended time to avoid overcooking and spoiling its tender flesh.

Once you have grasped the principle of microwave cooking, you must remember that, as with conventional cookers, you should adapt the cooking times to your own particular model of microwave oven. The timer control is most important as microwave cooking is judged by *time* only – not by time and temperature. Cooking times and power levels will be given in the instruction book supplied with your particular model of oven. Remember that, when cooking large whole fish, the microwave energy may penetrate unevenly, and unless your microwave has a turntable, you should turn the fish from time to time.

The microwave oven is also invaluable for quick de-frosting. If your microwave does not have a de-frosting facility, it is possible to de-frost by giving short one-minute bursts of microwave energy with intervening standing times, and continuing until the fish is completely thawed. It is most important not to toughen (or even partly cook) the fish by over-de-frosting.

Bear in mind, too, the standing time when the tissue heat continues to rise. It is wiser to remove the fish from the oven while still slightly icy.

Microwave techniques

COOKING FISH AND SHELLFISH

1   As with all microwave cooking, always cook fish and shellfish in non-metallic containers, and avoid dishes which have gold or silver patterns.

2   Always cook fish and shellfish for the minimum recommended time to avoid overcooking, remembering that cooking continues during the standing time after it has been removed from the oven. Always cover the fish with kitchen paper or a plate.

3   When cooking whole fish – e.g. herring, mackerel or sole – lightly score the skin two or three times on each side to speed up cooking and to prevent the skin bursting. Remove the head and tail from large fish to enable them to fit in the oven. Turn them over halfway through cooking.

4   Brush the fish with a sauce or added stock according to your recipe, put the fish in a suitable dish and cover with kitchen paper.

5   The dish will not need turning around during the cooking process if your microwave has a turntable. Otherwise turn the fish halfway through cooking and turn the fish over too. Rearrange whole small fish halfway through cooking by moving fish in the centre of the dish to the outside and vice versa.

6   When cooking fish fillets, steaks and cutlets, season, add a little lemon juice, oil or stock according to your recipe, and arrange them in a suitable dish, securing any flaps with wooden cocktail sticks. Cover with kitchen paper or a lid or plate. The dish will not need turning around during the cooking process if the microwave has a turntable. Otherwise turn halfway through cooking. Arrange cutlets in the dish with the thinner parts towards the centre.

7   When cooking braises or stews, the dish will need an occasional stir during the cooking process; alternatively, give the dish a half- or quarter-turn from time to time.

8   Fish cannot be deep-fried in a microwave. It could be shallow-fried using a browning dish, but in practice it is as easy and quick to do this in the conventional way, especially as you will want to turn the fish and keep in close contact with it as it cooks.

9   To re-heat boiled shellfish in the microwave (or re-cook it in a made-up dish), follow the guide for fillets, steaks and cutlets given in point 6 (above). Lobster or crawfish tails will need turning half-way through the cooking time. A whole lobster will need standing time before serving.

DE-FROSTING FISH AND SHELLFISH

1   The timing of de-frosting depends on the size – and most importantly the *thickness* – of the whole fish, fillets or cutlets.

2   De-frosting should be carried out on a 50% (de-frost) setting, or on 30% in cookers with a variable power control.

3   Whole fish, fillets or cutlets should be placed in a single layer in an appropriate dish. Alternatively, an unopened paper or plastic package of commercially frozen whole fish, fillets or cutlets can be placed intact on to the base of the oven – in this case, de-frost for half the recommended time, then give the package a quarter-turn before completing the remaining de-frosting time.

4   Fish should always feel completely cold when thawed. If it feels warm – even just in parts – set it aside from the cooker until it is completely thawed.

5   Packs of fillets or cutlets can be held under cold running water in order to separate them, and in the same way icy particles can be washed away from whole de-frosted fish – especially around the head and belly cavity.

6   Small shellfish, like prawns or scallops, should be spread out on a shallow dish, turned over once during the minimum recommended de-frosting time, and should feel cool and soft to the touch. Similarly, larger shellfish, such as lobster tails and crab claws, should be de-frosted for half the recommended time before being turned over to finish the de-frosting.

7   Whole packages of shelled shellfish, like crab meat, prawns, scallops and so on, can be de-frosted intact in their plastic tubs or blocks, or turned out into a suitable dish. Half-way through the recommended de-frosting time, turn over the package or block and gently stir or fork through to allow even penetration of microwave energy.

8   Fish pies, stews, flans and other pre-cooked frozen fish dishes can be de-frosted in the microwave using a 50% setting. It is important to re-heat the dish *gently* when cooking – if full power is used to re-heat pre-cooked dishes, there is a danger that the sauce, pastry or topping will overcook before the main body of the dish is heated through: therefore use a 60–70% setting to continue the cooking process.

Equipment and utensils

Good sharp knives! These are the most important utensils you will need when preparing fresh fish. Pots, pans and a colander are basic to most kitchens, but you may also like to consider buying some of the equipment which is special to fish and shellfish.

Filleting knife: The long flexible blade is designed for easing around the bones and flesh of the fish. An 8in (20cm) blade is the most versatile.

Broad heavy knife: Use to slice steaks and cutlets.

Small flexible knife: This should have a sharp point for cutting through fish skin. Use it for filleting small fish such as plaice, sole or herring: it is good for following the bone very closely.

Sharpener: Depending on the type of blade edge a knife has, you can sharpen it up on a steel, stone or patent sharpener. For the sake of safety, and your knives' well-being, store them in a knife block or special rack, so that they do not jostle and become blunted against other cooking paraphernalia in your kitchen drawers.

Oyster knife: A most useful, cheap and effective implement. The short, stout, stubby blade can also be used for opening other shellfish, such as scallops.

Fish scaler: There are several types available, all inexpensive and effective, but the back of a stout knife works just as well.

Scissors: All-purpose kitchen scissors are invaluable for cutting off fins and snipping out backbones and rib bones. The attractive pointed Chinese scissors are useful for fiddly snipping jobs.

Tongs: These are essential for turning fish on the barbecue or grill.

Fish slices: Also essential for general fish cookery and you will need two for lifting out cooked whole fish.

Perforated spoon: Use this for fishing out quenelles and dumplings, or fritters and croquettes from hot oil, and for skimming stock.

Large skimmer: A wire-mesh skimmer can be used in the same way as a perforated spoon, and is the best way of lifting fish from poaching liquid or cooking oil.

Pastry or basting brush: This is especially effective when grilling and barbecueing, and more thorough than using a spoon.

Kebab skewers: These should be flat rather than round so that the cubes of fish or shellfish stay in place as you turn them.

Shallow wire sieve: Use for straining stocks and sauces and removing deep-fried fish from the pan.

Large colander: This should be metal rather than plastic. Use it for straining fish stocks or court bouillon.

Wok: A round-bottomed wok is best for a gas cooker; the flat-base type is best for an electric cooker or solid-fuel stove. If the wok is used over a gas flame, a metal collar or trivet keeps it standing firmly. A small rack placed in the centre of the wok can support a plate for steaming fish, and a semi-circular rack clipped on the rim is used for draining fried morsels of fish as you cook them in batches.

Fish kettle: Use for poaching large whole fish, or boiling large shellfish (watch out for splashes, as the pan is shallow), or as a bain marie for keeping sauces warm. A perforated rack with lifting handles accommodates a large fish in the kettle, and you will need to use two burners on a gas or electric stove. A fish kettle is not an essential item to buy as you can hire them from some kitchen or catering shops or improvise with a large roasting tin lined with aluminium foil (see page 40). Consider storage space before buying a fish kettle as they are large – 24in (60cm) – and unwieldy.

Liquidiser or food processor: Most people are familiar with these time-saving appliances, which are wonderfully versatile for making sauces, mousses, pâtés and pastes for marinades. I have a personal preference for preparing some things by hand when I have the time – you can achieve different and varying textures, rewardingly unlike the uniform consistency of whizzed-up ingredients.

Paella: This is the name of the shallow two-handled pan used for making the traditional dish named after it. It is not expensive, and can be used for all kinds of seafood and rice dishes – or for gentle poaching. It is an excellent all-purpose pan for cooking risottos or similar complete meals, and can be taken straight from the stove to the table.

Picks and crackers: Most usually for crab and lobster, these can be bought at specialist kitchen shops. But you can improvise and make a thorough job of picking out all the precious meat with butcher's skewers and small teaspoons. A wooden mallet or rolling pin with which you can give the claws a smart thwack is better than crackers or hammers, which tend to splinter the shell rather than producing a clean crack.

Cutlery: Why special fish knives and forks – currently rather unfashionable – for eating fish? A fish knife is perfectly designed, with its gently curved tip and soft-edged blade, for manipulating fish served on the bone.

Barbecue: Hibachis are the smallest portable barbecues. They come in various shapes and sizes and are very adaptable. They can stand low on the ground, or on a garden wall or window ledge. The brazier-type barbecue, with tubular legs or pedestal stand, is the essential colour-supplement patio barbecue. But if you have a sheltered area in your garden, the ultimate barbecue must be a permanent brick or stone affair.

Miscellaneous: Ramekins, soufflé dishes, gratin dishes, casseroles and tart and pie dishes.

Fish-shaped grid: This is effective for barbecueing whole fish, which will not break up when turned and any stuffing will stay in place. It is available in various fishy shapes and sizes and is usually cheap – although good-quality nickel-plated grids are expensive. Remember to oil the grid before use.

Home smoker: An interesting alternative to buying ready-smoked fish and shellfish, is to obtain one of these, available from good kitchen shops. You can buy various 'hot' or 'cold' smokers. The most useful for the average household is probably a standard compact smoker which takes four to six whole fish. Full instructions and recipes are supplied with good-quality smokers, and the main advantage of owning one is the pleasure gained from experimenting with and eating fish smoked to your personal liking as well as avoiding commercial colorants and additives.

General notes on basic ingredients

Oils

Fresh fish deserves to be cooked in good-quality oil. Safflower, sunflower and corn oil are all suitable: they are polyunsaturated, and their lightness does not compete with the flavour of fish. The superb flavour of olive oil is more suited to robust fish dishes. Avoid lard and blended vegetable oils.

Butter

Ideally, butter should be clarified for sautéeing. This eliminates the salt, and any moisture, although you can, of course, buy unsalted butter in the first place.

To clarify butter, gently heat it in a heavy pan. Do not let it colour as it melts and cooks: skim off any scum or impurities, then strain through a fine mesh seive lined with muslin or cheesecloth into a basin. Let it settle, then pour it into another basin, leaving any sediment behind. It can now be stored in the normal way, and used as required.

Butter is a saturated fat and should be used cautiously and in moderation. Fish swimming in butter is neither pleasant nor necessary. However, the flavour good butter imparts to a dish is incomparable – for example, when small nuts of it are dotted on white fillets before grilling, or when it is used exquisitely *à la meunière*. Margarine does not work successfully for frying or sautéeing – it is better to dry- or shallow-fry using oil.

Herbs and spices

Try to use fresh herbs wherever possible. Good-quality dried or freeze-dried herbs are an acceptable substitute, but they must be stored in a cool dark place – throw away musty old herbs that have been kept for longer than six months.

Use a subtle touch with herbs – their flavour should enhance rather than overwhelm the fish. Bland fish can be transformed with a spicy herb, like fresh coriander leaves or dill.

You will appreciate the flavour of spices if you grind them freshly when cooking. Most spices will keep for years, if stored whole. Ready-ground spices lose their flavour after a few months. Here are some herbs and spices that are particularly good with fish.

anise (or aniseed): A little of this distinctive flavour goes a long way. Do not confuse it with star anise, which is a different plant.

Basil: Use only the fresh herb. There are many varieties, and the sweet aroma and taste varies in strength. It is suitable for fish and pasta dishes, in sauces and soups.

Bay: The leaves are effective dried or fresh – they can be used in many fish dishes: whole or crumbled. Their sweetish flavour is good in marinades, and they add flavour and a decorative flourish to fish kebabs.

Cardamom: A pale green pod containing little black seeds – one of the ingredients of an authentic 'curry'. I use it lightly crushed in oil-based marinades. Dried cardamom loses its flavour quickly.

Cayenne: A fierce pepper, pale orange-red – use with discretion.

Chervil: A delicately flavoured herb which looks like parsley but tastes completely different, this makes a pretty garnish, and interesting mild sauces for white fish.

Chillies: Do not wipe or touch your eyes after finely chopping or de-seeding these fiery peppers. They vary in strength and size, can be fresh or dried, red or green, and are an essential ingredient in Indian cooking. They are good in some marinades. Tabasco (chilli sauce) can also be used sparingly to pep up a fish dish.

Chives: Always snip chives with scissors as chopping with a knife squashes and bruises the leaves. They are an attractive garnish and have a milder taste than onion.

Coriander, fresh leaves: Also known as Chinese parsley, this herb does indeed look rather like parsley but the leaves are flatter and the taste is strong, spicy and lemony. It combines superbly with fish, but use it with discretion as it can be overpowering.

Coriander seeds: Good crushed for use in marinades, and whole or ground for spicy sauces. The flavour is mild and orangy.

Dill: Dill weed and seeds are very popular with fish. Dill weed is essential for Gravad Lax, the Scandinavian salmon dish (see page 234). The leaves make a pretty garnish, and both leaves and flowers may be used to give a mild spicy flavour in cooking fish. The seeds are used for pickling.

Fennel: The feathery fronds have a strong taste of aniseed. Use the chopped leaves in sauces and dressings, sprigs for tucking into the belly of a whole fish or as a garnish. The bruised and cracked branches of wild fennel will flavour and scent a whole fish.

Garlic: Crushed in marinades, dressings and sauces, its pungent flavour is good with many fish dishes – I particularly like a hint of it with shellfish.

Ginger: Fresh root ginger should be pale brown with a silky smooth skin. It must be peeled before being very finely sliced or grated to use in marinades, in dishes like stir-fries, or in parcels of fish for steaming. The taste is strong and sharp, so use it with discretion. Dried ground ginger has a completely different taste and is usually used for cake making.

Marjoram: The fragrant flavour of this herb is especially good with blander types of fish. It is closely related to oregano: dried oregano is a good substitute for fresh marjoram.

Mint: There are many varieties. Used in stuffings, it gives a fresh fragrant taste to fish; it is good combined with fruit sauces and helps offset the richness of oily fish.

Nutmeg: Use freshly grated nutmeg when baking white fish, in crumbled toppings for pies or in sauces.

Oregano: Available fresh and dried, its distinctive taste is excellent with baked fish and in seafood sauces with pasta.

Paprika: This spice is made from ground red peppers, and often confused with the much hotter cayenne pepper. I don't think it does a lot for fish, except as a colourful garnish on sauces, salads or dips.

Parsley: The most commonly used herb with a marvellous flavour – compatible with all kinds of fish and shellfish, in sauces, stuffings, salads and as a garnish. There are two varieties – the familiar, dark green, curly-leaved parsley and the stronger, paler, flat-leaved variety.

Peppercorns: Black, white or green, these are always best freshly ground. White peppercorns are the inner part of the fully ripe berry; black peppercorns are the whole immature berry, milder but more aromatic than white pepper. Green peppercorns are soft – undried and unripe – with a fresh pungent taste.

Rosemary: This spiky-leaved evergreen herb is good with oily fish. Throw branches or sprigs on to the barbecue embers to scent the fish.

Saffron: The wonderful flavour and colour of saffron is incomparable in rice and fish dishes. It is expensive, but you need to use only a little of the thread-like stigma (from the crocus flower) – infuse before adding it to your recipe. A powdered form is available in small sealed sachets – also expensive, but a satisfactory and convenient substitute.

Sage: A popular and pretty herb with velvety silver leaves. Good with baked fish and in stuffings.

Tarragon: Two kinds are available but only 'French' tarragon has the fine flavour. Avoid the bland, tasteless 'Russian' tarragon. Tarragon is the classic herb to use with fish in sauces, stuffings or as a garnish.

Thyme: A good herb to use with oily fish, especially when combined with lemon. It is also good with blander types of fish, and in fish sauces for pasta. I use wild thyme branches on my barbecue.

Herbed oils for barbecueing and grilling

Fish needs a protective brushing with oil when exposed to the intense heat of the barbecue or grill. Using a herbed oil will produce wonderfully aromatic or pungent results.

Use any favourite fresh herbs, one single variety or a mixture: not too many. About one third herbs to two thirds oil is the right proportion. Sterilise and dry a wide-necked jar, and push a perfectly dry bunch of herbs inside (they can be slightly bruised or coarsely chopped if you wish). Fill the jar with a light oil, such as safflower or sunflower. Remember that olive oil already has its own distinctive flavour. Cover tightly – there should be no air gap at the top of the jar. Store in a cool place for three or four weeks, giving the jar a gentle shake from time to time. You can then strain the oil through a muslin-lined funnel into another sterilised jar or bottle – and use as required.

Oil can be creamed with garlic paste to make a quick, easy coating for grilled or baked fish.

Flour, breadcrumbs, oatmeal and other protective coatings

Recipes for batters are given on page 83.

Dredging fish with flour, or rolling it in breadcrumbs, oatmeal, sesame seeds or ground nuts, are all effective methods of protecting its tender flesh during cooking.

Use a good-quality white flour, lightly seasoned – perhaps with a little grated lemon rind, a pinch of cayenne or a grating of nutmeg. Brown wholemeal flour gives a speckled appearance and a nutty taste, but does not adhere as well because of its grainy texture. Dip the fish in a little beaten egg or milk before coating with flour – the action of dipping and dredging should be quick, light, flowing and done immediately before cooking.

Do not use bright-yellow dyed packaged 'breadcrumbs': they are horrible. Home-made wholemeal or white breadcrumbs made from day-old bread are easy to prepare – and they can be stored in a jar in the refrigerator for a few days. Again, the fish will need swiftly and lightly dipping in beaten egg before coating.

Oatmeal or oatflakes are ideal coatings for herring and other oily fish. Sesame seeds or finely ground nuts add flavour to bland white fish, croquettes and cakes. They can also give a pleasant crunch and appearance when lightly spinkled over white fillets to be grilled, and make a tasty garnish or topping for simple fish dishes and pies.

Cream and milk

In my view, thick, rich, creamy sauces contradict and at times suffocate the light, delicate nature of most fish. Use a little cream now and then to thicken simple sauces; or try using low-fat dairy products such as fromage blanc, crème fraîche, quark or smetana. Skimmed or semi-skimmed milk is fine for poaching and gives excellent results in sauces.

Sea vegetables

In common with many people I prefer to call seaweeds 'sea vegetables' because the word 'weed' implies that they are plants of no value. Nothing could be further from the truth. Eating seaweed is not a new idea – nor a cranky fad. Two thousand years ago the Imperial Court of China was importing highly prized sea vegetables from Korea, and our Celtic and Viking ancestors used to chew on dulse as they travelled.

You may be familiar with regional specialities like Welsh laverbread and East Anglian samphire, and perhaps you know of the Irish blancmange made with carragheen. Dried seaweeds are mostly imported from Japan where some are grown commercially. They are becoming popular in the West and can be bought in health food shops or oriental supermarkets. These give a really original spark to fish soups, salads and stir-fry dishes, and I instantly developed a liking for their flavour when I first tried cooking with them.

All sea vegetables are a rich source of protein, vitamins and minerals. Most are also very salty. The following guide lists a selection of the most commonly found – fresh and dried.

Dried sea vegetables

These are almost exclusively from Japan and usually need soaking before use. You will find instructions on the packets.

Arame: An oriental sea vegetable with a soft texture and mild sweet flavour. The fine shreds are used as a vegetable or in soups.

Carragheen: Available dried and used as a setting or thickening agent (like agar agar). It also adds flavour to stews and sauces, and is well known in Ireland.

Dulse: Purple-red in colour, this is the richest in iron of all sea vegetables. It has a spicy flavour which is good in soups.

Kombu: Used to make basic Japanese stock, as well as being cooked as a vegetable in its own right. It is used in the Far East and also known around Atlantic shores by various names including wrack, tangle and oarweed. Instant kombu will add a refreshing piquancy to many fish dishes.

Mekabu: A relative of wakame, which on deep-frying in oil opens into a flower shape in seconds and can be served, like potato crisps, as a snack, sprinkled with fresh lemon juice.

Nori: Known in the West as laver, nori is entirely produced from cultivated plants. Usually sold in sheet form, it has a mild flavour, is very versatile and is the richest sea-vegetable source of protein and vitamins. It is thought to help decrease cholesterol in the body. Chiefly used to wrap sushi, it is also used as a garnish. Wild nori, or laver, has a stronger taste (see 'Laver', below).

Wakame: A leafy sea vegetable which can simply be soaked and added to a dressed green salad – it unfurls into a delicate green leaf – or used in soups or as a flavouring. It has a mild flavour, and is rich in calcium.

Fresh sea vegetables

Carragheen: Also known as Irish moss, the branched fronds, purplish in colour, are common on most rocky coasts – particularly Cornwall and Ireland – at deep tide level, so collect at spring tide. Carefully soak and clean this sea plant before using it chopped in fish and vegetable soups, or as a gelling agent in a fish mousse.

Dulse: The dark red fronds can be found growing profusely around rocky shores from spring to autumn. They can be eaten raw, or simmered until tender and combined in small quantities in seafood salads and stews. Try a little with steamed or stir-fried potatoes.

Laver: Known as sloke in Ireland, slake in Scotland, blackbutter in Devon and nori in Japan (where it is cultivated), it is found at middle to high tide level on rocks. It is higher in protein (percentage by weight) than the soya bean – and is most commonly cooked down to a thick purée called laverbread. This is often coated with oatmeal and served with bacon and cockles.

Oarweed: Also known as wrack or tangle, this is very common around our coasts. It can easily be dried and used in the same way as wakame or mekabu.

Sea lettuce: Found at middle to high tide level on rocks, this thin translucent green sea vegetable can be used in seafood salads, or as a dressing or flavouring.

Wild vegetables

Everyone can sample the original flavour – wild and intriguing – of the cultivated vegetables we buy or grow. Many so-called weeds are the ancestors of cultivated vegetables – for instance, Alexanders was introduced to Europe by the Romans and cultivated up to the seventeenth or eighteenth century, when it was displaced by celery.

Plants growing near the sea, like fennel and samphire, seem to have a special affinity with fish. Take an illustrated guide with you when out foraging, and only pick plants which have a strong foothold in the environment. Do not pick rare or endangered species – all plants are protected under the law, and 62 of them (none listed here) may not be picked under any circumstances. The Nature Conservancy Council (address on page 297) will send details on request.

Cornsalad: The cultivated variety, also known as lamb's lettuce, is popular in France, Italy and the USA, and it is now available in many greengrocers in this country. In its wild form (it grows commonly all over the British Isles) it has a tangy sharpness and is rich in vitamin C. I find it an excellent salad herb, and it makes a mixed seafood salad a pleasing starter.

Good King Henry: Also known as mercury or Lincolnshire spinach, this is best in the springtime, cooked like spinach. The raw young leaves may be used in salads. It is delicious served with fish.

Horseradish: We think of this perennial herb mainly as an accompaniment to roast beef – but a suggestion of its fiery flavour is excellent with some of the blander species of fish. Fresh horseradish sauce is far superior of the ready-made varieties. The complex root system is fiddly to clean, peel and grate but well worth the effort. Once added to mayonnaise or a sauce, it can be refrigerated in the normal way. The plant, which has large, long, shiny leaves, is common in fields and on roadsides and waste land from May to September; it is not so common in the South West.

Fennel: The delicate fronds of wild fennel grow in profusion around the sea shore. You can use its feathery leaves in stuffings, salads and sauces. The stems (which can also be dried and stored ready for tossing on to an aromatic barbecue fire) can be bruised and used as a base for baking whole fish – like grey mullet. Wild fennel has a more decisive flavour and bite than the bulb and leaves of the cultivated Florentine fennel, which is the one sold in shops.

Samphire, marsh samphire: This is special to East Anglia, although it does grow elsewhere. It can be used as a vegetable or pickled. It is best collected at low tide in high summer and needs careful washing. It is extremely salty, deliciously crunchy – rather like cucumber in texture – and I have seen it, imported from France, on London fish stalls, ready to eat raw as a marvellous side dish with fish or shellfish. Soak it first to lessen the saltiness, rinse it well, then cook it very briefly (about 5 minutes) in lavish quantities of boiling water.

Samphire, rock samphire: This is not related to marsh samphire but does bear some resemblance to it with its fleshy succulent leaves. It is prolific in the south of Britain and found clinging on cliffs or in the crevices of rocks. Most people find it too strange-tasting to enjoy raw, but cooked or pickled it is very good indeed, and is a rich source of iron and vitamin C. It is at its best in spring and early summer.

Sea kale: Where I live there are just a few sparse patches of sea kale, so I have tried it only once or twice – and the tender stalks have a most delicate flavour. It is plentiful on shingle beaches elsewhere, and the stalks are blanched as they grow through layers of pebbles and sand. Cook it like asparagus, and serve it with fish and a simple sauce or dressing.

Sorrel: This has a lemony taste, pleasantly sour, and is very popular in France where it is cultivated. Wild sorrel is common throughout the British Isles, and you need only a handful or two to make a sorrel sauce or stuffing, both of which are classic accompaniments to fish. Wild sorrel is tougher and more acid than cultivated sorrel, so choose only young tender leaves. Cook it like spinach, though it wilts more dramatically. The chemicals in the plant react to iron, so use only stainless steel knives and pans to prepare and cook it. It can be used raw in salads.

Stocks, sauces, dressings and marinades

Let the flavour of fish speak for itself. Aim only to enhance it with complementary sauces and dressings – bear in mind the character of the fish when making your choice. Oily fish respond well to tart fruity sauces, white fish of all kinds are lovely with simple sauces enhanced with their cooking juices. Sauces based on reduction – long-simmering vegetables or fruit with herbs or spices – puréed and lightened with yoghurt or fromage blanc, and with a tablespoon or two of the fishy cooking juices added, are fresh-tasting, pretty and delightful.

Nevertheless, the classic béchamel or 'white' sauce and hollandaise remain standard favourites. I suggest, however, that you use them sparingly, cook them with care and make them with only the best ingredients. Do not spoil a fine fresh fish with a badly made sauce.

The consistency of sauces should vary according to the part they play in the recipe. A sauce served separately needs to be flowing, whereas a sauce that is an integral part of the dish needs to be slightly thicker and of coating consistency. Thicker sauces can be used to bind or hold together made-up fish dishes such as rissoles and fish pies.

When using wine in cooking fish or sauce making, it is often fine to use a cheap bottle or left-overs; but if you are cooking a really superior fish, it is wise to use a better-quality wine.

It is fine to resort to good-quality vegetable or bouillon stock cubes if you are in a hurry. There are also one or two satisfactory fish stock cubes appearing in shops which are quite acceptable for the occasional speedy fish dish.

Marinades

The flesh of fish is naturally tender and (with the exception of octopus) does not need beating, boiling or marinating to tenderise it further. The usual purpose behind marinating fish, therefore, is to impregnate the flesh with subtle infusions of aromatic or rather more pungent flavours, and it is particularly good for fish which has a mild or bland flavour. A marinade can also enhance and emphasise the flavour of more superior fish, and helps to keep the flesh from drying out when cooked by the high heat of a grill, barbecue or oven.

The combinations of ingredients which can be used in marinades are endless. They may be mixtures of herbs and spices, perhaps a little sliced onion or spring onion, garlic, wine or cider, oil or yoghurt, vinegar or juice from citrus fruits, mustard, soy sauce, tomato purée, Worcestershire sauce or rice wine. Sometimes the ingredients for a marinade can be cooked first to extract the flavours and aroma. Marinades containing citrus juice may be used to 'cook' and 'pickle' or 'cure' raw fish as in Gravad Lax (page 234), Sashimi (page 253) and Seviche (page 268). The marinade can also be used to baste the fish while it is cooking, and can be transformed into a sauce or dressing for the final dish.

The tender flesh of fish will become soggy and flaky if it is marinated for too long. As a general rule, it is only necessary to marinate whole fish for about 4 hours; fillets need a little less time and cubes of fish or shellfish only 30 minutes.

Use a glass or earthenware dish for marinating if you are using citrus juice. Turn the fish from time to time. If marinating a whole thick fish, make criss-cross slashes along the body so that the marinating mixture or paste can fully penetrate the flesh. Brush or spread the marinade into the cuts and turn the fish two or three times as it lies in a cool place.

Pickling, spicing or sousing fish is a particularly good method for oily varieties as the acid of the marinade offsets the richness of the fish. It is also helpful in softening the small bones of tiny fish like pilchards, sardines and sprats. Many spiced or pickled fish dishes are best kept for 3 or 4 days before eating – and will, in fact, remain fresh for some time. The simple procedure for Gravad Lax produces an exquisitely flavoured salmon dish, but it can be used with equal success for the more humble mackerel (see page 234). Always remember that fish is a most versatile food, so experiment and substitute different marinade ingredients and species of fish and shellfish, according to season and availability.

All-round marinade

My personal favourite 'all-round' marinade, given below, lends itself to countless adaptations.

Juice and a little of the grated rind of 1 orange

Juice and a little of the grated rind of 1 lemon

An equal amount of good olive oil

Coarsely crushed black peppercorns

Crushed coriander seeds

2 spring onions or 1 shallot, finely chopped

1 tablespoon parsley, finely chopped

Whisk all the ingredients together, place in an earthenware or glass dish (*not* metal) and marinate the fish in it for 30 minutes to 4 hours. The marinating time will depend on whether you are using small cubes of fish, fillets or a whole fish.

Stocks

Good stocks take very little time to make. They make a marked difference to the finished result of poached fish, and give body and taste to soups and sauces. They can be prepared a day or two in advance and stored in the refrigerator. Stocks may also be frozen in an ice-cube tray and stored in the freezer – particularly useful when you need just a tablespoon or two of fish stock.

You can take short cuts and surround the fish you are poaching with finely chopped vegetables, herbs and fish trimmings as it simmers in wine and water, thereby producing a well flavoured stock while cooking the fish at the same time. This stock can then be reduced to make a sauce, or added to a dressing.

Various different herbs and combinations of vegetables and other seasonings can be added to the following basic stocks, according to the character of the fish you are cooking.

Court bouillon

This, the most basic stock, can be used for poaching fish and shellfish. After the cooked fish has been removed from the court bouillon, it can be reduced by boiling down hard to half or one third of the original quantity, which concentrates the flavour and thickens the stock.

Makes about 2½ pints (1.4 litres)

2 pints (1 litre) water

8oz (250g) carrots, chopped

2 medium onions, sliced

1–2 sticks celery

1 bouquet garni (parsley, bay leaf and thyme)

Pinch of salt

10fl oz (300ml) white wine or cider

6 black peppercorns, crushed

Put everything except the peppercorns into a large saucepan. Simmer for 40 minutes, adding the crushed peppercorns for the last 15 minutes – if they are in the stock for the full simmering time they may make it slightly bitter. Strain well and allow to cool.

Stock for freshwater fish

Use the same ingredients as for the basic court bouillon but add 8fl oz (250ml) of white wine vinegar or tarragon vinegar. This is a good stock to use for trout, salmon and perch.

(Overleaf) Barbecueing is an excellent method of cooking fish either whole, as with the Red mullet with fresh lime and chives (page 134) shown here, or on skewers, like these Monkfish kebabs in baguettes (page 128).

Light and crisp, my favourite fried fish: Haddock and chips (page 117); Goujons of dogfish with herbed cheese mayonnaise (page 108); and Stir-fried sweet and sour ling (page 126).

Basic fish stock

Use the head, tail and bones of fish to make a good basic stock. Your fishmonger will give or sell you 'frames', which are the whole fish minus the fillets. Oily fish such as mackerel and herring are not suitable for stock making. If you happen to have them, add the shells of prawns or crab for an extra-tasty stock.

Makes about 2 pints (1 litre)

1½lb (750g) fish trimmings (head, bones, skin, scraps)

1½ pints (900ml) water

1 onion, sliced

1 carrot, chopped

1 leek, chopped

10fl oz (300ml) white wine or cider

Pinch of salt

Broken parsley stalks or bouquet garni

6 black peppercorns, crushed or bruised

Put everything except the peppercorns into a large saucepan, bring to the boil and simmer for no more than 30 minutes, skimming from time to time. Add the peppercorns for the last 10 minutes of cooking time.

Milk, lemon and herb stock

This stock, which needs no preliminary cooking, is excellent for white fish and smoked fish such as haddock or cod. The acidity of the lemon heightens the flavour of the fish.

Makes 1 pint (600ml)

10fl oz (300ml) full cream or semi-skimmed milk

10fl oz (300ml) water

2–3 lemons, peeled and sliced

Pinch of salt, freshly ground black pepper

Bouquet garni or crushed parsley stalks

Simply combine all the ingredients. To avoid curdling when poaching fish in this stock, it is more than usually important not to let it boil. Poach in the normal manner (see page 40). The strained liquid can form the basis of many different creamy soups or sauces.

Fish velouté

A well flavoured fish stock (see page 70) is used to make a smooth velouté which can be served as it is, but also provides the basis of countless other sauces and variations.

1oz (25g) butter
1oz (25g) white flour
1 pint (600ml) fish stock
Freshly ground black pepper

Melt the butter in a small pan over a gentle heat, stir in the flour and continue stirring for 1 minute – do not let the flour brown. Remove from the heat and stir in 1 or 2 tablespoons of the stock until you have a smooth paste, return to the heat and gradually add all the liquid, stirring continuously until the sauce is smooth and of a creamy consistency. Continue to cook the sauce gently for a further 5 minutes, then use as required.

Tomato velouté

Add 4 tablespoons of fresh tomato purée, a dash of Tabasco and 1 tablespoon of soured cream. Season to taste.

Spinach velouté

Beat in 2 tablespoons of very well drained and finely chopped spinach.

Onion velouté

Add 2 tablespoons of finely minced onion stewed in a little fish stock and 1 tablespoon of chopped parsley.

Fresh herb velouté

Add 2 tablespoons of finely chopped fresh herbs, e.g. tarragon with poached turbot, dill with baked halibut, or fresh coriander with hake or cod. A mixture of summer herbs could be added to enhance the flavour of blander white fish.

A miscellany of sauces

Simple purées of fruit or vegetables combined with a spoonful or two of the cooking juices of the fish, soured cream, fromage blanc, cream or yoghurt provide fresh, colourful and light sauces. Tart fruit sauces agree with oily fish, and a sauce based on a vegetable – for instance, fennel, watercress or tomato – can lift a plain dish of white fish into an interesting and attractive meal. Here are a few suggestions.

Watercress or spinach sauce

Makes about 10fl oz (300ml)

1–2 bunches watercress, trimmed, or 8oz (250g) blanched spinach, chopped

5fl oz (150ml) soured cream

Freshly ground black pepper

Squeeze of lemon juice

Whizz all the ingredients in a food processor or blender to make a pretty speckled sauce and add lemon juice to taste. This can be served chilled, or very gently warmed through.

Carrot, coriander and soured cream sauce

Makes about 15fl oz (450ml)

1lb (500g) carrots, chopped

15fl oz–1 pint (450–600ml) fish or vegetable stock (pages 66–70)

1 tablespoon coriander leaves, finely chopped

Freshly ground black pepper

2–3 tablespoons soured cream or natural yoghurt

Simmer the carrots slowly in the stock for about 30 minutes, or until they are really tender. Tip them into the bowl of a food processor or blender and whizz until very smooth – add more or less of the cooking liquid to achieve the consistency required, then add the coriander, a dash of freshly ground pepper and the soured cream or yoghurt. Whizz briefly again and check the seasoning. Serve the sauce warm.

Saffron sauce

Makes 10fl oz (300ml)

1 small onion or 2 shallots, very finely chopped
5fl oz (150ml) dry white wine
5fl oz (150ml) double cream or fish stock (page 70)
Pinch of saffron powder

Put the onion or shallots in a saucepan with the wine. Bring up to the boil and simmer until reduced to 2 tablespoons. Strain into another pan and stir in the cream or fish stock and saffron. Warm through gently and serve.

Cucumber and yoghurt sauce

Makes about 10fl oz (300ml)

½ cucumber, peeled and grated
8oz (250g) natural yoghurt, lightly beaten
Freshly ground black pepper
½ tablespoon finely chopped mint, dill, or fennel
Pinch paprika (optional)

Combine all the ingredients in a bowl, cover and chill. Garnish with a light sprinkling of paprika if you wish.

Rhubarb sauce

Makes about 8fl oz (250ml)

12oz (350g) rhubarb, cut into 1in (2.5cm) pieces
Squeeze of orange juice

Cook the rhubarb in a little water until tender. Purée until smooth using a food processor or blender. Add orange juice for extra piquancy.

Many other fruit sauces can be made in the same way. I like blackberries with mackerel and plums with herring. A plain apple sauce is very good with both oily and white fish – add lots of lemon juice or 1 or 2 teaspoons of prepared horseradish sauce (or a little less of fresh horseradish).

Tartare sauce

This sauce is particularly good with fried fish.

Makes about 10fl oz (300ml)

10fl oz (300ml) home-made mayonnaise (see below)

2 teaspoons gherkins, chopped

2 teaspoons capers, chopped

1 teaspoon green olives, stoned and chopped

1 teaspoon herbs, chopped

Mix all the ingredients together. The sauce can be kept in a covered jar in the refrigerator.

Mayonnaise

A good mayonnaise provides the basis of many sauces and dressings. Its character will mainly depend on the oil you use, and can be enhanced with the addition of herbs, spices and other flavourings. When serving a mayonnaise dressing with fish, thin it down with a little natural yoghurt or soured cream and 2 or 3 tablespoons of the cooled cooking juices from the fish or a little fish stock. This is a simple foolproof method of producing a well-flavoured dressing which is distinctly superior to, and much lighter than, commercially prepared dressings. Making mayonnaise by hand, which produces the authentic texture of classic mayonnaise, is an enjoyable art worth mastering. Blender mayonnaise takes seconds to make and gives good, although different, results from 'real' mayonnaise.

Blender mayonnaise

Makes about 10fl oz (300ml)

2 egg yolks or 2 whole eggs

½ teaspoon English or French mustard

2 tablespoons white wine vinegar or 2–3 tablespoons lemon juice

10fl oz (300ml) olive or sunflower oil

Pinch of salt and freshly ground black pepper

Put the egg yolks (or whole eggs), mustard and 1 tablespoon of vinegar into the bowl of a food processor or blender and process for 20 seconds.

With the machine still running, slowly trickle in the oil through the feed tube or hole and continue processing for 1 minute or until the mayonnaise is thick and creamy. Now add the remaining vinegar, season to taste and process for a further 20 seconds. If you like, whisk in a tablespoon of hot water to make the sauce lighter.

Hand-made mayonnaise

Only the yolks of the eggs are used in hand-made mayonnaise. It can be a rather temperamental sauce to make but, generally speaking, if the ingredients are at room temperature and the mixing basin is absolutely dry, the mayonnaise will be perfect. Very fresh eggs (that is, only a day or two old) will not perform well.

Makes about 10fl oz (300ml)

2 egg yolks

½ teaspoon Dijon mustard

10fl oz (300ml) good-quality olive or sunflower oil

1–2 tablespoons white wine vinegar or lemon juice

Pinch of salt, freshly ground black pepper

Pinch of cayenne pepper (optional)

Put the egg yolks and mustard into a small mixing bowl and beat well for 1 to 2 minutes. Now stand the bowl on a damp dishcloth or teatowel to prevent it skidding over the work surface and pour in a trickle of oil, beating well until it is incorporated into the egg. Add a trickle more oil, beat again, then start very slowly to pour in a continuous thin trickle of oil as you beat vigorously and rhythmically. You will see the mixture become thick and creamy, but if by any chance it starts to curdle, stop mixing. Start the process again in a clean basin, beating the egg and mustard, then trickle in the curdled mixture and you should regain a fine mayonnaise.

When all the oil is used, beat in the vinegar or lemon juice and season to taste. If you like, you could also add a pinch of cayenne or a squeeze more lemon juice.

Aïoli

*This famous mayonnaise of Provence is almost overwhelming, and for garlic lovers only.
It is the essential ingredient of La Bourride (see page 250), is very good served with other
fish soups or stews and is the classic accompaniment to salt cod. Of course, you can use a
little less garlic if you like.*

Makes about 10fl oz (300ml)

6 cloves garlic (or to taste)

Pinch of salt

2 egg yolks

10fl oz (300ml) good-quality olive oil

Squeeze of lemon juice

Freshly ground black pepper

Pound the garlic with a pinch of salt until thoroughly mashed – use a pestle
and mortar, or the end of a wooden rolling pin or back of a wooden spoon in a
sturdy bowl. Add the egg yolks and beat with a wooden spoon. Now add the
oil drop by drop, beating all the time, and continue until the sauce thickens
and all the oil is incorporated. When the mixture is smooth and creamy, beat
in a little fresh lemon juice and freshly ground black pepper to taste.

Remoulade sauce

It is the anchovy paste which gives this sauce its distinctive flavour.

Makes about 10fl oz (300ml)

10fl oz (300ml) mayonnaise (pages 74–75)

2–3 teaspoons anchovy paste, or to taste

1 teaspoon capers, finely chopped

1 pickled gherkin, finely chopped

½ tablespoon fresh herbs, finely chopped

Whisk together all the ingredients and serve. You can whisk in 2 tablespoons
natural yoghurt to lighten and thin the sauce if you like.

Rouille

This fiery sauce is not a mayonnaise, but the method of making it is rather similar. It gives an authentic touch to Bouillabaisse (see page 247) and other Mediterranean fish stews or soups.

Makes about 5fl oz (150ml)

2–3 fat cloves garlic, chopped

1 slice white bread, crust removed

A little fish stock or water

2 red chilli peppers, finely chopped

3 tablespoons good-quality olive oil

Pound the garlic to a paste with a pestle and mortar (or use the end of a wooden rolling pin or the back of a wooden spoon in a sturdy bowl). Squeeze out the slice of bread in a little fish stock or water and pound this and the chilli peppers into the garlic paste. Now add the olive oil drop by drop, beating all the time, until you have a smooth and creamy red sauce.

Hollandaise

Blender hollandaise sauce

Although this method is supposedly foolproof, I suggest that if you are using it for the first time you make it in advance in case anything goes wrong. A successful hollandaise, made in advance, can be kept warm in a warmed vacuum flask. As with mayonnaise, the texture of blender hollandaise is different from that of the hand-made sauce. Flavourings such as finely chopped herbs can be added according to the character of the fish.

Makes about 10fl oz (300ml)

6oz (175g) unsalted butter

4 eggs

2 tablespoons water

2 tablespoons lemon juice

Freshly ground white pepper

First, melt the butter over a gentle heat in a pan with a pouring lip.

Put the eggs, water, lemon juice and a grinding of pepper into the bowl of a food processor or blender and whizz for 20 seconds. With the motor still running, slowly pour the melted butter through the feed tube or hole until the sauce is thick and creamy. Check the seasoning and serve immediately.

Classic hollandaise sauce

Makes about 10fl oz (300ml)

3 tablespoons white wine vinegar

2 tablespoons water

6 white peppercorns

4–6oz (125–175g) unsalted butter

3 egg yolks

Squeeze of lemon juice

Pinch of salt

Put the vinegar, water and peppercorns into a small heavy saucepan, bring to the boil and cook until the liquid is reduced to about 1 tablespoon. Strain this liquid into a bowl (the bowl should be of a size which you can later fit over a pan of simmering water) and leave to cool.

Now melt the butter over a gentle heat. Beat the egg yolks until frothy.

Rest the bowl of reduced vinegar over a pan of simmering water, making sure that the bowl does not touch the water. Very gradually beat in the egg yolks. Now very gradually trickle in three quarters of the melted butter, stirring all the time until the sauce thickens to a creamy consistency. Add a squeeze of lemon juice, and if the sauce is too sharp add a little more of the reserved melted butter. Season to taste with salt. If the mixture thickens too quickly as you are cooking, remove it from the heat for a few seconds, then return to the heat and continue to beat. Ideally, the sauce should be served immediately, but you can keep it warm in a warmed vacuum flask or in the bowl over a pan of simmering water.

White (béchamel) sauce

A well-made creamy-textured white sauce is a good versatile standby for binding or coating white fish: herbs, spices or grated cheese can be added for variations. Try using skimmed or semi-skimmed milk for lighter healthier results.

Makes about 15fl oz (450ml)

1½oz (40g) butter

1½oz (40g) white or wholemeal flour

15fl oz (450ml) skimmed or semi-skimmed milk

1 blade mace (optional)

1 bay leaf

1 shallot, very finely chopped

Pinch of salt, freshly ground black pepper

Melt the butter in a heavy saucepan, stir in the flour and cook for 2 minutes on a very low heat. This stage is very important because if the flour is not thoroughly cooked, the sauce will have a strong floury flavour.

Slide the pan off the heat and whisk in a little milk with a ballon whisk. Add the rest of the milk a little at a time, whisking constantly so that there are no lumps. Now return the sauce to the heat, add the mace (if using), bay leaf and finely chopped shallot, bring up to just under simmering point and cook for 10 minutes, stirring all the time. Season to taste and remove the bay leaf.

Variations:

Easy Curry Sauce: Add 1 to 2 teaspoons of curry powder to the melted butter and flour when you begin to make the sauce.

Mustard Sauce: Simply whisk 2 or 3 teaspoons prepared English mustard or wholegrain mustard in to the sauce 1 minute before the end of the cooking time.

Quick Mushroom Sauce: Gently cook 4oz (125g) sliced button mushrooms in a scrap of butter until soft but not brown. Add them with their juices to the finished sauce with a pinch of cayenne pepper and cook through for a further 30 seconds.

Simple Cheese Sauce: Add 4oz (125g) grated Gruyère cheese, or good Cheddar cheese, or a combination of freshly grated Parmesan and Cheddar to the sauce 2 minutes before the end of the cooking time. Add a teaspoon of prepared mustard too, if you wish. Cook, stirring, until the cheese is melted and the sauce is smooth and creamy.

Onion Sauce: Cook 1 large very finely chopped onion in a little butter or oil until soft but not brown, and add to the basic sauce. Alternatively, simmer the finely chopped onion in a little fish stock, purée in a blender and whisk into the finished sauce.

Anchovy Sauce: Add 6 pounded anchovy fillets, or a few drops of anchovy essence to the finished sauce.

Caper Sauce: Add 2 tablespoons of capers to the finished sauce.

Herb Sauces: Add 2 tablespoons (adjust this amount to your taste) of finely chopped herbs to the basic sauce 2 minutes before the end of the cooking time: for example, dill, parsley, tarragon, fennel leaves, chervil, coriander.

Spicy Sauce: Add 1 to 2 teaspoons of your favourite crushed or ground spice when you are cooking the butter and flour.

Prawn or Shrimp Sauce: Add 4–6oz (125–175g) peeled chopped prawns or shrimps, a squeeze of lemon juice and, if available, 2 tablespoons of stock in which the prawns were cooked.

Sorrel sauce

Makes about 15fl oz (450ml)

2 shallots, finely chopped

5fl oz (150ml) fish stock

5 tablespoons dry white wine

3 tablespoons dry vermouth

10fl oz (300ml) cream or fromage blanc

4oz (125g) sorrel leaves, ribs removed, finely chopped

2oz (50g) spinach or watercress leaves, ribs removed, finely chopped

1oz (25g) butter

Squeeze of lemon juice, freshly ground black pepper

Put the shallots into a saucepan with the stock, wine and vermouth. Cook over a high heat until the liquid reduces (almost disappears) to a syrupy glaze. Stir in the cream or fromage blanc and cook at just under boiling point, stirring all the time, until the sauce has slightly thickened. Now add the chopped leaves (thoroughly patted dry with kitchen paper after washing and before chopping) and cook for a further 30 seconds, adding scraps of the butter in the final stage. Season to taste with the lemon juice and pepper and serve straight away. You can process the sauce in a blender or food processor for a smoother texture if you prefer.

Fresh tomato sauce

Makes 10fl oz (300ml)

1–1½lb (500–750g) ripe, juicy tomatoes, peeled and deseeded

1 tablespoon olive oil

½ tablespoon finely chopped fresh herbs

1–2 teaspoons tomato purée

Freshly ground black pepper

Place all the ingredients in a large heavy pan and simmer for 15 minutes, stirring occasionally, until the sauce is reduced. If the colour is pale, add a little more tomato purée. Serve the sauce hot or cold. You can process it in a food processor or blender if you want a smoother texture.

Pesto

There are many versions of this aromatic sauce, but the most important ingredient, giving Pesto its characteristic flavour, is fresh basil. It is an excellent dressing for all kinds of plain grilled or baked fish, especially any in which the flesh tends towards dryness. Try also adding a little Pesto to fish soups or stews.

Makes about 10fl oz (300ml)

2–3 fat cloves garlic

2 tablespoons pine-nuts

Pinch of salt, freshly ground black pepper

4 tablespoons grated Parmesan cheese

10fl oz (300ml) good-quality olive oil

2 tablespoons water

1 large bunch basil (say, 60 leaves, depending on their strength and your taste)

Put all the ingredients, except the basil, into the bowl of a food processor or blender and whizz until smooth. Now add the basil leaves, and whizz for a further 15 seconds, or until the dressing has a green speckled appearance.

Alternatively, in a pestle and mortar, pound the garlic, then add the pine-nuts, salt, pepper, Parmesan cheese and basil. Slowly add the oil, stirring all the time, and finally mix in the water.

The sauce can be stored in the refrigerator for a week or two.

Lemon sauce

Serve this powerful sauce warm or cool with grilled, baked or steamed white fish.

Makes about 10fl oz (300ml)

10fl oz (300ml) fish stock (see page 70)

4 egg yolks

Juice of 2 lemons

1–1½ teaspoons arrowroot

Freshly ground white pepper

First warm the fish stock over a gentle heat. Meanwhile, whisk together the egg yolks and lemon juice in a basin. Pour a little of the warm (*not* boiling) stock into this mixture, whisk, then tip back into the pan of stock. Cook gently, whisking all the time, at just under simmering point (do not boil or the eggs will scramble).

Mix the arrowroot with 1 or 2 tablespoons of cold water, then stir in 2 or 3 tablespoons of the sauce to make a smooth mixture. Add to the pan of sauce and continue to cook, stirring all the time, until the sauce has thickened and is smooth and glossy. Season to taste with pepper and pour into a jug to serve.

Batters

1   Tempura batter

This very light batter gives a crisp snowy appearance and is suitable for coating deep-fried small pieces of fish and shellfish. It does not need a 'resting' time and should be made just before it is needed.

1 egg

8fl oz (250ml) iced water

4oz (125g) white flour, sifted

Using a balloon whisk or fork, lightly mix together all the ingredients until smooth. Do not beat or overmix. Use straight away.

2   Simple blender batter

You may adjust the amount of milk used in this traditional batter, depending on whether you need a thin or slightly thicker mixture.

4oz (125g) plain flour, sifted

1 egg

Pinch of salt

5–6 tablespoons skimmed milk

Put all the ingredients into the bowl of a food processor or blender and whizz for about 45 seconds or until the mixture is smooth. Leave the batter to rest for an hour before using.

3   *Beer batter*

4oz (125g) plain flour, sifted

3 tablespoons olive oil

About 8fl oz (250ml) beer or water

1–2 egg whites

Put the flour into a mixing bowl and make a well in the centre. Pour in the oil and, using a balloon whisk or wooden spoon, beat it thoroughly into the flour. Add the beer gradually, beating from the outside of the bowl towards the centre. Set aside until you are ready to cook, then whisk the egg whites fairly stiffly and fold them into the batter. Use straight away.

Spring onion garnish

Spring onions go well with many types of fish and this pretty garnish can be used with any oriental-style dish, e.g. the bass recipe on page 86.

1   Trim off the green parts and bulb from the spring onion to leave a section about 3 inches (7.5cm) long.

2   With a sharp knife make two cuts in the shape of a cross about 1 inch (2.5cm) down into one end of the section and do the same at the other end.

3   Soak the section in iced water and the ends will soon curl up into frills.

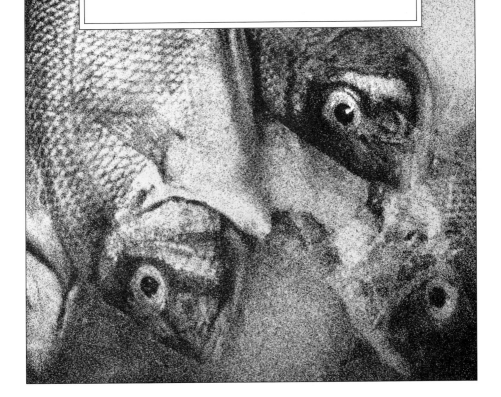

Round White Fish

M any of the fish in this general group, which is dominated by the cod and its relations, are highly versatile. They may be interchanged in the recipes and will always respond to an individual adventurous touch.

Bass

Steamed bass with ginger and spring onions in Chinese-style

The bass must be very fresh for this dish. It may seem sacrilege to add the distinctive flavour of ginger, spring onions and soy sauce to such a fine fish, but this traditional Chinese method of steaming perfumes rather than overwhelms the bass. The method can be used for other whole fish, such as large rainbow trout, snapper perch or mullet. Serve with a garnish of frilled spring onions.

Serves 3 to 4 as starter or light lunch, or 2 as main meal

1½–1¾lb (750–850g) bass, gutted and with gills removed

1 teaspoon salt

1 tablespoon fresh ginger, very finely chopped

2 spring onions, very finely sliced, including all the good green parts

1 tablespoon sesame oil

1 tablespoon soy sauce

4 spring onions, frilled (see page 84), to garnish

Wash the fish thoroughly and pat it dry with kitchen paper. Rub the salt all over the fish inside and out, and leave it in a cool place for 20 minutes.

Now set up the steamer. For this size of fish it is best to steam the fish between two plates. Alternatively, wrap it loosely in lightly oiled foil and place on the steaming rack of a wok or fish kettle (see page 42 for steaming methods). Put a little of the ginger and spring onion inside the belly of the fish, scatter the rest all over and steam for 15 to 25 minutes depending on the size of the fish.

Transfer to a warmed serving dish. In a small sauce pan quickly heat up the sesame oil and soy sauce to boiling point and pour sizzling over the fish. Garnish with the frilled spring onions and serve immediately.

To microwave
Remove the head, then slash the fish twice on each side. Prepare as above. Wrap in a double sheet of greaseproof paper and cook on HIGH for 7–9 minutes, turning the fish over halfway through cooking.

Baked bass with sorrel sauce

Such a graceful dish is best served simply with an elegant selection of julienned steamed vegetables. Time the cooking of the sauce and vegetables so that the fish can be taken straight to the table.

Serves 4

1 bass, about 2¼lb (1.1kg), gutted and with gills removed

Pinch of salt, freshly ground black pepper

1 lemon, sliced into rounds

4 sage leaves

2 tablespoons dry vermouth or dry white wine

1 quantity Sorrel Sauce (see page 81)

Pre-heat the oven to gas mark 6, 400°F (200°C).

Wash the fish thoroughly and pat it dry with kitchen paper.

Lightly oil a sheet of aluminium foil and place the fish on this. Lightly season the inside of the belly and tuck in 2 slices of lemon and 2 sage leaves. Now season all over the outside and cover the fish with the remaining slices of lemon in an overlapping line along the body, with the 2 remaining sage leaves tucked between the slices in the middle. Bring up the sides of the foil, add 2 tablespoons of vermouth or white wine, then fold and crimp the foil into a loose parcel. Bake in the oven for about 30 minutes, or until the fish is just cooked.

Using two fish slices or spatulas, carefully lift the bass on to a warmed serving platter. Pour the cooking juices all over and serve immediately. Hand the sauce separately.

Variation: This is a good method for very fresh small whole haddock or codling.

To microwave
Remove the head and tail from the fish, then prepare as above. Wrap in a double sheet of greaseproof paper and cook on HIGH for 10–12 minutes, turning over halfway through cooking.

Bream

Herbed grilled sea bream

The red sea bream is one of many breams, or porgies. Make sure you do not buy redfish by mistake. Red sea bream has a faint thumbprint just behind the gills. It is a tasty fish. Although it is bony, the bones are not fiddly or wispy but are easy to negotiate.

Serves 4 as starter or light lunch, or 2 as a main meal

4 small red sea bream, about 12oz (350g) each, scaled and gutted

Herbed oil (see page 59)

1 lemon, quartered to garnish

When gutting the fish, you may find the membrane where the gut is attached rather tough to pull away, so snip it out with small scissors if necessary. Wash the fish and pat it dry with kitchen paper.

Heat the grill or barbecue until very hot and oil the grill rack. Brush each bream generously inside and out with the herbed oil. Grill for 3 to 4 minutes on each side, until the fish is just cooked, basting with more herbed oil as you go. Serve straight away with quarters of lemon.

Variation: You can also cook the excellent gilt head bream in this way.

Baked sea bream

Tomatoes, fresh herbs and olives mingle with the juices of the bream as it bakes. Plain steamed rice goes well with this moist dish.

Serves 4

1 bream, about 2¼lb (1.1kg), scaled and gutted

Olive oil

1 large onion, sliced into rings

2 cloves garlic, finely sliced

4 ripe tomatoes, thickly sliced

12 black olives

Freshly ground black pepper

Juice of ½ lemon

1–2 tablespoons parsley, finely chopped

Pre-heat the oven to gas mark 6, 400°F (200°C).
   Wash the fish and pat it dry with kitchen paper.
   Heat a little oil in a heavy pan and gently fry the onion with the garlic until it is soft but not brown. Lightly oil a shallow baking dish and spread half the softened onion, garlic and tomato slices over the base of the dish. Put the fish on top and surround with the olives. Season generously with freshly ground black pepper. Sprinkle the lemon juice over the fish, cover with the remaining tomatoes and softened onion and garlic, season again with pepper and sprinkle with the chopped parsley. Drizzle a little olive oil over the dish, cover loosely with foil and bake in the oven for about 20 minutes. Then remove the foil and check the fish before returning it to the oven for a final 10 minutes or until it is cooked.

Variation: This is also a good method for red gurnard or small whole monkfish tails.

Catfish

Euphemisms like 'rock salmon' or 'rock turbot' are used to describe the skinned filleted catfish. The appearance of the whole fish is considered too fierce for most people as it has long chisel-like teeth and crushing molars for munching on the diet of small crustaceans and sea urchins which colour its flesh a delicate pinkish white.

The firm, almost boneless flesh responds very well to baking and is good for mixed seafood dishes like Couscous (see page 263) or stews. It can be treated like veal.

Baked catfish spiked with garlic and fresh tomato sauce

This baked dish should be served with bright, lively-looking green vegetables.

Serves 4

1½–2lb (750g–1kg) thick catfish fillets or tail piece

2 fat cloves garlic, cut into fine slithers

Olive oil

Pinch of salt, freshly ground black pepper

1 bay leaf

2 tablespoons parsley, chopped

1 lemon

1 quantity Fresh Tomato Sauce (see page 81) to serve

Pre-heat the oven to gas mark 6, 400°F (200°C).

Wash the fillets or tail piece of catfish and pat dry with kitchen paper. Make several slits in the fish and poke in the garlic slivers. Lay the fish on a lightly oiled shallow baking tray, season with a pinch of salt, freshly ground black pepper, crumbled bay leaf and 1 tablespoon of the chopped parsley. Sprinkle with the juice of half the lemon and a little olive oil. Bake in the oven, uncovered, for 15 to 20 minutes, or until just cooked.

Transfer the cooked fish to a warmed serving plate, adding any cooking juices to the Fresh Tomato Sauce. Pour the sauce over and around the fish and garnish with the remaining half of lemon, thinly sliced, and the remaining tablespoon of chopped parsley. Serve immediately.

Variation: A good fish for pies and braising, or cook as for Poached Cod with Special Lemon and Parsley Sauce (page 97).

To microwave
Prepare as above. Put the fish in a large shallow dish, cover and cook on HIGH for 8–10 minutes for fillets and 10–12 minutes for a tail piece.

Cod

It is a pity that we take the fine firm flesh of cod so much for granted. When really fresh and kindly cooked, the big sweet flakes just fall off the bone and need little more than a squeeze of fresh lemon, a dash of pepper and a trickle of the cooking juices. Cod is also excellent when marinated, cooked, then chilled, and served with an elegant summer salad.

Smoked cod's roe appetiser

This is a very simple and pretty starter, which makes a winning introduction to a summery supper party.

Serves 4

6–8oz (175–250g) smoked cod's roe

Selection of salad leaves: for instance, curly endive, radicchio (red lettuce), frissé, dandelion leaves, ribbons of cos lettuce, watercress

1 stick French bread

1 lemon, thinly sliced

Vinaigrette dressing

Chives to garnish

Peel the skin off the roe and soak the roe in water for 1 hour to lessen the saltiness. Drain, pat dry and slice.

Prepare the salad leaves, and arrange attractively around the border of four plates. Cut four thick slices of bread on the slant of the stick, warm them or toast them very lightly and place one in the centre of each salad arrangement. Top with a slice or two of smoked cod's roe and garnish with thin slices of lemon. Sprinkle the vinaigrette over the leaves, add more slices of lemon for squeezing and scatter with snipped chives.

Variation: Add smoked mussels or oysters, or ribbons of smoked halibut to the salad leaves as a boost to a special supper.

A warm summer salad with piquant cod

The cloves used in the following marinade, which also serves as the final dressing, do not dominate the taste of the fish but give an unusual piquant suggestion to the dish. You can use more or fewer cloves, as you prefer, and substitute the fish with other members of the cod family, such as ling, pollack, hake, whiting or coley (saithe). (For more about marinating see page 65.)

Serves 4

4 cod steaks or cutlets

Sunflower or olive oil

10fl oz (300ml) dry white wine

10fl oz (300ml) white wine vinegar

2–4 fat cloves garlic, finely chopped and crushed

12 whole cloves

Grated rind and juice of 2 large oranges

Grated rind and juice of 2 large lemons

Bouquet garni of parsley, tarragon, thyme and bay

Freshly ground black pepper

Summer salad:

Crisp lettuce or endive

Radicchio

2 bunches watercress *or* 2 handfuls spinach

6 spring onions

4 courgettes

4oz (125g) button mushrooms

12 round red radishes

1 tablespoon parsley, finely chopped

Wash the cod steaks and pat dry with kitchen paper. Heat a little oil in a large heavy frying pan or skillet and lightly cook for 2 minutes on each side. Carefully lift out the steaks with a slotted spoon and put them in a heatproof glass or china dish suitable for marinating.

Add all the other marinade ingredients to the fishy juices in the pan and bring up to simmering point. Continue to cook for about 5 minutes, drawing out the flavours of the herbs and spices – the aroma is sensational! Then pour the hot marinade over the cod steaks and leave to cool. Cover the dish with cling-film and leave in a cool place to marinate for about 4 hours.

Meanwhile, prepare the salad. Wash, pat dry and shred the lettuce and radicchio. Wash the watercress and remove the stalks, or wash the spinach and tear the leaves into pieces. Place all the leaves in a polythene bag in the fridge to chill and crisp. Trim the spring onions and slice diagonally, including the green parts. Wipe and trim the courgettes and slice them very thinly – also diagonally. Wipe the mushrooms and slice thinly. Wash and thinly slice the radishes.

Remove the cod steaks from the marinade and, with a knife and fork, ease the flakes off the bone. Pour the marinade juices into a saucepan, return to the heat and warm gently.

Combine the salad ingredients and heap a good portion on to each of four dinner plates: the colours and shapes will look summery-fresh and elegant. Distribute a helping of the flaked fish among the salad on each plate. Strain the warmed marinade and pour a little over each plate. Scatter a generous handful of roughly chopped fresh parsley on top and serve immediately with plenty of fresh bread to mop up the juices.

Variation: Also good with other firm white fish or salmon steaks.

Cod steaks with lemon and parsley sauce

Choose chunky steaks for this soothing dish: you can, of course, use cutlets or steaks of any white fish – hake, grey mullet or monkfish, for instance. A well-made old-fashioned white sauce (or béchamel) still has its place in fish cookery, especially when well flavoured with herbs or spices complementary to the fish.

Steamed greens and parsleyed potatoes are good accompaniments.

Serves 4

4 chunky cod steaks, trimmed

Freshly ground black pepper

1 tablespoon sunflower oil

Grated rind and juice of 1 lemon

1 quantity White Sauce (see page 79)

4 tablespoons parsley, finely chopped

Sprigs of parsley to garnish

Pre-heat the oven to gas mark 6, 400°F (200°C).

Wipe the fish steaks, and pat dry with kitchen paper. Season with a good shake of freshly ground pepper. Lightly oil a shallow baking dish, put in the steaks and pour over the juice from half the lemon mixed with half the grated rind and the tablespoon of oil. Bake for about 15 minutes, according to the thickness of the steaks, basting, if necessary, during the cooking time.

While the steaks are cooking, prepare the sauce. Add the parsley and remaining lemon rind and cook gently. Whisk in the remaining lemon juice in the final stage – taste as you go, and adjust the seasoning as required.

When the steaks are cooked, transfer them to warmed plates. Add the cooking juices to the lemon and parsley sauce and quickly stir. Pour a little sauce over each steak and garnish with a sprig of parsley. Serve the rest of the sauce separately.

To microwave
Prepare as above. Put the fish in a large shallow dish with the lemon rind and juice and the oil. Cover and cook on HIGH for 8–10 minutes.

Savoury cod crumble

This favourite family dish can be cooked in advance and gently re-heated at supper time. It is also ideal for freezing. Serve with a crisp green salad.

Serves 4

1–1½lb (450–700g) fillets of cod

Semi-skimmed milk for poaching

1–2 tablespoons sunflower oil

4 leeks, trimmed and sliced diagonally, including the tender green parts

4 ribs of celery, scrubbed and finely sliced

6oz (175g) mushrooms, wiped and quartered

4 hardboiled eggs, peeled and quartered

6 anchovy fillets, each sliced in two lengthways

1 quantity White Sauce, made with poaching milk (see page 79)

Crumble topping:

6oz (175g) wholemeal breadcrumbs

4oz (100g) Cheddar cheese, grated

2 tablespoons fresh green herbs (e.g. parsley, coriander, tarragon), finely chopped *or* 2 teaspoons mixed dried herbs

1oz (25g) butter (optional)

Poach the cod fillets in the milk (see page 40 for poaching instructions), remove them from the pan with a slotted spoon and set aside to cool. Reserve the poaching milk for the white sauce. Using a large heavy pan, heat the oil and gently fry the leeks, celery and mushrooms until they are soft but not brown. Allow to cool. Remove any skin and stray bones from the cod fillets, cut into small pieces and gently combine with the vegetables, taking care not to break up the fish or the softened leeks.

Lightly oil a shallow pie or gratin dish, slide in the fish and vegetable mixture, and top with the quarters of hardboiled egg and anchovy strips.

Set the oven to gas mark 5, 375°F (190°C). Now make the white sauce, using the reserved poaching milk (see page 79), and pour this all over the dish. While the sauce is 'settling' into the dish, prepare the crumble topping by combining the breadcrumbs, grated cheese and herbs and scatter over the top of the pie. Finally, dot with a few scraps of butter if you wish. Bake in the oven for 35 minutes and serve immediately.

Variations: Use scraps of smoked salmon, or strips of kipper fillets instead of the anchovies. Cheaper kinds of white fish, such as coley, whiting or grey mullet, can be substituted for the cod.

To microwave
Put the fish and 2 tablespoons of milk in a shallow dish. Cover and cook on HIGH for 4–6 minutes. Cook the vegetables and sauce as above. Cook the crumble on HIGH for 5–6 minutes until hot, then brown under the grill.

Melting pots of cod and brie

Individual soufflé dishes or ramekins of fish with a bubbling toasted topping and creamy fondue sauce makes an excellent starter. Serve with slices of wholemeal toast.

Serves 4

8–10oz (225–275g) cooked cod

1 tablespoon sunflower oil

4oz (100g) button mushrooms, wiped and thinly sliced

4 spring onions, trimmed and finely sliced including all good green parts

2 cloves garlic, peeled and very finely chopped

4 ripe tomatoes, peeled and sliced

Freshly ground black pepper

8–10oz (225–275g) firm brie, sliced

Remove any skin or bones from the cooked cod, and flake the flesh. Heat up the oil in a small saucepan and gently fry the mushrooms, spring onions and garlic for 1 or 2 minutes until they are soft but not brown.

Light the grill and set to medium heat. Lightly oil 4 individual soufflé dishes or ramekins. Fill them with layers of the softened vegetables, slices of tomatoes and flakes of cod, seasoning each layer with a little freshly ground black pepper and finishing with a layer of tomatoes. Cover each pot with slices of brie and place under the grill for 4 to 5 minutes until the cheese has melted down through the layers and the tops of the dishes are bubbling and golden. Serve immediately.

Variation: Use flakes of any well flavoured firm white fish, and combine with 4oz (100g) prawns if you like.

Poached cod with special lemon and parsley sauce

Cod with parsley sauce is a classic (see Cod Steaks with Lemon and Parsley Sauce, page 94), but here the sauce is an integral part of the dish: superb, glossy and bursting with lemony flavour. The success of it depends on using home-made fish stock (see page 70).

The method is a blueprint for all good firm white fish – I have cooked nuggets of monkfish, fillets of John Dory and cutlets of hake in this way with excellent results.

The dish is lovely served with tiny pink new potatoes and mushrooms.

Serves 4

4–6 thick very fresh cod cutlets, trimmed

15fl oz (450ml) semi-skimmed milk

15fl oz (450ml) fish stock

2 bay leaves, broken in half

Juice of 1 lemon

6 tablespoons parsley, very finely chopped

Freshly ground black pepper

2oz (50g) beurre manié (1oz (25g) butter creamed with 1oz (25g) flour)

Wipe the cutlets and pat them dry with kitchen paper. Gently warm the milk, stock, bay leaves in a shallow poaching pan – a paella pan would be suitable. Then place the cutlets in the warm liquid, heat until just under simmering point and poach for about 2 minutes. Carefully turn the cutlets over and poach for another 2 minutes, depending on the thickness of the fish. Using a spatula, transfer the cutlets to a warmed serving dish and keep warm.

Now bring the liquid up to simmering point and let it reduce a little. Drop in little nuts of beurre manié and stir with a wooden spoon or balloon whisk until the sauce has thickened and is smooth. Add the parsley and a little pepper and cook gently for 1 more minute. Turn off the heat, then add the lemon juice, stirring it in quickly. Pour this over and around the cutlets and serve immediately.

Cod kebabs with basil sauce

Very fresh steaks of cod or other firm white fish should be used for these kebabs. Served on a bed of herbed rice, they are just right for a summer lunch, or make a delicious starter with warm bread rolls. The sauce can be prepared well in advance and kept warm in a vacuum flask or over a pan of simmering water. Adjust the amount of basil to taste.

Serves 4

2lb (1kg) chunky cod steaks, skinned and boned

2 red or yellow peppers

Juice of 1 lemon

4 tablespoons olive oil

Pinch of salt, freshly ground black pepper

Basil Sauce:

3 tablespoons olive oil

1 tablespoon white wine vinegar

1 clove garlic, crushed

2–3 tablespoons basil leaves, chopped

3 tablespoons cream or fromage blanc

1 egg yolk

Pinch of salt, freshly ground black pepper

Wash the fish, pat dry with kitchen paper and cut into cubes. Scorch the peppers over a gas flame or under a hot grill until the skins are black, then peel, quarter, remove the seeds and ribs and cut each quarter in half again.

Combine the lemon juice, oil and seasoning in a basin, turn the fish and pepper pieces in this mixture and leave to marinate for 20 minutes.

Meanwhile, make the sauce. Put the oil, vinegar, crushed garlic, chopped basil and cream or fromage blanc into a saucepan and heat very gently, stirring all the time. Remove the sauce from the heat, beat in the egg yolk and season. Return to a low heat and stir the sauce constantly as it thickens to a nice creamy consistency. Do not let it boil. You can keep the sauce warm by resting the pan over another saucepan of simmering water; alternatively, pour into a warmed vacuum flask.

Heat the grill until very hot and oil the grill rack. Lightly oil the kebab skewers – this prevents the fish sticking to them. Thread the cubes of fish and pieces of pepper alternately on to the skewers and cook under the grill for about 4 minutes, turning them occasionally and basting with the marinade mixture. Serve immediately on a bed of herbed rice, or with warm rolls. Pour a little of the pretty green-flecked sauce in a line over each kebab, and serve the remainder separately.

Variation: Dogfish (huss) and fresh tuna or shark make excellent kebabs.

Grilled cod fillets with fresh tomato and basil sauce

Make the sauce in advance (it will keep in the refrigerator for two or three days) and you have a quick simple meal. The sauce is long-simmered so that it thickens by reduction. You can easily adjust its consistency to your taste. In the summer, use fresh very ripe tomatoes; otherwise tinned tomatoes are a good substitute. Fresh basil is essential (see 'Herbs', page 56), but if it is not available try oregano or marjoram instead.
  Fillets of hake, haddock or whiting may be substituted for the cod.
  This dish is good served with plain potatoes, and frozen petits pois or peas.

Serves 4

4 cod fillets, trimmed

Juice of ½ lemon

1–2 tablespoons olive oil

Freshly ground black pepper

4 basil leaves to garnish

Fresh Tomato and Basil Sauce:

1½lb (750g) very ripe tomatoes, plus 1 tablespoon tomato purée (optional) *or* 2 × 14oz (397g) tins tomatoes

2 Spanish onions, finely chopped

3 cloves garlic, finely chopped

4 tablespoons olive oil

½ tablespoon basil leaves, chopped

1 strip lemon peel

Pinch of salt, pinch of sugar, freshly ground black pepper

First make the sauce. If you are using fresh tomatoes, peel and de-seed them. Plunge them into boiling water for a minute; then, using a fork, lift them out, make a small incision in the skin to peel them. Slice them open and squeeze out the seeds, then coarsely chop the flesh. If the tomatoes are pale and lack flavour, add 1 tablespoon of tomato purée for colour and body.

If using tinned tomatoes, de-seed and coarsely chop them, reserving the juice.

Gently soften the chopped onions and garlic in the oil in a heavy pan over gentle heat. Now add the tomatoes, basil, lemon peel and seasoning and simmer for about 20 minutes, stirring occasionally. If you wish for a very smooth sauce, whizz the sauce in a blender or food processor, or rub it through a sieve. The sauce can be gently re-heated when you are ready to serve the fish.

Heat the grill and oil the grill rack. Rinse the fish fillets, pat dry with kitchen paper and brush with a mixture of the lemon juice and 1 or 2 tablespoons of olive oil. Sprinkle with freshly ground black pepper and grill for about 4 minutes, or until the flesh is just opaque.

Pour a puddle of the sauce on to each of four warmed plates and place the fillets on top. Serve straight away, garnished with basil leaves.

To microwave
Prepare as above. Put the fish in a large shallow dish, sprinkle with the lemon juice, cover and cook on HIGH for 8–10 minutes.

The simplicity of flat fish, whole or in fillets: Baked plaice with lemon and parsley (page 151); Rolled fillets of sole with salmon mousseline (page 157): Fillets of dab with prawns and mushrooms (page 144); and Poached chicken turbot with saffron sauce (page 163).

(Overleaf) Three versions of classic Italian dishes: Fresh clams or cockles with pasta (page 197); Fresh anchovies baked with oregano (page 167); and Baked stuffed squid in tomato sauce (page 222).

Taramasalata

There is hardly a better example of the astonishing difference between a commercially made food product and the real thing than taramasalata. Smoked fish roe (arguably grey mullet is the correct fish, but cod is more usual) is used to make this marvellous creamy dip.

A pleasing authentic texture is achieved by making taramasalata by hand. However, the results are smoother and quicker if you use a blender – simply follow the steps for making Blender mayonnaise (see page 74).

Serve the taramasalata with warm fingers of pitta bread or toast, or with scrubbed sticks of celery, carrot and peppers.

Serves 4

8oz (250g) smoked cod's roe

3–4 thick slices bread

2–3 cloves garlic (to taste), crushed

10fl oz (300ml) good-quality olive oil

Juice of 1 lemon

Freshly ground black pepper

Black olives to garnish

Peel the skin away from the roe and soak the roe in water for an hour to lessen the saltiness. Cut the crusts off the bread and soak the slices in a little water. Now pound the roe and the crushed garlic – use a large pestle and mortar, or a sturdy basin and the rounded edge of a wooden rolling pin. Squeeze the moisture from the softened bread and add to the mixture as you continue to pound. Now start to add the oil, a little at a time, beating continuously, until you have a creamy consistency: add more oil if necessary. Season with lemon juice and freshly ground black pepper. Tip into a pretty, shallow serving dish and garnish with black olives.

Variation: Try substituting 8oz (250g) smoked cod, skinned and flaked, for the bread. Use the juice of 2 lemons instead of 1 and decrease the oil to about 8 tablespoons. Add the lemon juice and oil by alternate tablespoons as you pound or process the mixture. Garnish with lemon slices and green olives.

Cod's roe and smoked ham fritters

These scrumptious fritters make a nutritious tea-time snack or light supper served with oven-baked chips (see page 117) and a crisp green salad. Cold, they can be offered on a platter of mixed appetisers – or included in a picnic hamper.

Serves 4 to 6

1½lb (750g) cod's roe

2 eggs, lightly beaten

3 tablespoons mayonnaise (see page 74)

Freshly ground black pepper

8oz (225g) smoked ham, finely chopped and with visible fat removed

3 tablespoons finely chopped parsley

Sunflower oil for frying

To serve:

Wedges of lemon

Tartare sauce (see page 74)

If the roe is uncooked, simmer it in water for 5 minutes and allow to cool. Remove the skin and place the roe in a large mixing bowl. Beat in the eggs, mayonnaise and season with freshly ground black pepper. Mix in the smoked ham and parsley. The mixture should be like a thick batter but the consistency will vary according to the size of the eggs and nature of the mayonnaise.

Now heat up a little oil in a large heavy frying-pan. When you can barely detect a slight haze, drop in tablespoons of the fritter mixture, turn down the heat slightly and fry for two minutes. Flip the fritters over and fry for a further two minutes until they are all golden brown. Using a fish slice, remove them from the oil and drain on absorbent kitchen paper. Transfer to a warmed serving plate and keep warm while frying more batches of fritters. Serve immediately with wedges of lemon and tartare sauce.

Variation: Roe from ling, or hard roe from herring can be substituted.

To microwave
If the roe is uncooked, put it in a large bowl with 10fl oz (300ml) boiling water. Cover and cook on HIGH for 4–5 minutes until tender, turning over halfway through cooking. Complete the recipe.

Creamed salt cod bake

This dish has a distinctive taste which is not particularly salty. 'Tow rag' (salt cod) was important in the Cornish fish preserving industry not so long ago. Now it is popular mainly on the continent and in the West Indies. This recipe is adapted from a homely traditional Portuguese dish. The salt cod is well soaked to lessen its saltiness; but, even so, beware of adding more salt during cooking. I like this dish with steamed greens and/or chunks of freshly cooked beetroot.

Serves 4 to 5

1½–2lb (750g–1kg) salt cod

1½–2lb (750g–1kg) potatoes

4 fat cloves garlic, crushed

5 tablespoons good-quality olive oil

Freshly ground black pepper

1 tablespoon parsley, chopped

1 tablespoon breadcrumbs

½–1oz (15–25g) butter

First soak the stiff, dry cod in several changes of cold water for at least 4 hours but preferably overnight. Then place it in a poaching pan of cold water, heat until just under simmering point and poach until tender. Strain and, when cool, remove all the skin and bones and flake the fish.

Meanwhile, boil the potatoes and mash them in the usual way.

Pre-heat the oven to gas mark 4, 350°F (180°C).

Add the crushed garlic to the mashed potatoes and slowly pour in the oil, beating all the time, then beat in the flakes of fish and continue until you have a light mixture. Season to taste with freshly ground black pepper. Turn into a lightly oiled or buttered baking dish, fork the mixture down, scatter with the chopped parsley and breadcrumbs and dot with scraps of butter. Bake in the oven for about 30 minutes until the crust is a light golden colour and serve the dish.

To microwave
Prepare as above. Cut the fish into 4 pieces, put in a shallow dish with 10fl oz (300ml) water, cover and cook on HIGH for 8–10 minutes. Complete as above.

Conger eel

Have you ever tried to skin an eel? I don't recommend it, especially if it is live, although that is how some experts do it. I remove the skin after cooking – the easy solution. Conger eels have huge fierce jaws and put up a considerable fight when they are caught. The last conger that I gutted had a perfectly intact velvet blue swimming crab inside it.

Conger eel is a good-flavoured versatile fish with firm flesh. The middle cut is best; the tail end is bony but good for stock.

A casserole of conger eel

This casserole is rich and filling. I like to serve it in shallow soup bowls, providing a fork and spoon. A garlic mayonnaise (Aïoli, page 76) could be served separately if you like.

Serves 4

4 thick conger eel steaks weighing about 7–8oz (225–250g) each

12 tiny onions or shallots

2 cloves garlic, finely sliced

1–2 tablespoons olive oil

1 × 14oz (397g) tin tomatoes

1 glass red wine

2 small strips orange rind

1lb (500g) potatoes, diced

4 sticks celery, finely sliced

15 black olives

Freshly ground black pepper

Bouquet garni

Pre-heat the oven to gas mark 4, 350°F (180°C).

Wash the conger eel steaks and pat dry with kitchen paper.

Heat a little olive oil in the bottom of a heavy flameproof casserole dish and gently turn the whole onions and sliced garlic in this until they begin to soften. Now add the conger steaks and allow to cook for 2 minutes on each side before adding the tomatoes and their juice, the wine and orange rind. Pack the diced potato, sliced celery and olives all round, season with black pepper and push in the bouquet garni. Cover the casserole tightly and cook in the oven for a good 35 minutes, or until everything is tender.

Before serving, lift out the conger steaks with a perforated spoon and remove the skin. If necessary, continue to simmer the vegetables until the sauce reduces. Serve immediately.

Variation: This kindly braise or casserole is also suitable for freshwater eels, or large monkfish steaks.

To microwave
Put everything except the eel in a large bowl, cover and cook on HIGH for 12 minutes until the potato is tender. Add the eel, pushing it down into the liquid. Re-cover and cook on HIGH for 8–14 minutes, depending on the thickness of the fish.

Coley

Some people buy coley (or saithe) for their cats, yet I know others who feed their cats on prime smoked salmon. As cats are the ultimate food snobs, perhaps we should not be too dismissive of coley. In texture and flavour it is not as good as other members of the cod family but, because of its relatively low price, it is useful for padding out the family fish pies or mixed fish stews. Wherever you see a recipe for mixed white fish, try using some coley as an economical option. It also gives body to fish stock.

Dogfish

This member of the shark family (also known as flake, huss or rigg) is another fish deemed too ugly to be seen whole on the fishmonger's slab. Its rough leathery skin (used in the past to polish alabaster and wood) is usually removed as soon as the catch is landed. It is a tasty fish which lends itself particularly well to goujons. Steaks are good marinated and grilled.

Goujons of dogfish with herbed cheese mayonnaise

These goujons can be served with a home-made Tartare Sauce (see page 74) or simply with wedges of lemon and a crisp salad. We enjoyed them one lunchtime with this pleasing sharp mayonnaise.

Serves 4 to 5

1½lb (750g) dogfish fillets

2 large or 3 medium egg yolks

2 tablespoons olive oil

2 tablespoons water

4–6oz (125–175g) breadcrumbs

Sunflower or safflower oil for deep-frying

Lemon wedges to garnish

Herbed Cheese Mayonnaise:

1 egg

1 teaspoon Dijon mustard

1 fat clove garlic, chopped

Pinch of salt, freshly ground black pepper

5fl oz (150ml) safflower oil

1 tablespoon boiling water

1 scant tablespoon lemon juice

4oz (125g) low-fat soft cheese

2 good tablespoons chopped herbs (a mixture of parsley, thyme, etc., as available)

First prepare the Herbed Cheese Mayonnaise. This can be done by hand using the traditional method (see page 75) and then incorporating the cheese and herbs with a balloon whisk, or by using a blender or food processor. Break the egg into the liquidiser bowl, add the mustard, garlic and a little seasoning and whizz. Slowly pour in the oil with the machine running until you have a thick mayonnaise, then dash in the boiling water and lemon juice and whizz again for 10 seconds. Finally add the remaining ingredients and process just a few seconds more until everything is creamy and well mixed. Adjust the seasoning, if necessary, and refrigerate until needed.

Wash the fish fillets, pat dry with kitchen paper and cut into thin strips about 2½–3in (6–7.5cm) long by ½in (1cm) thick. Beat the egg yolks and whisk in the olive oil and water.

Heat 2–3in (5–7.5cm) oil in a wok or frying pan until a cube of bread dropped in sizzles and floats immediately to the surface. Dip the strips of fish in the oil mixture, and coat with breadcrumbs. Fry the goujons in batches, nudging and turning them around in the pan for about 2 minutes until crisp and golden. Drain on crumpled kitchen paper and keep warm in the oven until the frying is completed. Garnish with lemon wedges and serve immediately with Herbed Cheese Mayonnaise in a dipping dish.

Variation: Use strips of any firm white round fish, or flat fish like plaice, dab or witch.

Dogfish (huss, flake) braised with olives and tomatoes

This delicious braise takes only a few moments to prepare and lends itself to countless adaptations. Add your favourite herbs in season, or use other dense-fleshed fish like monk, swordfish, shark, tuna or shellfish.
    I like to serve it with a dish of steaming herbed potatoes and courgettes.

Serves 4

1½–2lb (750g–1kg) huss, cut into 1in (2.5cm) thick pieces across the bone

2 tablespoons olive oil

3 fat cloves garlic, finely chopped and crushed

2 large Spanish onions, peeled and sliced

1 green pepper, sliced

1 × 14oz (397g) tin tomatoes

Bay leaf, broken in half

4 parsley stalks

20 green olives

Freshly ground black pepper

1 tablespoon natural yoghurt or single cream

Coarsely chopped parsley to garnish

Wash the fish and pat it dry. Pre-heat the oven to gas mark 5, 375°F (190°C).

Heat 1 tablespoon of the oil in a heavy frying-pan over a low heat, and gently fry the garlic, onion and pepper until they are soft but not brown. Transfer to a shallow oven-to-table baking dish. Add the remaining oil and carefully turn the pieces of huss until they are golden. Use a slotted spoon to transfer them to the baking dish, then pour the tinned tomatoes into the pan, stir and heat through, scraping up all the fishy juices from the base of the pan. Tip the bubbling tomatoes over the fish in the baking dish, add the broken bay leaf, parsley stalks and olives and season with freshly ground black pepper. Cover with a lid or aluminium foil and bake for 15–20 minutes or until the fish is tender. Stir in the yoghurt or cream, scatter with parsley and take the dish to the table to serve straight away.

Variation: Just before serving, scatter 4oz (100g) freshly grated Parmesan cheese and chopped anchovy fillets over the braise and flash under the grill until bubbling and golden.

To microwave
Prepare as above. Cover and cook on HIGH for 5–8 minutes until the fish is tender, stirring occasionally. Stir in the yoghurt or cream, scatter with parsley and serve straight away.

Gurnard

Baked stuffed gurnard

The red gurnard is marvellously flamboyant when it appears in such dishes as bouillabaisse and soups. It has firm white flesh and responds well to baking whole. It is easy to take the fillets off larger fish, but small ones are best stuffed and baked. Grey gurnard may be cooked in the same way.

Serves 4

4 red gurnard, gutted

1 large onion, thinly sliced

A little olive oil

5fl oz (150ml) fish stock

1 glass dry white wine

1 tablespoon cream (optional)

Stuffing:

8oz (250g) lean smoked bacon, de-rinded and finely chopped

1 small onion, grated

1 large egg

6 tablespoons breadcrumbs

1 teaspoon thyme, finely chopped

2 teaspoons parsley, finely chopped

1 tablespoon lemon juice

Freshly ground black pepper

Pre-heat the oven to gas mark 6, 400°F (200°C).

First make the stuffing. Fry the bacon gently in a heavy pan until the fat runs. Add the grated onion to the sizzling bacon so that it cooks in the bacon fat until soft but not brown. Beat the egg in a mixing bowl, add the breadcrumbs, bacon, onion, thyme, parsley and lemon juice to make a moist stuffing – add a little fish stock to moisten more if necessary – and season to taste with pepper.

Wash the fish and pat dry with kitchen paper. Fill the belly cavities with the stuffing. Scatter the sliced onion over the base of a lightly oiled casserole or baking dish. Arrange the gurnard on top and pour in the stock and wine. Brush the backs of the fish with oil and bake for between 25 and 30 minutes, or until the fish are cooked.

Transfer the fish to warmed plates and keep warm while you boil the baking juices and onion down to a thick creamy consistency. Remove from the heat, whisk in the cream if using, and spoon a little of the sauce alongside each fish. Serve straight away.

To microwave
Prepare as above but remove the heads from the fish. Scatter the onion in a large shallow dish and arrange the stuffed fish on top with the stock and wine. Cover and cook on HIGH for 10–15 minutes until tender, rearranging once during cooking. Complete the sauce as above.

Steamed gurnard with sweet and sour ginger sauce

Would you believe that this charming little fish is commonly used as bait around the south west? Red gurnard is cheap and plentiful and, in my opinion, its delicate flavour and stylish appearance deserves more recognition. Yellow and grey gurnard may be cooked in the same way, and served with this arresting sweet and sour sauce.

Serves 2

2 medium red gurnard

2 tablespoons sunflower oil

6 spring onions, trimmed and finely sliced including all the good green parts

2 cloves garlic, peeled and finely chopped

2in (5cm) cube of fresh ginger, peeled and grated

2oz (50g) pineapple chunks, finely diced

1 tablespoon unsweetened pineapple juice

1 tablespoon dark soy sauce

1 tablespoon white wine vinegar

5fl oz (150ml) water

Chopped spring onion greens to garnish

Set up the steamer. Remove the innards from the gurnard, then wash the fish and pat dry. Place in the steamer and cook for about 15 minutes according to the size of the fish, until the flesh is opaque and eases off the bone.

Meanwhile, make the sauce. Heat up the sunflower oil in a large pan or wok, and stir-fry the spring onions, garlic and ginger for 1 minute. Draw the pan off the heat, add the pineapple, juice, soy sauce, vinegar and water, return to the heat and stir briskly.

Transfer the gurnard to warmed plates and pour over the hot sauce. Garnish the fish with chopped spring onion greens and serve immediately.

Variation: Small snappers or bream may be substituted.

To microwave
Slash the fish twice on each side and arrange in a large shallow dish with 2 tablespoons of water. Cover and cook on HIGH for 7–9 minutes. Complete the recipe.

Haddock

Baked spicy haddock Indian-style

This light, spicy Indian dish is adapted from a popular recipe at the Star of India Restaurant in London. You could use other white fish, such as cod, brill or whiting: fresh is best, but frozen fillets perform well in this sort of dish.

Don't let the long list of spices deter you. Once you have assembled them, the cooking is easy – and the aroma is unbelievable. Serve hot with plenty of boiled rice or chilled with a green salad.

Serves 6

6 × 8oz (250g) haddock fillets

4 tablespoons oil

Whole spices:

4 cloves

4 cardamom pods

1in (2.5cm) stick of cinnamon

1 teaspoon fennel seeds

2 teaspoons cumin seeds

1 teaspoon mustard seeds

5 cloves garlic, finely chopped

4 Spanish onions, sliced in rings

½ teaspoon salt

1 teaspoon ground cumin

1 teaspoon ground coriander

2 teaspoons turmeric

1 teaspoon garam masala

4 whole green chillies (or to taste), de-seeded and finely chopped

1 pint (600ml) natural yoghurt

Pre-heat the oven to gas mark 5, 375°F (190°C).

Heat the oil in a heavy pan over medium heat and throw in all the whole spices. Wait for the cardamom pods and mustard seeds to pop and the fennel and cumin seeds to turn golden brown (this takes just a few seconds).

Now add the garlic, onions and salt and continue to fry until the onions turn a deep amber colour. Add the ground cumin and keep stirring. Add the ground coriander, turmeric and the garam masala as the mixture reduces, then add the chillies and continue to fry. Turn down the heat and gradually incorporate the yoghurt into the mixture, a tablespoon at a time.

Wash the haddock fillets and pat dry with kitchen paper. Place them in a lightly oiled baking dish and pour over the spicy yoghurt sauce. Bake in the oven for about 30 minutes, or until the fish is cooked. The yoghurt sauce may have separated slightly, but this does not matter. Serve hot or chilled.

To microwave
Prepare as above. Put the haddock in a large shallow dish, pour over the sauce, cover and cook on HIGH for 10–12 minutes, rearranging once during cooking

Steamed haddock with saffron sauce

Very fresh haddock is a fine-flavoured fish in its own right: many people think it better than cod. These lightly steamed fillets are complemented with a clean-tasting saffron sauce – a delicate dish which may be elegantly presented with florets of broccoli.

Serves 4

4 small or 2 large haddock fillets, trimmed and skinned

Juice of ½ lemon

1 tablespoon dry white wine

Freshly ground black pepper

Saffron Sauce (see page 73) to serve

If you are using 2 large haddock fillets, cut each into 2 pieces. Wash and pat dry with kitchen paper. Place each fillet on a square of aluminium foil, sprinkle with lemon juice and white wine and a grinding of pepper, and crimp the foil loosely into parcels. Set up a steamer (or wok) with a plate placed on the rack, and put in the parcels. Steam for about 15 minutes, or until the fish is just cooked.

Meanwhile, prepare the sauce. Unwrap the haddock fillets and keep warm on a warmed serving dish. Add all their cooking juices to the sauce to finish, and check the seasoning. Pour a puddle of sauce on to each of four warmed plates, put the fillets on top and serve straight away.

Variation: Use very fresh fillets of plaice or sole.

To microwave
Prepare as above. Place the fish in a large shallow dish with the lemon juice, wine and pepper. Cover and cook on HIGH for 6–8 minutes. Complete as above.

Old-fashioned smoked haddock breakfast

Finnan haddock, Arbroath smokies, Glasgow pales – there are several kinds of smoked haddock of varying cures. The one to avoid is the dubious bright-yellow dyed fillet, often not haddock at all. Look for the distinctive 'thumbprint' on the skin (see page 279).

When I was very young, I used to stay with a grand great aunt. At the breakfast table she would peer sternly at me over the silver service and starched lace tablecloth until I had finished up every scrap of poached smoked haddock. In spite of the constrained atmosphere in which I first enjoyed it, it remains one of my favourite breakfasts. Wholemeal toast should be on hand.

Serves 2

2 smoked haddock
15fl oz (450ml) skimmed milk
½ lemon, sliced
Freshly ground white pepper

Poach the haddock in the milk with 2 slices of lemon and a dash of white pepper (see page 40) until just cooked. Keep a watchful eye on them to ensure that they don't overcook. Using two perforated spoons, transfer the haddock to warmed breakfast plates (reserve the poaching liquid for a soup), and serve them with the remaining slices of lemon.

To microwave

Put the haddock, milk, lemon and pepper in a large shallow dish. Cover and cook on HIGH for 8–10 minutes. Complete as above.

Haddock and chips

The best crispiest chips are fried twice: once until they are soft and nearly cooked, then again at a much higher temperature for a crunchy golden finish. Always use a good-quality clean oil. I sometimes half-cook my chips, drain them, spread them on a baking sheet and complete the cooking in a really hot oven. (See page 43 for deep- and shallow-frying techniques.)

Of course, the haddock does not have *to be fried too; there is no reason why it could not be crisply baked in the oven, or steamed or cooked in a microwave oven.*

As my family lives on a remote island, fish and chips were almost unknown to my children, so I used to serve this 'classic' to them as a real treat in cones of newspaper . . . but, of course, they never had a rainy city street to walk along as they ate them – which is half the fun.

In time-honoured fashion, fish and chips should be served with brown vinegar and/or tomato ketchup.

Serves 4

4 thick haddock fillets, skinned

Juice of ½ lemon

Freshly ground black pepper

4 large potatoes

Oil for deep-frying

Seasoned flour

1 quantity Batter No. 2 or 3 (see pages 83–84)

Wash the haddock fillets and pat dry with kitchen paper. Sprinkle with a little lemon juice and pepper.

Peel the potatoes, cut them into thick chips, rinse well with cold water and pat them dry with kitchen paper.

Now gently heat up the oil in a deep-fryer (see page 45 for deep-frying). Use the chip basket to lower the chips into the hot oil.

Heat up a little oil in a shallow frying pan. Dredge the haddock fillets with flour, dip into the batter to coat, and shallow-fry for about 2 minutes on each side, depending on the thickness of the fish.

Meanwhile, when the chips are soft and nearly cooked, drain them well, raise the temperature of the oil slightly and lower the basket back in again for 1 to 2 minutes for the chips to crisp. Drain well on kitchen paper before serving.

Smoked haddock soufflé

This simple soufflé is just one example of the versatility of smoked haddock – it can be used in mixed fish dishes, quiches, soups and salads. If you prefer, the recipe can be used to make small individual soufflés instead of one large dish.

Serves 4

8–12oz (250–350g) smoked haddock

1½oz (40g) butter

10fl oz (300ml) skimmed milk

1oz (25g) flour

2oz (50g) Gruyère cheese, grated

Freshly ground white pepper

4 eggs, separated

Pre-heat the oven to gas mark 6, 400°F (200°C).

Using a scrap of the butter, lightly grease a 3–3½ pint (1.7–2 litre) soufflé dish.

Poach the haddock in the milk (see page 40) until just cooked, lift out with a perforated spoon, remove any skin and bones and flake the flesh. You need 8oz (250g) of fish, so save any extra for another dish, and reserve the poaching liquid for the sauce: the amount you use for the soufflé will vary according to the size of the eggs.

Now melt the remaining butter in a heavy pan and stir in the flour. Cook over a low heat without browning for 1 to 2 minutes, stirring all the time. Then gradually add the poaching milk and grated Gruyère, stirring constantly to make a creamy sauce. Season with a little pepper and stir in the flaked fish. Remove from the heat, and add the beaten egg yolks. Whisk the egg whites until they are stiff (forming small points which stand straight up) and fold (do not stir) into the sauce. Pour the mixture into the soufflé dish. To give the soufflé a decorative 'cap', lightly score a trench around the top, about 1in (2.5cm) in from the edge, and 1in (2.5cm) down. Bake in the middle of the oven for 25 to 30 minutes. Serve as soon as it is cooked – a soufflé cannot wait.

Variation: Substitute smoked trout or salmon.

To microwave
Put the haddock and half of the milk in a large shallow dish, cover and cook on HIGH for 3–4 minutes. Complete as above, adding the remaining milk.

Kedgeree

Kedgeree is a popular old-fashioned breakfast or lunch dish which originated in India – the Indian version has turmeric and other spices like chilli and ginger. Although many kinds of fish can be used, such as white sea fish or fresh or smoked salmon, smoked haddock is most commonly used. Kedgeree has a tendency to dryness: this recipe gives beautifully moist results, and the previously cooked brown rice provides a lovely nutty flavour. Add or substitute other fish and use spices if you wish – kedgeree is a versatile dish.

Serves 4

1lb (500g) smoked haddock fillets

Milk and slices of lemon for poaching

1½oz (40g) butter

1 small onion *or* 2–3 spring onions, finely chopped

8oz (250g) cooked brown rice

4 eggs, hard-boiled and chopped

1 tablespoon chopped parsley to garnish

First wash the fish fillets, pat them dry with kitchen paper and poach them in the milk and with the lemon slices (see page 40) until just cooked. Using a perforated spoon, lift out the fillets and set aside to cool. Reserve the poaching liquid. Remove all the skin and bones from the haddock, and flake the flesh.

Heat the butter in a large saucepan and gently fry the chopped onion or spring onions until soft and pale. Add the cooked rice and turn it around in the sizzling butter with the onion until all the grains are glistening. Now add the flaked fish and chopped hard-boiled eggs, gently stirring with a fork until well incorporated and heated through. At the last moment, stir in 1–2 tablespoons of the poaching liquid – just enough to moisten the rice slightly – and tip the kedgeree into a large warmed serving dish. Sprinkle with chopped parsley and serve immediately.

To microwave
Put the haddock, 3 tablespoons of milk and the lemon slices in a large shallow dish. Cover and cook on HIGH for 4–5 minutes. Complete as above.

Smoked haddock cooked with vinegar and mustard

This adaptation by Katie Stewart and Pamela Michael of an Arab recipe devised in the year 1226 so intrigued me that I had to try it straight away. The original medieval dish would have used salted fish, but smoked haddock is an excellent substitute. It is a very good recipe indeed – perfect on a winter's night for supper.

Serves 4

4 fillets smoked haddock, about 1½–2lb (750g–1kg)

2–3 tablespoons sesame oil

4 tablespoons white wine vinegar

¼ level teaspoon dry mustard powder

2 teaspoons ground coriander

Pinch of powdered saffron

Boiled rice to serve

Wash the fish and pat dry with kitchen paper.
　　Heat the oil in a frying pan and fry the haddock fillets until they are lightly browned on both sides. Discard any surplus oil and pour 3 tablespoons of the vinegar over the fish. Mix the remaining tablespoon of vinegar with the mustard and add to the fish, along with the coriander and saffron. Cook gently for a further 4 minutes. Serve the haddock on a bed of rice with all the cooking juices poured over.

Hake

Jenny's hake with coriander sauce

The hake must be really *fresh for this simple dish; the flavour of the fish is gently enhanced by the lemon rind. A pretty selection of lightly steamed vegetables makes a good accompaniment.*

Serves 4

4 hake cutlets

Finely grated rind of 1 lemon

2oz (50g) white flour

Freshly ground white pepper

Sunflower oil for frying

5fl oz (150ml) fromage blanc

1 teaspoon coriander leaves, finely chopped, plus whole leaves to garnish

First wash the fish cutlets and pat dry with kitchen paper. Combine the grated lemon rind with the flour and a little pepper.

Lightly coat the hake cutlets in the lemony flour and, using a very little oil in a heavy frying pan, quickly fry them for 2–3 minutes on each side, depending on their thickness, until cooked. Transfer them to a warmed serving platter and keep warm.

Now gently heat the fromage blanc and chopped coriander leaves in a small saucepan to just under simmering point. Trickle a little of this sauce over each cutlet and garnish with whole coriander leaves. Serve the remainder of the sauce separately.

Grilled hake fillets with cripsy cheese topping

These crisp yet moist fillets, with a hint of garlic, are lovely served with puréed spinach and new potatoes. You could use fillets of cod or haddock if hake is unavailable.

Serves 4

2 large or 4 small hake fillets

1 tablespoon sunflower oil

1 teaspoon garlic purée

Freshly ground black pepper

4 tablespoons dry white wine

4oz (125g) brown breadcrumbs

4oz (125g) Cheddar or Gruyère cheese, grated

Wash the fish and pat dry with kitchen paper. Leave the skin on, as this will help to keep the shape of the fillets. If you are using large fillets, cut each into 2 pieces. Cream the sunflower oil and garlic purée together to make a paste, spread over the top of each fillet and sprinkle with a little freshly ground black pepper.

Now heat the grill. Remove the rack from the grill pan and pour in the wine – just enough to cover the base of the pan. Put the fillets, skin side down, in the bottom of the pan. Top each fillet with the combined breadcrumbs and grated cheese and grill for about 4 to 6 minutes. When crisp and golden, serve on warmed plates with the cooking juices and wine poured over.

Variation: Also good with cod, haddock or ling, or if using a cheaper variety of fish, such as pollack or coley fillets, mix a handful of chopped fresh herbs in with the breadcrumbs.

A warm salad of tagliatelle and hake with tuna and capers

This is a wonderful way of using left-overs of firm white fish like hake, cod or monkfish – although the dish is so good that I think it is worth buying a fish especially for the recipe. It makes an excellent summer lunch, served with chilled dry table wine.

Serves 4

12oz (350g) cooked hake

1 × 6oz (175g) tin tuna, well drained and flaked

6 anchovy fillets, drained and chopped

Juice of ½ lemon

1 teaspoon capers

5oz (150g) natural yoghurt

5fl oz (150ml) home-made mayonnaise (see page 74)

Freshly ground black pepper

1 Webb's Wonderful lettuce

1lb (500g) green tagliatelle

1 teaspoon capers and slices of lemon to garnish

First make the sauce. Place the flaked tuna fish, chopped anchovy fillets, lemon juice, capers, yoghurt and mayonnaise into the bowl of a blender or food processor and whizz for 45 seconds or until smooth and creamy. Pour this sauce into a large mixing bowl, taste and add freshly ground black pepper if you like.

Cut the cooked hake into bite-size pieces – ensure that no bones remain – and set aside. Wash the lettuce, pat dry and arrange around the border of a large shallow serving dish.

Now cook the tagliatelle in boiling salted water. Drain it thoroughly and, while it is still very hot, tip it into the mixing bowl containing the sauce. Toss to combine, then carefully fork in the pieces of hake. Quickly tip into the centre of the serving dish, garnish with capers and slices of lemon and serve while still warm.

John Dory

John Dory poached with scallops

John Dory has a marvellous flavour. It is a difficult fish to handle because of the little sharp spikes which run all round the rim. However, there is a convenient pocket in the flesh near the belly which enables you to pick it up – that is why our local fisherman call John Dory 'handbags'! The firm-textured fillets are easy to lift off, and the large strange-looking head makes excellent stock. I like this way of poaching the fillets as the scallops add their own unique flavour.

Serves 4 as a starter, or 2 as a main meal

1 large or 2 medium John Dory

4 scallops, cleaned and trimmed

Warm stock made from the fish head and bones (see page 70)

2–4 tablespoons dry vermouth

Juice of ½ orange and 4 matchsticks of thinly pared orange peel, blanched

Freshly ground black pepper

Chervil to garnish

Although the John Dory is a round fish, lifting off the fillets is more like dealing with a flat fish (see page 23). Take off the 4 fillets and use the head and bones to make the stock. If you wish to skin the fillets, this is more easily done after cooking.

Wash the fish fillets and pat dry with kitchen paper. Slice the white lobe of each scallop in half. Place the fish fillets in a shallow pan suitable for poaching and pour the warm stock over, adding the vermouth, orange juice and matchsticks of peel and a grinding of black pepper. Bring slowly up to just under simmering point and poach for 2 minutes. Now add the scallops and continue to poach for a further minute, or until just cooked, adding the corals of the scallops for the final 30 seconds' cooking time: they cook very quickly.

Using a perforated spoon, transfer the fish fillets and scallops to a warmed serving dish and keep warm. Reduce the poaching liquid by half, until it is of a creamy consistency. Check the seasoning, trickle some sauce over and around the fillets and scallops, garnish each fillet with a clover pattern of chervil and place a scallop coral in the centre.

To microwave
Prepare as above. Put the fish fillets, 10fl oz (300ml) stock, the vermouth, orange juice and peel in a large shallow dish. Cover and cook on HIGH for 2 minutes. Add the scallops and put the corals in the centre of the dish. Re-cover and cook on HIGH for 1 minute. Transfer the fish to a serving dish. Cook the poaching liquid, uncovered, on HIGH for 5 minutes until reduced. Complete as above.

Ling

Baked ling and courgettes

You can use other white fish, such as fillets of cod, hake or coley, for this moist baked dish. It goes well with lemony rice, or simply with warmed bread rolls.

Serves 4

4 ling fillets, trimmed and skinned

1 tablespoon olive oil

1 medium onion, finely sliced

1lb (500g) courgettes, cut into ¼in (0.5cm) slices

Freshly ground black pepper

½ tablespoon oregano or basil, chopped

Juice of ½ lemon

4 tomatoes, thickly sliced

2 cloves garlic, crushed

4oz (125g) Gruyère cheese, grated

Pre-heat the oven to gas mark 5, 375°F (190°C). Wash the fish fillets and pat dry with kitchen paper. Lightly oil a shallow baking dish and place in it the onion and half the courgettes, then arrange the fish fillets on top. Sprinkle with a little freshly ground black pepper, half the herbs and a little lemon juice. Cover with the remaining slices of courgettes and all the tomatoes. Season with the remaining lemon juice and herbs, add the garlic and drizzle the rest of the olive oil all over. Scatter the grated Gruyère over the whole dish. Cover loosely with a sheet of oiled aluminium foil and bake in the oven for 20 minutes, or until the courgettes and fish are nearly cooked. Remove the foil and return the dish to the oven for a further 5 minutes or until the cheese is bubbly and golden. Alternatively, you could finish the dish by quickly flashing it under a hot grill to crisp and brown.

To microwave
Prepare as above, but omitting the cheese. Cover and cook on HIGH for 12–15 minutes until the fish and courgettes are tender. Sprinkle with the cheese, then brown under a hot grill.

Stir-fried sweet and sour ling

Ling is not so well flavoured as other fish in the order of cod, so this tingling stir-fry is an excellent way to cook it. You can substitute any other white fish or scallops if you like. Serve on a bed of hot noodles.

Serves 3 to 4

8–12oz (250–350g) ling fillets

4 spring onions

8oz (250g) baby corn

1 tablespoon tomato purée

1 tablespoon soy sauce

1 tablespoon wine vinegar

Juice of 1 orange

Juice of 1 lime

1lb (500g) thick noodles to serve

1 tablespoon olive oil

Freshly ground black pepper

Frilled spring onions to garnish (see page 84) – optional

For stir-frying, it is particularly important to do all the preparation before you start to cook. Trim the spring onions and slice on the slant, including all the good green parts. Wash the fish fillets, pat dry with kitchen paper, trim and cut into chunky pieces. Wash the baby corn and pat dry with kitchen paper.

To make the sweet and sour sauce, whisk together the tomato purée, soy sauce, wine vinegar and the orange and lime juices.

Cook the noodles in boiling water. When cooked, strain and keep warm in a serving dish.

Now heat up the oil in a wok and briskly stir-fry the onions and baby corn for 45 seconds. Keep stirring as you add the fish and continue to cook for a further 45 seconds to 1 minute; then add the sweet and sour sauce. As soon as it bubbles once or twice, pour the whole dish over the noodles and serve straight away. Sprinkle with a shake or two of freshly ground black pepper and garnish with frilled spring onions if you like.

Monkfish

Roasted monkfish tail

The French love monkfish. They like to roast it whole with a lot of garlic (like a leg of lamb). If you have left-over monkfish from this roast, use it in a mixed seafood dish (see pages 247–274).

I serve Roasted Monkfish Tail with Fresh Tomato and Basil Sauce, and steamed chunks of potato and fennel.

Serves 6

2½–3lb (1.25–1.5kg) monkfish tail, trimmed and skinned

1 fat clove garlic, cut into slivers

Freshly ground black pepper

Olive oil

Chopped parsley and lemon wedges to garnish

Fresh Tomato and Basil Sauce (see page 99) to serve

Pre-heat the oven to gas mark 7, 425°F (220°C).

Wash the fish and pat dry with kitchen paper. You can leave the bone in, but if you prefer to remove it, the tail will need re-shaping and securing with wooden toothpicks or cocktail sticks.

Make incisions in the fish and push in the slivers of garlic. Season with freshly ground black pepper and brush with olive oil. Place the fish in a lightly oiled roasting tin and roast for 20 to 30 minutes, or until cooked.

Garnish with chopped parsley and lemon wedges and serve the gently re-heated Fresh Tomato and Basil Sauce separately.

To microwave
Prepare the fish as above, cut in half if it won't fit in the microwave. Brush with olive oil and wrap in a double sheet of greaseproof paper. Cook on HIGH for 15–18 minutes.

Monkfish kebabs in baguettes

Monkfish is one of the most delightful fish to handle. Once the thick backbone has been removed, you will find the close-textured flesh firm and totally bone-free. The skin, trimmings and bone make exceptionally good stock – and so would the massive head if you could ever find one! Monkfish is excellent poached in the style of Poached Cod with Special Lemon and Parsley Sauce (see page 97), and good for Sashimi (page 253), kebabs and fine soups like La Bourride (see page 250).

　　These dashing kebabs, cradled in split baguettes, make splendid alfresco eating – they can be barbecued or grilled. Bear in mind that the quantities will vary according to the size of your skewers and the baguettes.

Serves 4 to 6

1½lb (750g) monkfish tail, skinned and with the backbone removed

1 large or 2 medium red peppers

For the marinade:

8 spring onions, chopped, including the good green parts

6 coriander seeds, crushed

4 cardamom pods, crushed

Juice of 1 lime

Juice of 1 orange

Freshly ground black pepper

6–8 tablespoons olive oil

To serve:

4 baguettes

1 bunch watercress, trimmed

2 lettuce hearts, cut into thin ribbons

Wash the fish, pat dry with kitchen paper and cut into 1–1½in (2.5–3cm) cubes.

Now prepare the marinade. Reserving 2 of the chopped spring onions to use as a garnish, combine the rest with all the other marinade ingredients in a glass bowl. Put the monkfish cubes into this, making sure that they are completely covered, and leave to marinate for 1 hour, turning them from time to time.

Cut the peppers in half, remove the ribs and seeds, and cut into pieces of a suitable size for the kebab skewers. Heat the barbecue or grill and oil the rack. Warm the baguettes. Oil the kebab skewers and thread on alternate pieces of fish and red pepper. Baste them with the marinade as you grill them, turning the skewers to ensure even cooking.

Meanwhile, slice open the baguettes lengthways along the top and half-fill them with the lettuce ribbons and watercress. Place the hot monkfish in the baguettes and scatter the reserved chopped spring onions and a few ribbons of lettuce over them. Drizzle over a little of the marinade and give each guest a large napkin when you hand them the baguettes.

Variation: Try using cod or tuna.

To microwave
Prepare as above, threading the fish and pepper onto wooden skewers. Arrange in a single layer in a large dish. Brush with marinade, cover and cook on HIGH for 4–5 minutes, repositioning the kebabs halfway through cooking. Complete as above.

Grey Mullet

You can *feel* when it is a good day to catch a grey mullet – early summer twilight, warm and still, a quiet cove with a tell-tale ripple breaking the surface of a sulky sea: that's the time to put out the net.

Grey mullet are herbivorous. There are more than 100 species. The sparkling deep-sea type caught around the Scillies are very clean and respectable inside – more commonly, the mullet that nose around the beds of shallow water on estuaries tend to be muddy. They can be unpleasant to gut and clean. Nevertheless, grey mullet is a good fish which lends itself well to baking – I recommend cooking it in this way with a moist breadcrumb stuffing. Home-smoked grey mullet is excellent. The smoked roe is then used for Taramasalata (see page 103).

Grey mullet steaks with oranges and fennel

This dish tastes just as good as it looks, and can be taken straight to the table to serve with a crisp green salad. It is equally successful with whole red mullet.

Fennel is simple to grow in a herb garden, but is also found in the wild. In this recipe I describe how to use both the stronger-flavoured wild fennel and Florentine fennel, which is purchased in bulb form.

Serves 4 to 6

1 grey mullet, about 2lb (1kg)

2 branches fennel *or* 1 bulb Florentine fennel

2oz (50g) butter

2 sticks celery, finely sliced

2 oranges, peeled and sliced into rounds

Pinch of salt and freshly ground black pepper

7–10fl oz (200–300ml) dry white wine

Pre-heat the oven to gas mark 6, 400°F (200°C).

Scale and gut the mullet, cut off the head and tail, and slice the fish into 4 or 6 rounds (cutlets and steaks), depending on its size. Break and bruise the branches of fennel, or thinly slice the bulb of Florentine fennel: reserve a few of the feathery leaves as a garnish. Lightly butter a baking dish with ½oz (15g) of the butter and cover the base with the celery, fennel and half the orange slices. Lay the cutlets of grey mullet on top and sprinkle with a pinch of salt and freshly ground black pepper. Dot with the remaining butter and smother with the remaining orange slices, then pour in the wine which should come about one third of the way up the cutlets. Bake in the oven for 20 minutes, or until the fish is cooked. Garnish with the reserved fronds of fennel and serve with a spoonful or two of the cooking juices.

To microwave
Prepare as above. Put the celery, fennel, half of the orange slices and the wine in a large shallow dish. Cover and cook on HIGH for 5 minutes. Slash the fish twice on each side and arrange on top. Cover with the remaining orange slices and dot with the butter. Re-cover and cook on HIGH for 10–12 minutes, turning the fish over halfway through cooking.

Baked stuffed grey mullet with sorrel sauce

Serves 3–4

1 grey mullet, about 2lb (1kg), scaled and gutted

1 lemon, sliced

6 bay leaves

1oz (25g) butter

Sorrel Sauce (see page 81) to serve

For the stuffing:

1oz (25g) butter

1 small onion, finely chopped

1 egg, beaten

2 tablespoons parsley, finely chopped

Grated rind and juice of 1 lemon

Freshly ground black pepper

4oz (125g) breadcrumbs

Pre-heat the oven to gas mark 6, 400°F (200°C).
   Wash the fish and pat it dry with kitchen paper.
   To make the stuffing, heat the butter and gently soften the onion in it. Add the beaten egg, parsley, grated lemon rind and juice, freshly ground pepper and breadcrumbs. Mix well.
   Place the fish on a sheet of lightly greased aluminium foil, fill the belly with the stuffing, and lay the slices of lemon, interspersed with bay leaves, along the outside of the fish. Dot with 1oz (25g) butter and sprinkle with pepper. Bring up the sides of the foil and crimp to make a loose parcel. Bake in the

oven for 20 to 30 minutes, depending on the size of the fish.

Meanwhile, prepare the Sorrel Sauce. To serve, place the fish parcel on a warmed platter and fold the foil back neatly. Hand the sauce separately.

Variation: This is also good with Fresh Tomato Sauce (page 81).

To microwave
Remove the head and the tail from the fish. Prepare as above, then slash twice on each side. Dot with the butter, then wrap in a double sheet of greaseproof paper. Cook on HIGH for 12–15 minutes, turning over halfway through cooking. Complete as above.

Red Mullet

Grilled diamonds of red and grey mullet with lime and spicy mayonnaise

The contrast of the silver-grey and rosy-hued skins of the two mullets makes a delectable dish – appealing both to the eye and the palate. Arrange the diamond-shaped pieces of fillet on elegant plates and garnish with the speckled mayonnaise and fronds of dill or fennel leaves. Serve as a starter, or as a main meal with a warm salad of new potatoes and dill or fennel leaves, and a dish of mange-tout.

Ask your fishmonger about where the grey mullet came from when you buy it. If from estuary waters, it may have a slightly muddy flavour – therefore, soak the fish in acidulated water for one to two hours before using.

Serves 4

1 × 2lb (1kg) grey mullet
2 × 1lb (450g) red mullet

Marinade:
Juice and grated rind of 1 lime
4 tablespoons olive oil
Freshly ground black pepper

Mayonnaise:

1 egg

5fl oz (150ml) olive oil

1in (2.5cm) cube of fresh ginger, peeled and grated

2 cloves of garlic, peeled and crushed

1–2 teaspoons of light soy sauce

Juice of ½ lime

½ teaspoon honey

½–1 teaspoon mild chilli powder (to taste)

Slices of lime, fronds of dill or fennel leaves to garnish

Scale the mullets, and take off the fillets (see pages 17 and 22). Reserve the liver of the red mullet and roe (if any) of the grey mullet – both are delicacies and can be used in other recipes. Wash the fillets and pat them dry. Using a very sharp knife, cut the fillets into pieces shaped like diamonds approximately 2 × 2in (5× 5cm). Smother with the combined marinade ingredients and leave in a glass or china bowl in a cool place for 1 hour.

Meanwhile, begin to prepare the mayonnaise in the usual way (see page 74) by hand, or using a food processor or blender. When all the oil is amalgamated, add the ginger, garlic, soy sauce, lime juice, honey and mild chilli powder. Taste and add more chilli powder if you wish.

Light the grill, and cover the grill rack with a double thickness of aluminium foil. Brush the foil with olive oil. Place the pieces of mullet, skin side down on the foil and grill for two minutes. Use a brush to baste the flesh with the remaining marinade mixture from time to time. Turn the pieces of fish over, and grill for a further two minutes or until the pink and grey skin is just beginning to blister and turn pale gold.

Arrange alternative pink and grey pieces of the grilled mullet, skin side up, in concentric circles on each of four warmed plates. Spoon a little of the mayonnaise in the centre of each arrangement, garnish with fronds of dill or fennel leaves and crescents of lime and serve immediately. Hand the remaining mayonnaise separately.

Variations: Combinations of very fresh, good-quality white fish can be marinated, grilled and served in a similar fashion, although you won't get the same stunning combination of colour as with the mullets. You could use the rouille on page 77 to serve, or other flavoured mayonnaises. Just remember that it is the freshness of the fish and the style of presentation that makes this dish so successful.

Grilled red mullet with fresh lime and chives

This is a colourful and mouthwatering starter. I have allowed 2 fish for each person – but as these red mullet are wonderful when barbecued, you could increase the amount of both marinade and fish for a summer lunch party and serve with tiny new potatoes and a fragrant green salad.

Serves 4

8 × 5–8oz (150–250g) red mullet, scaled but not gutted

Fresh chives, chopped

1 lime, quartered

Marinade:

Juice of 2 fresh limes

6 tablespoons olive oil

4 tablespoons chives, chopped

Freshly ground black pepper

Wash the mullet and pat dry with kitchen paper.

In a shallow glass or earthenware bowl combine the marinade ingredients and leave the fish in this for 15 minutes, turning them occasionally.

Meanwhile, heat the grill to high and lightly oil the grill rack. When you place the fish on the grill rack, make sure they are well coated in the marinade and chives as the latter are appealing to the eye as well as the taste buds. Grill the mullet 2 or 3 minutes, turning and basting them and heaping on more chives as they cook; continue to grill for a further 2 or 3 minutes.

The skin of the fish will be crisp and the tails slightly charred. When you serve them hot on warmed plates with quarters of fresh lime, they will look almost too good to eat!

The unbeatable flavour of really fresh mackerel grilled over a wood fire and served with chilled rhubarb and ginger sauce (page 183).

(Overleaf) Picnic fish for a British summer! Smoked mackerel tartlets (page 186); Monkfish and salmon terrine (page 254); Crab, mango and grapefruit salad (page 201).

Shark

Marinated grilled shark steaks

Shark is almost boneless, and excellent for grilling or barbecuing. Of the several kinds of shark available, the pinkish dense-textured flesh of the porbeagle and tope is the best and far superior to the cheaper white-fleshed shark meat. Shark steaks are superb when simply grilled and served with a squeeze or two of fresh lemon juice, but I also love them grilled or barbecued with this spicy marinade, and served with a chilled tomato salad and fresh bread.

Serves 4

4 × 1in (2.5cm) thick shark steaks, trimmed

Wedges of lemon

Marinade:

4 tablespoons good olive oil

4 tablespoons lemon juice

4 spring onions, trimmed and chopped

1–2 cloves garlic, peeled and chopped

1in (2.5cm) piece of fresh ginger, peeled and chopped

Dash of hot chilli sauce to taste

Freshly ground black pepper

Olive oil for basting

It is best to use a food processor or blender to prepare the marinade. Simply place all the ingredients in the bowl and whizz until you have a smooth paste. Alternatively, grate the ginger very finely and crush the chopped garlic before adding to the remaining ingredients and mixing well.

Wash the steaks, pat them dry and smother them with the marinade. Leave in a glass or china bowl for 1–2 hours.

When you are ready to cook, light the grill and get it good and hot, or prepare the barbecue fire. Oil the grill rack, brush one side of each steak with a little olive oil, place this side down on the rack and cook for 2 or 3 minutes. Brush with a little more oil and, using spatulas, turn each steak and cook for a further 2 or 3 minutes by which time the steak should be coloured with bubbling blisters of pale gold. Serve immediately with wedges of lemon.

Variation: This marinade is equally successful with other steaks of firm fish – swordfish, for instance, is an excellent alternative.

Whiting

Steamed minted whiting with soured cream

Whiting is a lovely fish – rather underrated, I think. It is a good fish to use for quenelles or little fish creams.

This dish is fresh, sweet and light. Serve it with a few plain potatoes, young garden peas and carrots. These quantities give you quite a minty meal – halve the quantity of leaves if you prefer.

Serves 4

4 whiting fillets, skinned

1 bunch mint

5fl oz (150ml) soured cream

½ lemon

Freshly ground black pepper

A little oil

Freshly grated nutmeg

Pinch of salt

Wash the fish and pat dry with kitchen paper. Finely chop 1 tablespoon mint leaves and stir into the soured cream – add a little squeeze of lemon juice and a grinding of pepper to taste.

Cut out and lightly oil four sheets of aluminium foil large enough to parcel up each fillet. Lay a fillet on each sheet, season lightly with a grating of nutmeg, a pinch of salt and a grinding of pepper, and sprinkle over a few bruised mint leaves and a squeeze or two of lemon juice. Bring up the edges of the foil and crimp into loose parcels. Steam for 8 to 10 minutes, according to the thickness of the fillets (see page 42). Meanwhile, gently *warm* the soured cream and mint mixture in a small pan: it should be just lukewarm.

The fish can be served in their parcels on warm plates – neatly fold back the foil and pour the lukewarm soured cream mixture around the fillets so that it mingles deliciously with the cooking juices. Garnish with whole mint leaves and serve at once.

To microwave
Prepare as above. Instead of parcelling in foil, put the fish in a large shallow dish with the nutmeg, mint and lemon juice, cover and cook on HIGH for 8–10 minutes, rearranging halfway through cooking. Complete as above.

Flat Fish

All flat fish are quick, simple and a joy to cook. What's more, their uncomplicated bone structure makes it easy to fillet them. Turbot and Dover sole shine out as having the most exquisite flavour, but brill and halibut are also meaty and well flavoured.

Brill

Baked brill with minted sauce

Brill is a very good fish, although it does not have the superb flavour of its cousin, the turbot, and its flesh is slightly softer. The pretty pale green sauce is fresh-tasting and light, and you can adjust the amount of mint to your preference.

Serves 4

4 brill fillets, trimmed

A little oil

Freshly ground black pepper

Juice of ½ lemon

½ onion *or* 1 shallot, very finely chopped

½oz (15g) butter

6oz (175g) frozen peas

1–2 teaspoons water

1 tablespoon mint, chopped

4 tablespoons natural yoghurt or fromage blanc

Whole mint sprigs or leaves to garnish

Preheat the oven to gas mark 5, 375°F (190°C).

Wash the fish fillets and pat dry with kitchen paper. Put them in a lightly oiled shallow baking dish and sprinkle with a shake of freshly ground black pepper and half the lemon juice. Cover with foil and bake in the oven for about 20 minutes, according to the thickness of the fillets.

Meanwhile, make the sauce. Gently sweat the onion or shallot in the butter in a covered pan over a very low heat. When it is pale and soft, add the peas and 1 or 2 teaspoons water and cook gently for a further 2 to 3 minutes. Tip the peas and onion into a food processor or blender, add the mint and yoghurt and process for 30 seconds until smooth. Add the remaining lemon juice and black pepper to taste. Transfer the fillets to warmed plates, pour a little of the sauce over each one and garnish with mint.

To microwave
Put the fish in a large shallow dish with the pepper and lemon juice. Cover and cook on HIGH for 5–7 minutes. Complete as above.

Steamed brill with mussel sauce

Mussel sauce also goes well with steamed halibut, turbot or sole. It can be prepared in advance and gently re-heated when you are ready to cook. A lightly cooked julienne of carrots, celery and leeks makes a colourful accompaniment to this dish.

Serves 4

4 brill fillets from 1 large brill

1½–2 pints (900ml–1.1 litres) fresh mussels

3–4 tablespoons dry white wine or dry vermouth

1 pint (600ml) Fish Velouté (see page 71)

1 lemon

Freshly ground black pepper

1 tablespoon soured cream

Chopped chives to garnish

First make the sauce. Scrub the mussels, discarding any that are cracked or open (see page 36) and steam them open in a large heavy pan in the wine or vermouth. Remove the mussels from the pan with a slotted spoon, reserving the cooking juices. Take the mussels from their shells, reserve 8 for garnishing the dish, and place the others in the bowl of a food processor or blender. Add the reserved cooking juices and a little of the velouté, if necessary, and whizz until smooth. Stir this purée into the remaining velouté.

Set up the steamer. Wash the fillets of brill and pat them dry, brush them with the juice of half the lemon and season with a little freshly ground black pepper. While they are steaming, gently heat up the sauce to simmering point, cook for 1 minute, remove from the heat and stir in the soured cream and juice from the remaining half of lemon to taste.

Pour a puddle of sauce onto each of 4 warmed plates, lay the fillets on the sauce, place 2 of the reserved mussels alongside each fillet, scatter the chopped chives over the top and serve straight away.

Variation: Frozen Japanese oysters in their liquid could be used in place of the mussels.

To microwave
Prepare the sauce as above. Put the brill, lemon juice and pepper in a large shallow dish, cover and cook on HIGH for 3–5 minutes. Complete the recipe.

Dab

Deep-fried dab in apple batter

A spicy apple batter gives unusual style to blander types of flat fish like dab, megrim, witch and so on. This makes a nice teatime dish for children, or a starter for a dinner, and I like to serve it with a dressing of mixed yoghurt and mayonnaise, wedges of lemon and slices of wholemeal bread.

Serves 4

1lb (500g) skinned fillets of dab, cut into pieces about 2in (5cm) square

Batter:

4oz (125g) plain flour

2 teaspoons baking powder

½ teaspoon ground mixed spice

Pinch salt

Freshly ground black pepper

5fl oz (150ml) apple purée

4 tablespoons cider

1 egg

2 tablespoons lemon juice

Sunflower oil or vegetable oil for frying

2 tablespoons flour

Freshly ground black pepper

First of all, make the batter. Sift the flour, baking powder, ground spices and seasoning into a bowl. Add the apple purée, cider and egg and beat well together for 1–2 minutes, then set aside for 30 minutes.

Place the pieces of fish in a bowl with the lemon juice and set aside for 20 minutes.

When you are ready to cook, heat up the oil in a large deep pan (see page 45 for notes on deep-frying). Coat the pieces of fish in the flour seasoned with black pepper, then dip in the batter and drop 5 or 6 pieces at a time into the hot oil. Cook for about 4 minutes until dark golden, then drain on kitchen paper and keep warm. Repeat with the remaining fish and serve straight away.

Variation: Dublin Bay prawns, scallops or monkfish are also very good cooked in this batter. You could try serving them with hot apple sauce.

Flounder

Fillets of flounder, dab or megrim with prawns and mushrooms

Some kinds of flounder are not so well flavoured as others, and dab and megrim definitely need a little boost to their flavour. This is a light, delicate dish, with a simple 'creamy' sauce and yet the dish is made entirely without cream, butter or flour. New potatoes and fresh green beans or mange-tout make good accompaniments.

Serves 4

2 medium to large flounder, dab or megrim, filleted and skinned

1 lemon

Freshly ground black or white pepper

8oz (250g) peeled prawns

1 tablespoon chopped tarragon, plus three whole sprigs to garnish

8oz (250g) button mushrooms

Oil for dry-frying

1 pint (600ml) warm fish stock (use trimmings from the fish – see page 70)

Dry white wine (optional) or water

2 tablespoons fromage blanc (optional)

Wash the fish fillets (you should have 4 from each fish) and pat dry with kitchen paper. Flatten them slightly (this will prevent them from shrinking when cooking) with the side of a knife blade and very lightly score them on the side that formerly had the skin on (see page 23 for method). Cut the lemon in half; use one half for squeezing and slice the other for a garnish.

Sprinkle each fillet with a little lemon juice and season with pepper. Cover half of each fillet with prawns, then sprinkle a little of the chopped tarragon over the other half. Fold the fillets in half and arrange them in a heavy poaching or frying pan. They should fit neatly in the pan so that the stock will easily cover them.

Now trim and wipe the mushrooms and halve or quarter, depending on their size. Dry-fry them briefly in an oil-brushed pan and then put them between and around the fillets. Sprinkle the remaining tarragon all over, together with a squeeze or two of lemon juice and a grinding of pepper. Pour in just enough warm stock to cover the fillets. Add more stock, or some white wine or water if necessary. Bring slowly and gently up to just under simmering point and poach for 3 to 6 minutes, depending on the size and thickness of the fillets.

Using a spatula, carefully transfer the cooked fish to a warmed serving dish. Use a perforated spoon to rescue stray prawns. Arrange the mushrooms around the fillets. Keep warm.

Bring the poaching liquid up the boil and reduce by half, or until you have a good quantity of slightly thickened sauce. Now take it off the heat and whisk in the fromage blanc, if using. Pour this sauce all over the fish and serve immediately, garnished with slices of lemon and sprigs of tarragon.

To microwave
Prepare the fish and mushrooms as above. Put in a large shallow dish with the lemon juice, pepper and only half the quantity of stock. Cover and cook on HIGH for 5–7 minutes. Transfer the fish to a serving dish, then cook the poaching liquid, uncovered, on HIGH for 5 minutes. Complete as above.

Skate and Ray

Wings of skate and ray have sweet and pleasant flesh which slides or shreds easily off soft ribs.

Skate with black butter

You need very fresh skate and a good court bouillon for this classic recipe. The butter is not in fact black but a deep golden sizzling brown. Have warmed plates and all your ingredients ready before you start to cook as the final stage before serving takes only seconds. Plain boiled potatoes are good with this dish.

Serves 4

1½–2lb (750g–1kg) skate wings, cut into 4 pieces if large

1–1½ pints (600–900ml) warm court bouillon (see page 69)

3oz (75g) butter

3 tablespoons white wine vinegar

Capers and chopped parsley to garnish

Wash the fish and pat dry with kitchen paper. If the skate wings are not already skinned, you will find this easier to do after the fish has been poached – the skin also adds flavour during the cooking.

Place the wings in a poaching or frying pan and add the warm court bouillon. Heat up to just under simmering point and poach gently until cooked. Carefully peel off the skin and transfer the fish to a warmed serving plate.

Now heat the butter in a small pan and, when it turns a deep golden brown, pour it all over the fish. Quickly return the pan to the heat and deglaze it with the wine vinegar – stir vigorously until it has reduced – and pour this over the fish too. Top with a scattering of capers and chopped parsley and serve straight away.

To microwave
Put the pieces of skate in a large shallow dish with 5fl oz (150ml) court bouillon. Cover and cook on HIGH for 9–12 minutes. Complete as above.

Tucker's skate

My friend Tucker tells me that skate is best fried, East-End-style – and I think he may be right – but leave out the chips and serve it with a mixed salad.

Serves 4

1½–2lb (750g–1kg) skate wings, cut into 4 pieces if large

Batter No. 2 (see page 83)

Sunflower oil for frying

Lemon wedges to garnish

Wash the fish and pat it dry with kitchen paper. Cut each wing in half so that you have 4 nice wedges of skate. Heat 1in (2.5cm) oil in a large frying pan or wok until you can just detect a slight haze. Dip each piece of skate into the batter and fry for 2 to 4 minutes on each side. Drain very well on kitchen paper before serving with lemon wedges.

Steamed ray with crispy herbed crust

This is a marvellous way to cook wings of ray or skate. After steaming, the wings are smothered with a crust of breadcrumbs, garlic, herbs, lemon juice and olive oil and flashed under a hot grill, producing a thin aromatic golden crust. I like to serve these wings with a dish of tomato salad garnished with more fresh herbs.

Serves 4

2½lb (1.25kg) ray or skate wings, cut into four pieces

Freshly ground black pepper

Juice of one lemon

4 tablespoons olive oil

1 clove garlic, crushed

2 tablespoons mixed fresh herbs (e.g. oregano, parsley, basil), finely chopped

4oz (100g) wholemeal breadcrumbs

Sprigs of fresh herbs to garnish

First, set up the steamer. Wash the skate or ray wings, pat them dry and place them, dark skin side down, on the steamer plate. Season lightly with pepper, sprinkle with a little lemon juice, cover and steam until barely cooked – about 12 to 15 minutes depending on the thickness of the wings.

Meanwhile, whisk together the olive oil, crushed garlic and 1 tablespoon of lemon juice. Combine the finely chopped herbs with the breadcrumbs.

Light the grill and cover the grill rack with a double thickness of aluminium foil, lightly brushed with olive oil. Carefully remove the dark skin from the fish – it will slide off quite easily – and place the pieces on the grill rack. Brush each wing generously with the olive oil, lemon juice and garlic mixture, scatter with the breadcrumbs and herbs, then drizzle over the remaining olive oil mixture. Place under the hot grill for about 1 minute, or until the crust is sizzling and golden. Serve on warmed plates, garnished with whole sprigs of fresh herbs.

Variations: Steaming gives superb moist results with fillets of other white fish, such as bass, John Dory, hake, perch, plaice or witch dab – all of which can be finished under the grill with the crispy herb crust.

Halibut

Baked halibut parcels served with aïoli

Use steaks from a large halibut, or fillets from smaller fish for these juicy parcels, and serve with steamed potatoes and fennel.

Serves 4

4 steaks or fillets of halibut

A little sunflower oil

2 leeks, trimmed and very finely sliced, including all the good pale green parts

Freshly ground black pepper

Juice and grated rind of 1 lemon, lime or orange

2 large ripe tomatoes, peeled and sliced

Sprigs of fennel leaves, if using as a side dish, or finely chopped parsley and snipped chives to garnish

1 quantity Aïoli (see page 76)

Pre-heat the oven to gas mark 6, 400°F (200°C). Cut out 4 pieces of aluminium foil large enough to make a generous parcel of each piece of fish. Brush the foil lightly with oil.

Wash the fish and pat it dry. Divide half the chopped leeks onto the base of each parcel, and place the fish on top. Season each lightly with freshly ground black pepper, sprinkle with a little of the citrus fruit juice and all the grated rind. Top with the remaining chopped leeks and arrange the sliced tomatoes on top. Season again with a little more pepper and sprinkle with the remaining juice. Draw up the sides of the foil and crimp to make loose but air-tight parcels. Place them on a baking tray and bake for about 25 minutes.

To serve, place the parcels on warmed plates, peel back the foil and garnish with the herbs. Or, if you prefer, allow your guests to open the parcels and savour the sudden wonderful escape and aroma of the mingled cooking juices. Hand the Aïoli separately.

To microwave

Prepare as above, making the parcels with double sheets of greaseproof paper. Arrange the parcels in a circle in the oven and cook on HIGH for 10–12 minutes depending on the thickness of the fish. Complete the recipe.

Halibut au gratin

Halibut has firm white flesh but tends to be rather dry. To remedy this problem, parcel the fish in foil with a dash of wine, herbs and seasonings and then bake or grill it. You could also try baking it according to this recipe, where the steaks are coated with freshly grated Parmesan cheese and topped with a light savoury custard. I serve it with grilled tomatoes in shallow soup bowls.

Serves 4

4 halibut steaks

A little oil

3 eggs

Freshly ground black pepper

4oz (125g) fresh Parmesan cheese, finely grated

6–8 tablespoons fromage blanc

Pinch of cayenne pepper (optional)

2 large or 4 small tomatoes, halved

Parsley, finely chopped

Pre-heat the oven to gas mark 4, 350°F (180°C).

Wash the halibut steaks and pat them dry with kitchen paper. Lightly oil a gratin or baking dish into which the steaks just fit in a single layer.

Beat one of the eggs thoroughly with a grinding or two of pepper and dip the fish steaks in this. Now coat them all over with the grated Parmesan cheese and put them in the baking dish. Cover with foil or greased greaseproof paper and bake in the oven for 10 to 15 minutes.

While this is happening, whisk together the fromage blanc and remaining 2 eggs – and add a pinch of cayenne pepper if you like. Remove the foil or greased greaseproof paper from the fish, pour the custard over the steaks and return the dish to the oven for a further 10 minutes, or until the custard is set.

Meanwhile, heat the grill. Scatter the tomato halves with freshly ground black pepper and a little chopped parsley and grill them until they are soft and juicy. Transfer the fish steaks to four warmed shallow soup bowls, put a portion of grilled tomatoes alongside each and sprinkle with parsley.

Megrim

Fillets of shallow-fried megrim with remoulade sauce

I do not consider megrim to be a particularly tasty fish, and yet I am always surprised at how good really fresh fillets taste when swiftly shallow-fried and served with parsley and wedges of lemon. Grilled mushrooms and tomatoes are pleasant with this dish. I am disappointed when I bake megrim, however, as the flesh is soft and the flavour is not outstanding. The fillets are very thin, so a large fish will be needed to serve two people.

Serves 4

2 × 2–2½lb (1–1.25kg) megrim, filleted and carefully skinned

2oz (50g) fresh brown breadcrumbs

1 egg

2 tablespoons skimmed milk

Freshly ground black pepper

Sunflower oil

Finely chopped parsley and lemon wedges to garnish

1 quantity Remoulade Sauce (page 76)

Wash the fish fillets (you should have 2 from each fish) and pat dry with kitchen paper.

Put the breadcrumbs on a large plate. Beat the egg with the milk in a shallow basin and season with black pepper. Heat up a little oil in a heavy frying pan, dip each fillet in the beaten egg, roll in the breadcrumbs and place in the hot pan. Fry 2 at a time if you have room. They will need 30 seconds to 1 minute on each side, depending on their thickness. When lifting the fillets from the pan, give them a gentle shake to drain, and serve straight away sprinkled with parsley and garnished with lemon wedges. Hand the sauce separately.

Plaice

In common with other flat fish (except Dover sole) plaice is at its best when very fresh. After that, its flavour deteriorates rapidly.

I like freshly caught plaice baked whole with a few scraps of butter and a squeeze of lemon juice – the glistening brown skin with its sprinkling of orange spots makes a beautiful presentation.

Plaice fillets are excellent for goujons and tempura (see pages 108 and 213).

Plaice fillets with lemon and sage

You can also use fresh fillets of sole for this delightfully simple dish.

Serves 4

4 plaice fillets, skinned

Butter

4oz (125g) button mushrooms, thinly sliced

Pinch of salt and freshly ground black pepper

4 sage leaves

1 lemon

1 tablespoon parsley, chopped

1–2 tablespoons dry white wine

1 tablespoon single cream or fromage blanc

Pre-heat the oven to gas mark 5, 375°F (190°C).

Wash the fish fillets and pat dry with kitchen paper. Lightly butter a shallow baking dish and lay the mushrooms over the base, seasoning lightly. Fold the fish fillets in half, tuck a broken sage leaf into the fold of each one and arrange them on top of the mushrooms. Cut the lemon in half. Squeeze the juice from one half over the fillets and mushrooms. Shake a grinding of pepper over each fillet, top with a nut of butter and a slice from the remaining lemon half and sprinkle parsley over the whole dish. Add the wine and bake in the oven for 15 minutes, or until the fish is just cooked.

Lift the fillets on to warmed plates. Stir the cream or fromage blanc into the hot juices and mushrooms, spoon over the fish and serve.

To microwave
Put the mushrooms and butter in a large shallow dish, cover and cook on HIGH for 3 minutes, stirring once. Prepare the fish as above, then arrange on top of the mushrooms. Sprinkle with the lemon juice, pepper and lemon slices, re-cover and cook on HIGH for 4–6 minutes or until the fish is cooked. Transfer the fillets to warmed plates. Stir the cream or fromage blanc into the mushrooms and cook on HIGH for 1 minute. Spoon over the fish.

Stuffed plaice fillets with sweet red pepper sauce

Large and slightly more elderly fillets are very good rolled around a stuffing, especially when contrasted with this startling red sauce. Plain rice and peas are a fine accompaniment to the dish.

Serves 4

4 whole or 8 halves plaice fillets, skinned

2 tablespoons dry white wine

Sweet Red Pepper Sauce:

4 red peppers, de-seeded and chopped

2 medium onions, finely chopped

4 cloves garlic, crushed

Juice of ½ lemon

2 tablespoons olive oil

Stuffing:

2oz (50g) breadcrumbs

2 tablespoons spring onions, finely chopped

2 tablespoons parsley, finely chopped

Juice of ½ lemon

2 teaspoons lemon rind, finely grated

1 small egg, beaten, to bind

Freshly ground black pepper

Wash the plaice fillets, pat dry with kitchen paper and prepare them for rolling (see page 60).

Now make the sauce. Place the chopped peppers in a saucepan with the onions, garlic, lemon juice and olive oil. Cook very gently over a low heat for about 1 hour – the peppers will make quite a bit of their own juicy liquid. Process the mixture in a blender until smooth, then set aside.

Combine the stuffing ingredients to make a moist mixture and spread some of this along each fillet, remembering that the side which formerly had the skin on must be on the outside of the roll so that it will contract and keep its shape when cooked. Heat the grill. Remove the rack from the grill pan and arrange the stuffed rolls on the base of the pan. Add the white wine. Grill under a medium heat for 3 or 4 minutes; then, using a spatula, carefully turn the rolls over and grill for a further 3 or 4 minutes, or until cooked.

Transfer the rolls to a warm serving platter, gently re-heat the sauce, adding the wine and cooking juices from the grill pan. Pour this *around*, not over, the plaice rolls and serve immediately.

Variation: Fillets of megrim, witch or flounder can also be used for this recipe, which is lovely with Watercress Sauce (page 72).

To microwave
Prepare the fish, sauce and stuffing as above. Put the stuffed fish in a shallow dish and pour over the wine. Cover and cook on HIGH for 5–7 minutes. Complete as above.

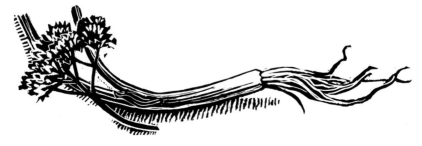

Tangy stir-fried plaice, flounder or megrim with prawns

This stir-fry can be served chilled on a salad of watercress and cucumber, or bubbling hot on a bed of noodles and beansprouts. Either way, the tangy marinade of ginger, pineapple and citrus will serve as a lovely hot or cold sauce.

Serves 3–4

1lb (500g) fillets of plaice, flounder or megrim, skinned

8oz (250g) peeled prawns

Marinade:

2oz (50g) tinned or fresh pineapple chunks

1in (2.5cm) cube of fresh ginger, peeled and grated

Juice and grated rind of 1 orange

Juice and grated rind of 1 lime or lemon

2 teaspoons coriander seeds, crushed

2 cloves garlic, crushed

Freshly ground black pepper

Sunflower oil

To serve:

Noodles or watercress and cucumber salad

Cut the fish into strips – about 2in × ½in (5cm × 1cm) is a good size. If the prawns have been frozen and thawed, pat and squeeze them thoroughly dry with kitchen paper.

Place all the marinade ingredients, except the grated rind of the orange and lime or lemon, in the bowl of a food processor or blender and whizz until smooth. Pour into a glass or china bowl, add the fish and prawns, cover and leave to marinate for 30 minutes.

If you are serving the dish hot, cook the noodles, drain and keep them warm on a serving dish.

Heat up a little sunflower oil in a wok or large heavy-bottomed frying-pan, remove the fish and prawns from the marinade, shaking off any excess liquid, and briskly stir-fry for one minute. Then add the marinade to the pan and gently stir as you cook for a further 2 minutes. Pour the bubbling mixture over the noodles, garnish with reserved grated rind and serve immediately. Alternatively, allow to cool, spoon onto a bed of watercress and cucumber, pouring over the juices as dressing and garnishing with the grated rind.

Variation: Use the sliced lobes of scallops in place of the prawns and garnish with the lightly steamed corals.

Steamed fillets of plaice Chinese-style

Very fresh plaice fillets are enhanced by a good-quality light soy sauce combined with fresh ginger and spring onions. I serve these fillets as a starter with a flourish of mange-tout or slices of fresh mango and garnished with frilled spring onions.

Serves 4

4 fillets of plaice, dark skin removed (see page 20)

4 spring onions, trimmed and sliced diagonally including all the good green parts

1in (2.5cm) cube fresh ginger, peeled and finely sliced

1 tablespoon good-quality light soy sauce

Frilled spring onions to garnish (see page 84)

First set up the steamer. Place half the spring onions and ginger all over a large plate. Lightly brush each side of the plaice fillets with soy sauce and lay them on top. Scatter with the remaining spring onions and ginger. Cover with an inverted matching plate to steam for 6 minutes, or until the fillets are *just* cooked.

Transfer to 4 warmed plates, garnish with the spring onions, pour any cooking juices over each fillet and serve immediately.

To microwave
Prepare as above. Cook on HIGH for 6–8 minutes. Complete the recipe.

Sole

With such a superb fish, it is important not to get your 'soles' mixed up. Dover sole is the true sole and not related to lemon sole, which isn't! It has a most wonderful flavour and needs little in the way of added ingredients. Dover sole is unusual among flat fish in that its flavour intensifies and is at its best when the fish is two or three days old. I prefer to keep the skin on as it adds to the flavour of the fish – but see page 20 if you prefer to skin it. In any case you may like to leave on the white skin (which should be scaled) to help the fish keep its shape and add to the flavour.

Grilled Dover sole

This is one of the simplest ways of cooking sole. I like to serve it with chopped parsley and new potatoes. Lemon sole, plaice and other flat fish can be grilled in the same way.

Serves 4

4 × 10oz (300g) Dover sole, skinned if preferred

1 tablespoon lemon juice

Freshly ground white or black pepper

1–2oz (25–50g) clarified butter (see page 56)

1 tablespoon parsley, very finely chopped

4 lemon wedges

Wash the fish and pat dry with kitchen paper.

Heat the grill and oil the grill rack. Season the soles on each side with lemon juice and pepper and brush with the melted clarified butter. Grill for about 4 or 5 minutes on each side, according to the thickness of the fish, brushing with a little more clarified butter if necessary. Carefully transfer to warmed plates, strew with chopped parsley, garnish with lemon wedges and serve immediately.

Rolled fillets of sole with salmon mousseline

Fillets rolled around a light fluffy filling, called a mousseline, are most appealing for a special lunch or dinner and far simpler to prepare than you might imagine. The rolled fillets, or paupiettes, can be served as a starter, or as a main course with asparagus and rice.

Serves 4

8 lemon sole fillets

1 tablespoon fromage blanc

Mousseline:

8oz (250g) fresh salmon, cut into cubes

Pinch of salt, freshly ground black pepper

Pinch of grated nutmeg

5fl oz (150ml) double cream

1 egg white

To poach:

5fl oz (150ml) good dry white wine

5fl oz (150ml) fish stock (see page 70)

First make the mousseline. Place the salmon in the bowl of a food processor and whizz for 30 seconds. Now add a pinch of salt and freshly ground black pepper, a pinch of nutmeg, the cream and egg white and process for a further 20 seconds. Alternatively, mince the salmon very finely and thoroughly beat in the seasoning, cream and egg white. This is a laborious method, and slightly rougher texture is achieved. Put the mousseline mixture into a bowl and chill for 1 hour.

Trim the sole fillets if necesary, then wash them and pat dry with kitchen paper. (See page 23 for preparing fillets for paupiettes.) Spread each lightly scored fillet generously with the mousseline. Roll them from the head to the tail end and place them in a poaching pan just wide enough to hold all the fillets snugly so that they do not unroll as they poach.

Carefully pour in the dry white wine and fish stock so that it almost covers the fillets, bring it up to just under simmering point, cover the pan and poach for 10 to 12 minutes or until the fish is cooked. For the best results, cover the poaching pan loosely with a sheet of lightly greased greaseproof paper punched with a few tiny holes. Transfer the fillets to a warmed platter.

Now boil down the poaching liquid to thicken and reduce by half. Take off the heat and whisk in 1 tablespoon fromage blanc. Pour over and around the fillets. If you are serving asparagus as an accompaniment, arrange a decorative criss-cross border of spears around the edge of the fish platter.

To microwave
Prepare as above. Put the fish and wine in a large shallow dish, cover and cook on HIGH for 6–8 minutes. Complete as above, adding the stock.

Sole meunière

Leave the heads and skin on the fish, if possible, for this classic dish. If you prefer, you can take off the dark skin, but leave the white skin on, as it becomes deliciously crisp and also helps keep the shape of the fish. Boiled new potatoes make a good accompaniment.

Serves 4

4 Dover sole

3oz (75g) butter

A little milk

2oz (50g) flour

Pinch of salt and freshly ground black pepper

Juice of ½ lemon

1–2 tablespoons finely chopped parsley to garnish

Wash the fish and pat it dry with kitchen paper.

When you are ready to cook, heat up half the butter in a frying pan. Dip the soles in the milk, then in the flour (seasoned with salt and pepper) in a swift, light, flowing action. Fry the soles for 4 to 5 minutes on each side, according to the thickness of the fish. Transfer them to warmed plates.

The butter used for cooking the soles should be golden brown. Now add the remaining butter and the lemon juice, swirl it around the pan, scraping up all the fishy juices, and pour this sauce over the soles. Scatter with the finely chopped parsley before serving. (I like sole served on the bone but, if you prefer, you can easily lift off the fillets just before serving.)

Sole St Agnes

A dish of blithe freshness; versatile and suitable for fillets of all flat fish, or slender fillets or cutlets of white fish such as whiting, haddock, or hake. It is good served with a delicate green salad and small herbed new potatoes.

Serves 4

4 fillets of lemon sole (or use flounder, plaice, etc.)

Sunflower oil

8oz (250g) wholemeal breadcrumbs

4oz (125g) peeled cooked prawns, finely chopped

1 tablespoon parsley, finely chopped

3oz (75g) mild Cheddar cheese, grated

Juice of ½ lemon

Freshly ground black pepper

Wedges of lemon

Wash the fillets and pat them dry. Line your grill rack with aluminium foil and brush this lightly with oil. Pre-heat the grill to a high setting.

Combine the breadcrumbs, finely chopped prawns, parsley and cheese. Moisten with a little lemon juice and season with freshly ground black pepper.

Place the fillets on the grill rack, brush with sunflower oil and sprinkle with a little lemon juice. Cover with the breadcrumb mixture, then drizzle over a little more oil. Grill until the topping is dark brown and bubbling. Serve straight away on warmed plates with wedges of lemon.

Sole baked with Parmesan cheese

Use only freshly grated 'real' Parmesan cheese for this beautiful dish, and serve it with braised celery hearts.

Serves 4

4 Dover or lemon sole, skinned

Freshly ground black pepper

1oz (25g) butter

3 tablespoons dry white wine

Juice of ½ lemon

3oz (75g) Parmesan cheese, finely grated

4 braised celery hearts, to serve

Pre-heat the oven to gas mark 5, 375°F (190°C).

Wash the fish and pat it dry with kitchen paper. Season each side of the fish with pepper and lay them in a lightly buttered shallow baking dish. Pour the wine and the lemon juice around (not over) the fish, and cover each one with finely grated Parmesan cheese. Bake in the oven for about 15 minutes or until the fish is cooked.

Towards the end of the cooking time, reheat the braised celery. When the fish are baked, flash the dish under a pre-heated grill to colour the melted Parmesan cheese. Now arrange the braised celery in the dish with the sole and take straight to the table and serve with the juices.

Baked sole with tarragon

This is a lovely way to cook any flat fish – whole or in fillets. Dover or lemon sole can be simply served with plain boiled or steamed potatoes and the cooking juices poured over, followed by a crisp salad.

Serves 4

4 small to medium Dover or lemon sole, skinned and filleted

A little oil or butter

Pinch of salt, freshly ground black pepper

4 tablespoons fish stock (see page 70)

4 tablespoons dry white wine

Juice of ½ lemon or orange

Tarragon leaves

Pre-heat the oven to gas mark 4, 350°F (180°C).

Wash the fish fillets and pat dry with kitchen paper. Lightly oil or butter a baking dish – choose a size in which the fillets will fit snugly. Season the fillets on both sides with a pinch of salt and freshly ground black pepper. Lay them in the dish and pour over the stock, wine and lemon or orange juice. Place a few leaves of tarragon over each fillet (reserve some for a garnish) and bake in the oven for 10 to 15 minutes, according to the thickness of the fish. Baste the fish once or twice as it bakes, and serve, garnished with the reserved tarragon, with the juices from the dish.

Turbot

Wonderful turbot – the flavour is so fine that it seems almost wicked to do more than simply poach or steam it. However, although the flesh is firm and tasty, a graceful sauce or dressing can enhance its otherwise plain and pale appearance.

Turbot is a huge fish, usually sold in steaks or fillets. Even the smaller ones – called chicken turbot – which are sold whole, are often quite big, and you need a very large frying pan or a turbotière (a specially shaped fish kettle) in which to cook it. The head, tail and bones of turbot make an excellent gelatinous stock.

A salad of turbot with lemon and marjoram dressing

Cold turbot makes a superb salad course. This simple dish, served with brown bread, can be an attractive light lunch or starter to a grander meal. You could substitute fresh coriander leaves for the marjoram or basil, but remember that coriander has a sharper taste.

Serves 4

1lb (500g) cooked turbot pieces, bones removed

Pinch of white sugar

Pinch of salt, freshly ground black pepper

1 teaspoon marjoram or basil, finely chopped

Grated rind and juice of ½ lemon

2 tablespoons good-quality olive oil

3fl oz (75ml) single cream

3fl oz (75ml) fromage blanc

1 firm lettuce

1 bunch round red radishes

Whisk the sugar, salt, pepper, herbs and lemon rind in the lemon juice with a fork until the sugar and salt have dissolved. Whisk in the oil, then stir in the cream and fromage blanc until you have a creamy sauce – be careful not to overstir or it will thicken too much.

Now arrange the washed crisp lettuce leaves on four plates, arrange the turbot and radishes among the leaves and pour over the sauce.

Poached chicken turbot with saffron sauce

Serves 4

1 × 2–3lb (1–1.5kg) chicken turbot

Milk and water for poaching (see page 40)

½ teaspoon saffron powder

1oz (25g) beurre manié – ½oz (15g) butter creamed with ½oz (15g) flour

Pinch of salt, freshly ground black pepper

Squeeze of lemon juice

1 tablespoon chopped parsley, or a few peeled prawns and lemon wedges to garnish

First wash the fish (it will already have been gutted at sea) and pat dry with kitchen paper. Prepare a pan large enough to poach the whole fish – you could improvise with a large roasting tin and lid of aluminium foil.

Place the fish in the warmed poaching liquid to which you have already added the powdered saffron. Bring up to just under simmering point and poach for 10 to 15 minutes, or according to the size and thickness of the fish. The flesh is firm, quickly turns white and eases from the bone when just cooked. Using two large fish slices or spatulas, carefully transfer the fish to a large warm serving platter.

Now simmer the cooking stock until it has reduced a little, at the same time dropping in tiny nuts of beurre manié and stirring vigorously until the sauce is smooth and creamy. Remove from the heat and stir in salt, pepper and a squeeze of lemon juice to taste. Pour the sauce over the fish, scatter with chopped parsley or prawns and serve with wedges of lemon. Hand the sauce separately.

Oily Fish

Unlike white fish, which store their rich and nutritious oil in their livers, the oil of these fish is distributed throughout their bodies and consequently they lend themselves well to grilling and barbecuing. All types of oily fish should be eaten very fresh as they deteriorate quickly.

Anchovies

The flavour of anchovies is unique and distinctive. Tinned anchovies are indispensable for pasta with fish sauces, for larding other species of fish, and for adding to some meat dishes, salads and pizzas. If they are too salty for you, soak them first in a little milk, rinse and then dry with kitchen paper.

Baked anchovy, tomato and basil rolls

These baked rolls are quick and easy to prepare. Serve them as a hot appetiser with cool white wine or cold with salad for picnics or summer lunches. Adjust the quantities according to the size of your loaf and your taste for anchovies.

Makes 12 to 16 rolls

1 × 1½oz (40g) tin anchovies, well drained

6–8 slices wholemeal or white bread

4 tablespoons good-quality olive oil

2–3 tablespoons tomato purée

2 teaspoons basil, finely chopped

2oz (50g) Parmesan cheese, grated

Pre-heat the oven to gas mark 6, 400°F (200°C).

Cut the crusts off the slices of bread. Mix together the oil and tomato purée and spread the slices of bread with this paste. Sprinkle with the finely chopped basil – which must be fresh for this recipe; dried is not suitable. Lay 2 or 3 anchovy fillets diagonally on each slice of bread.

Now carefully roll the bread slices, put them on a lightly oiled baking sheet, brush with a little olive oil – or any remaining oil and tomato purée mixture – then sprinkle with the grated Parmesan cheese. Bake in the oven for 15 to 20 minutes until the rolls are crisp and golden. Let them rest for 2 minutes before cutting each one in half to serve.

Variation: Use tinned sardines, or thin strips of smoked mackerel.

Family pizza with anchovies, cheese and olives

If you have time to make your own bread dough, a home-made pizza is unbeatable – fresh, springy and moist. It makes a robust lunch dish served with a crisp green salad and red table wine.

I use a 15 × 10in (37.5 × 25cm) baking sheet to make one large rectangular pizza, which gives 4 generous servings. Simply halve the ingredients for a pizza for 2. I like the base to be thin and crispy and the edge to puff up to a crunchy crust.

Serves 4

2 × 1½oz (40g) tins anchovies, well drained

Olive oil

1 × 14oz (397g) tin tomatoes, drained and coarsely chopped, *or* 1½lb (750g) ripe fresh tomatoes, sliced

Freshly ground black pepper

12oz (350g) mozzarella cheese, thinly sliced

About 20 black olives

1–2 tablespoons basil, marjoram or oregano, finely chopped

Pizza dough:

1lb (500g) plain flour

1½ teaspoons salt

2 teaspoons dried yeast

10fl oz (300ml) warm water

1 teaspoon sugar

3 tablespoons olive oil

First make the pizza dough. Dissolve the yeast in the warm water together with the sugar and leave to ferment. Sift the flour into a bowl with the salt. When the yeast mixture begins to froth, pour it into the flour. Stir in the olive oil and mix to a firm dough, first with a wooden spoon and then with your hands. Add a little more flour if the dough is too sticky. Knead well for 10 minutes until the dough is elastic and smooth, then roll it in a little oil to prevent a crust forming, cover with a damp cloth and leave to rise. When the dough has doubled in size, and just before you are ready to cook, pre-heat the oven to gas mark 8, 450°F (230°C). Oil a baking sheet.

Knock down the dough on a floured board, roll it out, then flatten it into the oiled baking sheet, pushing up the edges very slightly to form a rim. Now cover the rectangle with the chopped tinned tomatoes or the sliced fresh tomatoes and give a good shake of freshly ground black pepper all over. Top with slices of mozzarella cheese, criss-crossed with the anchovy fillets. Dot the olives all over in a decorative way and sprinkle with the chopped herbs. Drizzle a little olive oil all over the pizza and bake in the top part of the oven for 20 to 30 minutes, or until the olives are beginning to wrinkle and the cheese is melted and golden. Eat hot or warm.

Variation: Use mussels or fresh sardines instead of anchovies. If you do not have time to make your own bread, try frying thick slices of fresh bread (or split baguettes), in a little olive oil, then spreading them generously with the pizza topping and browning them under a hot grill.

Fresh anchovies baked with oregano

Fresh anchovies, with their characteristic flavour, are unusual but not impossible to find. They are occasionally caught off our coasts; or, if you are on holiday, you may find them in Mediterranean fishing ports.
Serve this recipe with fresh crusty bread to mop up the juices and salad greenery. Sprats or fresh sardines can be baked in the same way.

Serves 4

2–2½lb (1–1.25kg) fresh anchovies, gutted, with heads left on

Olive oil

Freshly ground black pepper

2–3 tablespoons oregano, chopped

Juice of 1 lemon

Pre-heat the oven to gas mark 7, 425°F (220°C).
Wash the anchovies and pat them dry with kitchen paper. Lightly oil a shallow baking dish with olive oil and lay the fish in it side by side. Sprinkle over a good grinding of black pepper, the oregano and the lemon juice. Drizzle a little olive oil over the fish – just enough to give a glaze – then bake in the oven for 10 to 15 minutes, or until they are cooked.

Variation: This is a good way to cook sardines.

Herring

Herring roes on toast

My sister and I were weaned on herring roes, or so I am told. When you think of it, it must be the ideal natural introduction to solid food.

Serves 4

8oz (250g) soft herring roes

4 slices wholemeal bread or wholemeal muffins

1–1½oz (25–40g) butter

Pinch of cayenne pepper

Freshly ground black pepper

1 lemon, quartered, to garnish

Wash the roes carefully and pat dry with kitchen paper.

Toast the bread or muffins, and meanwhile heat the butter in a pan and gently turn the roes in this. Sprinkle them with cayenne and black pepper as you cook them for 2 or 3 minutes until nicely browned. Serve them on the lightly buttered toast or muffins garnished with quarters of lemon, and with more cayenne and black pepper to hand.

Three exotic treatments of shellfish: King prawns in their shells with coriander and chilli (page 212); Mussels served on the half-shell with special mayonnaise (page 218); and Prawn tempura with nori (page 213).

(Overleaf) Suggestions for a mid-summer lunch table: A warm salad of tagliatelle and hake with tuna and capers (page 123); Dressed crab (page 199); Seviche (page 268); Steamed haddock with saffron sauce (page 115); John Dory poached with scallops (page 124); and Marinated kippers (page 177).

Grilled herrings with mustard, dill and yoghurt sauce

Now that the 'herring ban' is relaxed, these fish are once again plentiful and cheap – and wonderful for breakfast, lunch or supper. Children served with whole herring will need a little help with the bones!

Serves 4

4 medium to large herrings, gutted

A little sunflower oil

Freshly ground black pepper

1 lemon, quartered, to garnish

Mustard, Dill and Yoghurt Sauce (see page 189) to serve

If the herrings have roes, keep these for another dish. Wash the fish under running cold water and pat dry with kitchen paper. Heat the grill and lightly oil the grill rack. If the fish are large and plump, make two diagonal slashes on both sides of the body of each fish to allow the heat to penetrate.

Brush the herrings with a little oil and place them under the hot grill. Cook for about 4 to 5 minutes on each side, until the skin is crisp and the flesh cooked through. Serve sprinkled with black pepper and garnished with lemon quarters, and hand the Mustard and Dill Sauce separately.

To microwave
Prepare as above. Slash the fish twice on each side and remove the heads. Put in a large shallow dish, brush with olive oil, cover and cook on HIGH for 10–12 minutes, rearranging halfway through cooking.

Herring fillets in oatmeal

You can use coarse oatmeal or porridge oats for this classic Scottish way of cooking herring. The fillets can be shallow-fried or grilled.

Serves 4

4 medium to large herrings, gutted and filleted (butterfly fillets, page 25), with heads removed

3oz (75g) coarse oatmeal or porridge oats

Pinch of salt, freshly ground black pepper

2–4 tablespoons sunflower oil

Chopped parsley and lemon quarters to garnish

Tartare or Fresh Tomato Sauce (see pages 74 and 81) to serve (optional)

Wash the herring fillets and pat dry with kitchen paper. Season the oatmeal lightly with salt and pepper and press the fillets into it so that they are well coated on both sides. Heat the oil in a large frying pan or skillet, and fry the fillets (skin side up first) for about 3 minutes on each side, depending on the size of the fish. Drain the cooked fish on kitchen paper. Scatter chopped parsley over the herring and garnish with lemon quarters. Serve with Tartare or Fresh Tomato Sauce if preferred.

Rolled stuffed baked herring with cucumber and yoghurt sauce

In this dish the roes are returned to the herrings combined with a moist herby stuffing. Served in shallow dishes in the light sauce, it is a colourful starter or light lunch.

Serves 4

4 large herrings, gutted and filleted (butterfly fillets, page 25), with heads and tail fins removed

Chopped parsley to garnish

Stuffing:

2 tablespoons onion, finely chopped

A little oil

8oz (250g) soft roes (from the herrings), chopped

1 tablespoon parsley, finely chopped

Freshly ground black pepper

1 thick slice bread, crust removed, soaked in a little skimmed milk

Cucumber and Yoghurt Sauce (see page 73) to serve

Pre-heat the oven to gas mark 5, 375°F (190°C).

Wash the herring fillets and the roes and pat dry with kitchen paper.

Now prepare the stuffing. Cook the chopped onion in a little oil over a low heat for 8 to 10 minutes until it is transparent but not browned. In a mixing bowl combine the chopped herring roes with the softened onion, chopped parsley and a little black pepper. Squeeze the milk out of the bread and fork the bread into the stuffing to give an even mixture.

Open out the butterfly fillets and place them skin side down on a board. Divide the stuffing between them and roll up the fillets from the head end to the tail end, securing with wooden cocktail sticks or toothpicks. Put them in a lightly oiled baking dish in which they fit together closely in a single layer. Brush the fish with a little oil and bake in the oven for 15 to 20 minutes.

Meanwhile, prepare the Cucumber and Yoghurt Sauce. Pour some sauce into the base of four warmed shallow soup bowls. Place a stuffed herring roll in each bowl and garnish with a little chopped parsley.

To microwave

Prepare as above. Put the fish in a shallow dish, brush with oil, cover and cook on HIGH for 12–15 minutes. Complete as above.

Herrings baked in red wine and mango chutney with apple and ginger

This recipe reduces the oiliness of the herring and produces sweet-tasting fillets which are served chilled with mayonnaise and yoghurt flavoured with the cooking juices.

I arrange the fillets, silvery skin side up, on a platter of salad leaves, garnish them with chopped apple and gherkins and serve a cold potato salad in a separate dish.

Serves 4

4 medium herrings

10oz (275g) mango chutney

2–3 glasses dry red wine (to cover fish)

1 teaspoon powdered ginger

1 large cooking apple, not peeled but cored and cut into small chunks

Dressing:

4oz (100g) yoghurt

4oz (100g) mayonnaise (see page 74)

2–3 tablespoons cooking liquid from the herring

Fronds of fennel leaves, dill, or other green herbs in season to garnish

Pre-heat the oven to gas mark 6, 400°F (200°C).

Wash the herring, pat dry and reserve the roes for another recipe. Place the fish in a shallow baking dish of a size so that they fit in quite snugly. Mix together the chutney, red wine and ginger, add the apple and pour over the fish. Add more wine if the fish are not entirely covered. Cover the dish with aluminium foil or a lid, and bake in the oven for 15 minutes or until the fish are nearly cooked: leave them to cool in the liquid.

Whisk together the yoghurt and mayonnaise, and mix in 2 or 3 tablespoons of the cooking liquid to produce a pale pink dressing.

Lift the fish out of the dish using 2 spatulas. You will now find it easy to remove the head and tail, lift off the top fillet, and remove the bones to leave the bottom fillet. Arrange the fillets and garnish as described above.

To microwave

Remove the heads and tails from the herrings. Put the fish in a shallow dish with the remaining ingredients. Cover and cook on HIGH for 8–10 minutes, rearranging halfway through cooking. Complete the recipe.

Baked stuffed herrings in dry cider

This simple homely dish is very good indeed and can be served hot or chilled. Serve with parsleyed potatoes.

Serves 4

4 medium herrings, boned into butterfly fillets (see page 25)

Freshly ground black pepper

2 shallots, peeled and finely chopped

Grated rind and peeled and finely chopped flesh of 2 oranges

10fl oz (300ml) dry cider

Pre-heat the oven to gas mark 5, 375°F (190°C).

Wash the fillets and pat them dry. Lay them skin-side down on a board and season with freshly ground black pepper. Cover the flesh of each fillet with the finely chopped shallots and orange flesh, and roll the fillets up from the head to the tail end. Place them snugly in a baking dish, tucking under the tail ends so that the fillets do not unroll. (You can secure them with cocktail sticks if you wish.) Cover with the cider and three quarters of the orange rind and bake, uncovered, for about 25 minutes. Transfer to warmed plates, pour over a little of the delicious cooking juices and garnish each fillet with a little of the remaining grated orange rind.

Variation: Cold, the fillets may be served with a crisp green salad incorporating chopped apple, celery and peppers. Whisk a little of the cooking juices into a yoghurt and mayonnaise dressing, or soured cream. You could also serve them on a platter of mixed cold seafood as a starter, or part of a buffet. Mackerel can be cooked in the same way.

Rollmops

Herrings are superb when simply grilled, but for some people the oiliness is too rich and hard to digest. A delicious way to overcome this is by marinating them in a spiced vinegar for 3 or 4 days to create rollmops. Serve with a green salad and yoghurt dressing.

Serves 4 to 6

6 herrings, gutted and filleted, with heads removed

1 large onion or 2 shallots, finely chopped

4 gherkins, finely chopped

Marinade

1 large onion, roughly chopped

1 blade mace

1 bay leaf

4 cloves

4 allspice berries

Pinch of salt

8 black peppercorns

1 teaspoon brown sugar

5fl oz (150ml) water

5fl oz (150ml) wine vinegar

Wash the herring fillets and pat dry with kitchen paper. Finely chop the onion or shallots and the gherkins and mix together. Lay each herring fillet skin side down on a board and place a little of the onion and gherkin mixture on each. Roll up from head end to tail end and secure with a cocktail stick. Place all the herring rolls into a shallow heatproof dish or glass jar.

Put the remaining onion with all the other ingredients into a saucepan. Bring the liquid to the boil and simmer for a few minutes to allow the flavours to infuse. Then pour this liquid over the herring rolls, allow to cool, cover and set aside in a cool place or the refrigerator for 3 or (preferably) 4 days.

Variation: Try using mackerel fillets to create 'rollmacs'.

To microwave
Put the marinade ingredients in a large heatproof jug. Cook on HIGH for 2–3 minutes until boiling, then cook on HIGH for 1 minute. Complete as above.

Kippers

The versatile and ubiquitous kippered herring makes an excellent Sunday breakfast. It can be added to all manner of mixed seafood salads, tarts and soufflés, and also makes good pâtés and spreads for toast or muffins.

The best way to cook a plain kipper for breakfast is to 'jug' it. The virtue of this method is that there are no cooking smells. Stand the kipper, tail up, in a heatproof jug and cover it completely with boiling water. Five minutes later, lift the kipper out by its tail and serve straight away with toast and lemon wedges or mustard. Do not add any butter as the kipper is naturally oily. Kippers can also be gently grilled, or heated in a moderate oven, or in a microwave oven.

Marinated kippers

If you have a shallow rustic brown-glazed baking dish, use it for this recipe – the colours blend perfectly. Once marinated, the fillets and their marinade are deliciously pungent served on a bed of cold cooked green beans and chopped tomatoes with plenty of warm crusty bread and hearty red wine.

Serves 4

4 kipper fillets, skinned

Freshly ground black pepper

1 Spanish onion, thinly sliced

2 bay leaves, broken

3–4 whole cloves, crushed

2 tablespoons parsley, coarsely chopped

10fl oz (300ml) good-quality olive oil

4–6 tablespoons white wine vinegar

Lay the kipper fillets in a shallow dish, sprinkle with pepper and cover with the sliced onion, bay leaves, cloves and parsley. Combine the oil and vinegar and pour over the fillets. Cover with cling-film and put in the refrigerator for at least 8 hours, but preferably overnight. If the fillets are not entirely covered, turn them occasionally in their marinade.

Quick kipper pâté

You can make this tasty pâté in a food processor or blender, but I prefer the coarser texture and flecked appearance achieved when it is made by hand.

Serves 4 to 6 as a starter

8oz (250g) kipper fillets, cooked

4oz (125g) low-fat cream cheese

Juice of ½ lemon, plus lemon slices to garnish

1 tablespoon tomato purée

Freshly ground black pepper

Toast or water biscuits to serve

Make sure that there are no bones in the cooked kipper fillets. Roughly flake the flesh, mix with all the other ingredients and pound together. Pack the pâté into a pretty dish, fork the top up and lay halved lemon slices along it. Serve with slices of dry toast or water biscuits. You could also cut out thick rounds of bread with a scone cutter, toast them, spread generously with pâté and decorate with cucumber slices – children like these.

Variation: For a more luxurious pâté use smoked salmon.

Mackerel

Dill-pickled mackerel with mustard sauce

Sliced very thinly on the bias, these almost transparent slices of mackerel make a delicate starter, and the taste has a most distinctive quality – particularly highlighted by the sauce. The dish makes a delightful and simple presentation when the mackerel slices are fanned out on small plates garnished with a few sprigs of dill. Florentine fennel or wild fennel can be substituted for dill – the taste is different, but also exquisite.

This method of 'curing' mackerel is also used to create Gravad Lax or Gravlax (page 234), the Scandinavian salmon dish. You could serve it with a potato salad dressed with soured cream or yoghurt and chopped dill.

Serves 4 to 6

4 large mackerel, filleted

Curing mixture:

1 tablespoon black peppercorns, crushed

2 tablespoons sea salt

1 tablespoon caster sugar

1 bunch dill, coarsely chopped

Sauce:

2 tablespoons Dijon or German mustard

1 tablespoon sugar

1 large egg yolk

5fl oz (150ml) good-quality olive oil

1 tablespoon lemon juice or white wine vinegar

Freshly ground black pepper

1 tablespoon dill, finely chopped

Wash the mackerel fillets and pat dry with kitchen paper.

Prepare the curing mixture. Crush the peppercorns using a pestle and mortar, or the back of a wooden spoon or rolling pin, and combine with the salt and sugar.

Place one fillet of each pair skin side down, rub in an eighth of the curing mixture, then cover with the chopped dill. Adjust the amount of dill to your preference, but use a generous amount to achieve the characteristic flavour of this recipe. Rub another eighth of the remaining curing mixture into the corresponding fillet of each pair and place it skin side up on its mate, forming 4 'sandwiches'. Lay these in a shallow glass or earthenware dish, scattering over any remaining dill. Cover with aluminium foil, then search for a suitable plate or inverted lid with which to weigh down the mackerel – place on top a heavy stone or brick from your garden, or any heavy object you can lay your hands on.

Leave the fish for at least 36 hours, or up to 4 days, in a cool place or refrigerator, turning the fillets every 12 hours or so as they become compressed and the curing mixture permeates them.

For the sauce, beat together the mustard, sugar and egg yolk and add the oil as for mayonnaise (see page 75). The sauce is easily made by hand, or you can use a food processor or liquidiser. When you have added the lemon juice or white wine vinegar, check the taste and add a grinding of pepper, if you like, before folding in the chopped dill.

To serve, scrape off nearly all the dill and curing mixture (the odd peppercorn and green of the dill forms an attractive fringe to the slices). Using a very sharp knife, cut paper-thin slices across the fillets. Serve the sauce in a separate dipping dish.

Baked fillets of mackerel with fresh mint and apples

The fresh-tasting filling offsets the richness of the mackerel and makes an economical light lunch. This is a perfect dish for a summer barbecue.

Serves 4 as a starter

4 small to medium mackerel, filleted (butterfly fillets, page 25)

A little oil

1 large lemon

Freshly ground black pepper

1 bunch mint, finely chopped

2 apples (Cox or Russet), thinly sliced but not peeled

Soured cream to serve (optional)

Pre-heat the oven to gas mark 7, 425°F (220°C).

Wash the mackerel fillets and pat dry with kitchen paper. Lightly oil four squares of foil, cut to the size of the fish, and place a fillet skin side down on each one. Season with a good squeeze of lemon juice and a shake of pepper, and scatter over the mint to taste – but remember that mackerel has a strong rich flavour which is not easily overwhelmed. Arrange the apple slices along the fillets and sprinkle on more lemon juice.

Bring up the edges of the foil squares and at the same time roll up the fillets neatly. Crimp the foil parcels to seal them fairly firmly and twist the ends so that they look rather like large sweet wrappings. Bake in the oven for 15 to 20 minutes, serve with a dash of soured cream if you like.

To microwave

Prepare as above, using a double layer of greaseproof paper instead of foil. Put the fish in a large shallow dish, cover and cook on HIGH for 10–15 minutes, rearranging halfway through cooking.

Baked fillets of mackerel with lemon and spices

This spicy dish is good served with potatoes and mushrooms in soured cream.

Serves 4

4 small mackerel, filleted (butterfly fillets, page 25)

Pinch of salt and freshly ground black pepper

Juice of 1 lemon

1 chilli pepper

½ teaspoon coriander seeds, crushed

Sunflower oil

Wash the mackerel fillets and pat dry with kitchen paper. Place them on a board, skin side down, and season with salt, pepper and half the lemon juice.

Cut the chilli pepper in half lengthways, de-seed (wash your hands after this, and do not touch your eyes), then finely chop the flesh. Scatter the chilli and coriander over the mackerel and lightly rub into the flesh of the fish. Leave for 30 minutes.

Pre-heat the oven to gas mark 5, 375°F (190°C).
Lightly oil a baking dish. Close the fillets, as you would an open book, place
in the baking dish, sprinkle with the remaining lemon juice and a little oil
and dust with pepper. Bake uncovered for 20 to 30 minutes until the fillets
are cooked. Serve immediately.

To microwave
Prepare as above. Put the fish in a large shallow dish, cover and cook on HIGH
for 10–12 minutes, rearranging halfway through cooking.

Pan-fried mackerel with gooseberry sauce

*There are many variations of gooseberry sauce, traditionally served with mackerel to offset
its richness. This one is simple to make and effectively tart.*

Serves 4

4 small to medium mackerel, gutted

Freshly ground black pepper

Oil for frying

Sauce:

8oz (250g) gooseberries, plus 12 to garnish, topped and tailed

1 teaspoon honey, or to taste (optional)

Wash the mackerel and pat dry with kitchen paper. Cut off the heads if you
prefer, or if the fish are too long for your pan. Season the fish inside and out
with a sprinkling of pepper.
   Now make the sauce. Cook the gooseberries gently in a little water until
they are tender. Reserve 12 of the cooked gooseberries to use as a garnish,
then process or blend the remainder to a smooth purée. The quantity will
reduce down to 5fl oz (150ml). If this unsweetened sauce is not to your liking,
add honey to taste when simmering.
   Brush the bottom of a heavy frying pan or skillet with oil, then add 1
teaspoon more. Heat, then put in the fish (you will probably have to fry 2 at a
time). They will cook very quickly – after 2 minutes use tongs or two spatulas
to turn them. You should not need to use more oil unless you have a
temperamental pan that sticks.

Lift the mackerel out and briefly drain them on crumpled kitchen paper before placing them on warmed plates. Spoon a little gooseberry sauce alongside each fish and garnish with the reserved whole gooseberries.

Barbecued mackerel with rhubarb and ginger

There is a tendency for large whole fish to break up when barbecued. Inexpensive fish-shaped grids, well oiled, are an invaluable way of preventing this happening (see Equipment, page 55). If you cannot get hold of one of these grills, make sure that the barbecue rack is very well oiled. Cutting the head off the fish will make it less unwieldy when turning, although I think this spoils the appearance.

Serves 4

4 medium or 8 small mackerel, gutted

Freshly ground black pepper

A little oil

Sauce:

Juice of 1 orange, plus 1 matchstick of rind

1in (2.5cm) piece fresh root ginger, peeled and sliced

1 tablespoon honey, or to taste

8 sticks pink rhubarb, chopped

First make the sauce. In a heavy pan, warm the orange juice and matchstick of rind, the ginger and honey. Add the rhubarb and simmer for 5 to 8 minutes until the fruit is soft. Purée the sauce in a food processor or blender. Place it in the refrigerator until chilled through.

Light the barbecue (or heat the grill). Wash the mackerel and pat dry with kitchen paper. Make two or three diagonal slashes on both sides of each fish to allow the heat to penetrate. Season inside and out with a sprinkling of pepper, brush with a little oil and place over the hot barbecue. Cook for about 4 minutes on each side, depending on the distance of the rack from the fire and the size of the fish. (If grilling, the cooking time will be about the same.) The silvery skin will blister, brown and become crunchy. Serve straight away with the chilled rhubarb sauce.

Soused mackerel with samphire

A few years ago, I could drop a hook over the side of our boat and catch a mackerel a minute. 'Oh no, not mackerel again!' the family would groan, so I used to do a fair bit of sousing. It is a good way to cook mackerel because it will keep for 3 or 4 days in the refrigerator and the white wine vinegar reduces its natural oiliness. A warm potato salad goes well with this dish.

Serves 4

4 medium-sized mackerel, gutted

1 large onion, thinly sliced into rings

2 bay leaves, broken in half

12 black peppercorns, crushed

About 5fl oz (150ml) white wine vinegar

About 5fl oz (150ml) water

1 Webbs Wonderful lettuce, washed

1 bunch red radishes, sliced

Samphire, spinach or other green vegetable to garnish

Potato salad or brown bread and lemon wedges to serve

Pre-heat the oven to gas mark 4, 350°F (180°C).

Wash the mackerel and pat dry with kitchen paper. Place them snugly in a baking dish and scatter over the onion rings, bay leaves and peppercorns. Pour the wine vinegar and water over the mackerel, cover the baking dish with a lid or aluminium foil and bake for 30 to 45 minutes, depending on the thickness of the dish and the size of the fish.

When the fish are cooked, allow them to cool, then carefully lift them out using two spatulas so that they drain as you transfer them to a large plate. Cut the head and tail off each one and lift off the top fillet. Now remove the backbone, which will come away very easily exposing the other fillet.

Arrange the lettuce and radishes on a platter and lay the soused mackerel, skin side up, along the centre. Garnish with your chosen leaves.

Variation: Beer or cider can be used in place of vinegar.

To microwave
Remove the heads and prepare as above. Cover and cook on HIGH for 10–15 minutes, rearranging halfway through.

Warm smoked mackerel with lemon minted potato and spring onion sauté

If you have ever home-smoked your own fresh mackerel, you will know how succulent it tastes when eaten warm, straight from the smoker: the flesh is moist and velvety, quite unlike the dry, harsh-flavoured, highly coloured, cling-film species. (See page 48 for information on home smoking.) Good-quality commercially smoked mackerel can be gently warmed through in aluminium foil parcels with very good results. This is a lovely, if rather filling, supper dish; so, after a pause, serve fresh fruit to complete a simple summer's evening menu.

Serves 4

4 small to medium good-quality smoked mackerel

1 Webbs Wonderful lettuce

4oz (125g) button mushrooms, very thinly sliced

Vinaigrette dressing

Sunflower oil for frying

1lb (500g) potatoes, boiled in their skins, cubed or sliced

6 spring onions, sliced diagonally, including all the good green parts

1 lemon

1 tablespoon mint leaves, finely chopped, plus a few whole leaves to garnish

Freshly ground black pepper

Pre-heat the oven to gas mark 3, 325°F (170°C), or heat the grill or barbecue.

Wrap the smoked mackerel in individual foil parcels (you can take the fillets off if you prefer) and warm them gently in the oven, under the grill or over the barbecue.

Wash and dry the lettuce, and make it look sprightly in your best salad bowl. Scatter with the sliced mushrooms and drizzle over some vinaigrette – not too much as the salad is intended to be a foil to the lemony potatoes and naturally oily mackerel.

Now heat up the oil in a wok or large heavy frying pan. Add the potatoes and stir-fry them until they are crisp and golden. Toss in the spring onions and stir-fry for a further 2 minutes. Add the juice of half the lemon (reserve the other half to use as a garnish) and briskly stir-fry, then scatter over the chopped mint and a sprinkling of pepper and give a few final turns over the heat until the stir-fry is fragrant.

Place a smoked mackerel on each of four plates and garnish with thin halved slices cut from the reserved lemon half. Arrange the stir-fried lemon potatoes alongside and garnish with whole mint leaves. Serve with the green salad.

To microwave
Put the mackerel in a shallow dish and dot with butter. Cover and cook on HIGH for 2–3 minutes or until hot.

Smoked mackerel tartlets

Serve these melting, warm and fresh from the oven. I use 4in (10cm) patty or Yorkshire pudding tins, as these make tartlets of a size suitable for a starter or light lunch. You could use smoked trout or smoked salmon instead of mackerel if you wish.

Serves 4

8–10oz (250–300g) smoked mackerel fillets

6oz (175g) shortcrust pastry

8oz (250g) fromage blanc or cream

1 egg and 3 yolks

2 tomatoes, peeled and sliced

Freshly ground black pepper

1 tablespoon parsley, finely chopped

Pre-heat the oven to gas mark 4, 350°F (180°C).
Roll out the pastry to line 4 patty or tartlet tins and bake blind for 15 minutes. Remove them from the oven, then reduce the temperature to gas mark 3, 325°F (170°C).
Meanwhile, remove the skin and any stray bones from the mackerel and flake the flesh. Beat together the fromage blanc or cream, whole egg and egg yolks to make a custard.
Put some mackerel into each tartlet, cover with 2 slices of tomato, season with a grinding of black pepper and the parsley, and spoon in the custard. Bake in the oven for 15 minutes, or until the custard is set, and serve warm garnished with the chopped parsley.

Quick smoked mackerel pâté

Chill this simple pâté thoroughly. Serve it spread on crackers or warm soda bread, garnished with slivers of lemon.

Serves 4 to 6 as a starter

12oz (350g) smoked mackerel fillets

1 lemon

5oz (150g) low-fat cream cheese

2–3 teaspoons prepared horseradish sauce

Freshly ground black pepper

Skin and flake the mackerel, making sure that no bones remain. Squeeze the juice from half the lemon (reserve the other half to use as a garnish), add to all the other ingredients in the bowl of a food processor and whizz for 45 seconds. Alternatively, mix thoroughly together by hand, using a fork – this gives a more rough-textured pâté. Check the seasoning and add more lemon juice, pepper or horseradish if necessary. Turn the mixture into a pretty glass bowl, fork up the top and lay paper-thin slices of lemon, cut from the reserved half, all over in an attractive pattern. Chill for several hours before serving.

Variation: Use smoked trout or smoked salmon scraps if your budget permits.

Pasta salad with smoked mackerel, avocado and apple

This lovely combination mingles the smokey flavour of mackerel with a creamy sauce and spring onions, avocado and apple. The dish can be prepared in advance and served chilled in boats of Chinese leaves or chicory, or served warm on a bed of crispy lettuce, shiny round red radishes and chopped fresh herbs.

8oz (250g) smoked mackerel fillets

1lb (500g) pasta shells or spirals

6 tablespoons natural yoghurt

2 tablespoons mayonnaise (see page 74)

2–3 teaspoons lemon juice

1 avocado pear, ripe but firm, peeled and diced

2 Cox's eating apples, cored and diced

6 spring onions, trimmed and sliced diagonally, including all the good green parts

1–2 teaspoons dill seeds

Freshly ground black pepper

Chopped fresh dill or other herb to garnish

First cook the pasta in a large pan of lightly salted boiling water to which you have added a drop of oil to prevent the pasta from sticking.

While it is cooking, whisk together the yoghurt, mayonnaise and lemon juice in a large mixing bowl, then stir in the avocado, apple, spring onions and dill seed. Remove the skin from the smoked mackerel fillets, cut into strips and set aside.

Drain the cooked pasta thoroughly and tip into the mixing bowl, turning all the ingredients with a large spoon to combine them. Season with freshly ground black pepper. Allow to cool slightly before very carefully adding the smoked mackerel strips – mix the flakes in gently so that they do not break up. Serve straight away on a shallow serving dish or platter, garnished with fresh dill, or other chopped herbs in season. Sprinkle with a little more lemon juice and dill seeds before serving if you wish.

Variation: Use smoked trout, or salmon for a special buffet, and if avocado pears are not available, try using peeled cubed melon or mango. Seedless grapes are nice too.

Sardines, Pilchards and Sprats

Grilled sprats with mustard, dill and yoghurt sauce

Sprats (tiny ones are called brisling) are a member of the herring clan and rich in nutritious oil. If you see smoked sprats, buy them and serve them as part of a mixed seafood starter.

Fresh sprats are excellent little fish for grilling or barbecueing; it is best to clean them through the gills (see page 19) although they are perfectly all right if cooked ungutted. Try them with this super-sharp dressing.

Serves 4

Olive oil for grilling

1½–2lb (750g–1kg) sprats, gutted if preferred

Juice of ½ lemon

Pinch of salt, freshly ground black pepper

Mustard, Dill and Yoghurt Sauce:

5fl oz (150ml) natural yoghurt

1–2 teaspoons Dijon mustard (to taste)

1 tablespoon dill, finely chopped

First make the sauce. Whisk together the yoghurt and mustard and stir in the chopped dill. Put in the refrigerator for 1 to 2 hours to allow the flavours to mingle.

Heat the grill or barbecue and lightly oil the grill rack.

Wash the sprats and pat dry with kitchen paper. Season them with the lemon juice, a pinch of salt and a dusting of pepper. Grill them for 1 or 2 minutes on each side until the skin is crisp, crunchy and brown. Serve immediately with the chilled sauce.

Star-gazey pie

Each year just before Christmas, Tom Bowcock's Eve is celebrated in Mousehole, Cornwall, with this unusual pie. There are variations on most traditional recipes, but in this dish the heads of the fish always peep out from the pastry, with their eyes gazing up to the heavens.

Serves 4 to 6

8 large fresh sardines, small pilchards or herrings, gutted and filleted (butterfly fillets, page 25), with heads left on but tail fins removed

8oz (250g) wholemeal breadcrumbs

1 teaspoon ground cloves

1 teaspoon ground allspice

Freshly ground black pepper

1 small onion, very finely chopped

1 egg, beaten

1½lb (750g) shortcrust pastry

4 hard-boiled eggs, roughly chopped

8 teaspoons double cream

8 teaspoons natural yoghurt

4 tablespoons parsley, finely chopped

1 egg, beaten, to glaze

Pre-heat the oven to gas mark 7, 425°F (220°C).

    Wash the fish fillets thoroughly and pat dry with kitchen paper. Check for any stray bones, especially around the head, and remove these with tweezers.

    Combine the breadcrumbs, ground cloves, allspice, pepper and onion and beat in the egg to make a moist stuffing. Pack the stuffing into the bellies of the fish, re-shape and set aside.

    Now roll out half the chilled pastry and line a large, lightly oiled, shallow or flat pie-dish (about 12in (30cm) in diameter). Arrange the stuffed fish on the pastry as if they were the spokes of a wheel, with their heads overlapping the rim of the pie and their tails meeting in the middle. Scatter the chopped hard-boiled eggs in between, and then drop little blobs of cream mixed with yoghurt all over. Cover with a generous 4 tablespoons of chopped parsley and sprinkle with a shake or two of freshly ground black pepper.

Roll out and cut a pastry lid for the pie. Brush the rim of the pastry base, between the fish, with water and place the pastry lid over the pie. Press the lid down between the fish heads using your thumb, at the same time rolling the edge of the pastry back and around each head.

Brush the top of the pie with beaten egg. Using pastry scraps, cut out eight fish shapes and stick these to the lid in a decorative pattern. Brush them with beaten egg.

Bake the pie in the oven for 15 minutes, then reduce the temperature to gas mark 4, 350°F (180°C) and continue to cook for a further 20 to 25 minutes until the pie is golden brown.

Variation: Instead of using hard-boiled eggs, beat 4 eggs with the cream, yoghurt and parsley and pour this over and around the fish before covering with the pastry.

Grilled sardines with watercress and ricotta stuffing

I love the astringent taste of watercress in this simple stuffing. It makes a wonderful contrast to the tasty but rather oily little sardines, and the crisp brown skins of the fish in their turn make an attractive contrast to the freshness of the stuffing. The sardines can be grilled or barbecued. Serve them with an orange and watercress salad.

Serves 4

12–16 fresh sardines, depending on size

Sunflower oil

Stuffing:

1 medium onion, grated or very finely chopped

4–6oz (100–175g) ricotta cheese

1 squeeze lemon juice

Freshly ground black pepper

1 bunch watercress, trimmed and coarsely chopped

1 clove garlic, crushed (optional)

Lemon wedges to garnish

Bone the sardines through the belly as described on page 24. Beat the onion into the cheese in a small mixing bowl. Add a squeeze of lemon juice and a grinding of black pepper to taste. Fork in the chopped watercress together with the crushed garlic if using.

Heat the grill and lightly oil the rack. Using a teaspoon, stuff the belly of each sardine with the stuffing mixture until it is all used up. Grill the sardines for 3 to 4 minutes on each side, depending on their size. The skin will be crisp and crunchy. Serve garnished with wedges of lemon.

Tuna

There are several kinds of tuna, and the dark fleshy steaks are increasingly found on the fishmonger's slab. If you have never tried fresh tuna, ask your fishmonger to order it. I think it is a fish that is best cooked briefly – when baked slowly it is hardly different from tinned tuna, but when served raw and fresh in sashimi, grilled briskly on kebabs or swiftly fried it is sensational.

Rare tuna steaks with anchovies

A fishmonger friend of mine told me to fry tuna steaks as you would rare fillet steaks of beef – the outer edges of the tuna steaks turn white and the juicy insides are a beautiful dark fleshy red. Do try this recipe, and serve the steaks absolutely alone. Follow with a refreshing salad.

Serves 4

4 thick steaks of tuna

8 anchovy fillets, drained

A little milk (optional)

1 tablespoon good-quality olive oil

1oz (25g) butter

2 fat cloves garlic, finely chopped

Wash the tuna steaks and pat them dry with kitchen paper. Make random incisions through each steak with a small, very sharp, pointed knife.

If you find tinned anchovies rather strong and salty, soak them in a little milk for an hour, then rinse and drain. Slice each anchovy fillet in half lengthways. Using your fingers and a skewer or cocktail stick, push the strips of anchovy into the holes in the tuna steaks.

Now heat the oil and butter in a heavy frying pan or skillet and fry the garlic for 30 seconds. Drop in the steaks and fry at a high temperature for 30 seconds to 1 minute on each side so that they are quickly sealed. Use a fish slice to transfer them to warmed plates and serve immediately.

Tuna kebabs

This is another way to enjoy very fresh tuna. Replace the cherry tomatoes with firm button mushrooms or chunks of cucumber, according to your preference. The kebabs need only warm bread rolls as an accompaniment.

Serves 4

1½lb (750g) tuna

Good-quality olive oil

1lb (500g) cherry tomatoes (see above)

Bay leaves

Pinch of salt, freshly ground black pepper

Lemon wedges to garnish

Wash the fish, pat it dry with kitchen paper and cut into ½in (1cm) cubes.

Heat the grill or barbecue and oil the grill rack. Now oil six kebab skewers and thread on the cubes of fish, placing a cherry tomato on one side of each cube and a bay leaf on the other. Season lightly with salt and pepper, brush with olive oil and grill for 10 minutes, turning and basting with a little more oil to ensure even cooking. Serve garnished with wedges of lemon.

Whitebait

I remember that in my youth avocado pear (the 'kiwi fruit' of the sixties) was offered in steak houses as a daring alternative to deep-fried whitebait as a starter. For me, there is really no other good way to cook them than this – and quite delightful they are too!

Deep-fried whitebait

A wok is an excellent alternative to a deep-frying pan for the speedy cooking of these fish. Frozen whitebait may be used with good results – but make sure that they are completely thawed and patted dry before cooking.

Serves 4

8–10oz (250–300g) whitebait

A little milk

2oz (50g) flour

1 teaspoon cayenne pepper (optional)

Sunflower oil for deep-frying

1 lemon, quartered, to garnish

Thinly sliced brown bread to serve

Wash the whitebait and pat dry with kitchen paper. Dip the fish into the milk, then gently shake them in a polythene bag containing the flour and cayenne pepper. Heat about 3in (7.5cm) sunflower oil in a wok or deep pan (see page 45 for deep-frying) and fry the whitebait in small batches. They take only 30 to 45 seconds to cook to crispy perfection. Keep the cooked batches on a warm plate spread with kitchen paper to drain the fish until all are cooked, then serve straight away with lemon quarters and brown bread.

Shellfish

Crustaceans and molluscs hold a particular fascination for all who love shellfish, from the simple charm of cockles and mussels to the romance of the oyster and the luxury of lobster. Wherever possible try to obtain live shellfish for the finest flavour and results.

Clams and Cockles

Clams in oyster sauce

There is a variety of clams available at good fishmongers from time to time (see page 16), so snap them up when you see them, because they are very good. They must be soaked in salt water for a few hours before cooking so that they can spit out their sand.

This method of cooking them is simple and, what is more, your guests have the work of scooping the clams out of their shells. A wok is the most suitable pan for cooking them for this recipe. The liquor from the clams mingles deliciously with the wine and oyster sauce, and the dish goes well with hot noodles. Bottled oyster sauce is available from larger supermarkets and Chinese shops.

Serves 4

1½lb (750g) clams, soaked and well washed

2 tablespoons sunflower oil

1 bunch spring onions, finely chopped, including all the good green parts

1 chilli pepper, de-seeded (see page 57) and finely chopped

1 teaspoon fresh ginger, finely grated

2 tablespoons oyster sauce

2 tablespoons rice wine or sherry

Heat the oil in a wok or heavy frying pan, toss in the spring onions (reserving some of the green parts to use as a garnish), chilli pepper and ginger and stir-fry for 1 minute. Now add the clams and continue stirring over a high heat until they have all opened. Then add the oyster sauce and wine and stir vigorously until all is mixed and heated through. Depending on the size of your wok or pan, you may have to stir-fry the clams in two batches.

Garnish with the reserved spring onion greens and serve immediately.

Fresh clams or cockles with pasta

There is a rather bewildering variety of small bivalves in the small clam or cockle class
that can be used for this dish (see page 290 for identification). You'll be lucky to find them
in the shell in this country – but persist! (You could substitute small mussels if necessary.)
The Italians could teach us a thing or two about shellfish: they have a great appreciation
of the variety available and enjoy many simple and versatile recipes like this.

Remember to let freshly harvested shellfish eject their sand by giving them a good
soaking in salted water before cooking.

Serves 6

2½lb (1.25kg) clams or cockles in their shells, soaked and well washed

2 tablespoons olive oil

1 large Spanish onion, finely chopped

3 fat cloves garlic, peeled and crushed

2 × 14oz (397g) tins tomatoes, chopped

Pinch of salt, freshly ground black pepper

1¼lb (625g) fresh or dried vermicelli, linguine or thin spaghetti

2 tablespoons chopped parsley to garnish

Heat the oil in a large heavy pan and gently soften the onion and garlic. Add
the chopped tomatoes with their juice, season with salt and pepper to taste,
and let the sauce simmer for about 15 minutes until soft and smooth.

Meanwhile, in another large pan, steam open the clams or cockles in a
little water. When they have all opened, reserve 12 intact to use as a garnish,
then remove the rest from their shells. Pour all the cooking liquor into the
simmering tomato sauce. Continue to simmer the sauce over a low heat as it
reduces a little and thickens.

Now cook the pasta in plenty of boiling salted water to which you have
added a drop of olive oil to prevent it sticking. Fresh pasta takes no more
than 2 minutes to cook al dente (firm to the bite); dried takes longer – follow
the directions on the packet. Drain the pasta thoroughly and put it into a
large shallow serving dish. Keep it warm while you add the shelled cockles or
clams to the reduced sauce and gently heat through. Pour the sauce over the
pasta and fork it well in. Scatter the reserved clams or cockles in their shells
over the dish, sprinkle with the chopped parsley and serve immediately.

Note: If you do not have time to shell the cockles or clams, just add them
whole to the sauce after steaming them.

Crab

Freshly caught and cooked crab is best eaten in the simplest possible way: with just a squeeze or two of fresh lemon juice, perhaps some home-made mayonnaise, a salad and brown bread.

Many of the lobster and crab fishermen I know vow that crab is the better for flavour and texture (I prefer lobster!). Either way, freshly cooked crab is a far superior animal to the frozen or canned species. If you live near a fishing port and can buy fresh crab cheaply and whenever you like, you can afford to be blasé and use it in sauces, stuffings and soups. Always bear in mind that crab meat is very rich, and a little goes a surprisingly long way.

Soft-shell crab

Soft-shell crabs – now imported from Canada and America, frozen or tinned – are very small crabs which are moulting. The newly forming shell is very soft, and therefore the whole crab is eaten. There are many variations on the classic way to cook them. Wash them, dip them in beaten egg, roll them in flour and fry in butter or oil until brown and crisp. Served with tartare sauce or mayonnaise, the crab is crisp and crunchy. A handful of slivered almonds is a pleasing addition: toss them into the foaming butter as you are cooking.

Spider crab

Spider crabs are caught off our shores but mainly exported – or even thrown back to the sea – as they are not well known in this country. They are very good indeed, although the flesh is fiddly to extract.

Boil them in the same way as other crabs (see page 29). After they are cooked, cut them in half, crack the legs (they do not have big main claws) and serve with mayonnaise, leaving your guests to pick or suck out the meat. They are an impressive addition to my Iced Seafood Platter on page 224.

Swimming crab

These small crabs are easy to find if you live near the coast. There are at least two small family firms who export them to France, where they are popular. The claw meat is sweet and good. This crab should be cooked in the same way as other crabs (see page 29) and served with mayonnaise or home-made Tartare Sauce (see page 74) thinned down with a little yoghurt, or included in my Iced Seafood Platter on page 224.

Dressed crab

The reason that a fresh dressed crab is expensive will soon become clear to you. It is time-consuming and fiddly to prepare, but well worth the effort. See page 14 for advice on buying cooked or live crab, and page 29 for cooking live crab and extracting the flesh.

Dressed crab can be the centrepiece of a mixed salad arrangement of seafood; small crabs can be served individually. Have plenty of lemon wedges, fresh bread and salad on the table and offer a good home-made mayonnaise (see pages 74–76) with a squeeze of lemon juice.

Serves 6 to 8

2 × 1½lb (750g) crabs, cooked and with meat extracted and legs reserved

Salt and freshly ground black pepper

A little lemon juice

Pinch of paprika (optional)

2 hard-boiled eggs

4 tablespoons parsley, very finely chopped

To serve:

Lettuce hearts

Marigold petals, nasturtium flowers and leaves, or gorse flowers if available

Lemon wedges

Be sure to keep the white and brown meat (cream) of the crabs separate. Thoroughly scrub out the empty shells in boiling water, dry them, and lightly oil them inside and out.

Now season the white crab meat with salt and pepper, add a squeeze or two of lemon juice, and paprika if you like. Separate the yolks and whites of the hard-boiled eggs and chop them very very finely. Spoon equal quantities of brown crab meat into each end of the shells; then, working inwards, place a strip of chopped egg white alongside each, then a strip of chopped parsley, then a strip of chopped egg yolk. Now heap the white crab meat in the centre. You can further garnish the dish with a thin sprinkling of paprika on top of the egg yolk each side of the white meat.

Arrange the prepared lettuce hearts on a large serving platter. Scatter them with the flower petals and tuck in some lemon wedges and the little legs of the crabs. Place the dressed crabs in the centre and serve.

Crab bisque

There are many versions of this soup, and you can use the same method for other shellfish: lobster or prawns, for instance. This is my method, which is somewhat simplified, but it still takes three saucepans and as many hours to make. However, you can centre a whole lunch or supper party around such a magnificent soup. Serve it in rustic soup bowls with hot garlic bread and soured cream or yoghurt on the side so that guests can dollop a spoonful into their soup if they wish. Then follow on with a crisp salad to refresh the palate.

Serves 6 to 8

2 × 1½lb (750g) crabs, cooked

1 medium onion, finely chopped

1 carrot, finely chopped

2 sticks celery, finely chopped

2oz (50g) butter *or* 2 tablespoons sunflower oil

1–2 tablespoons brandy

2 pints (1.1 litres) fish stock (see page 70)

5fl oz (150ml) dry white wine

2oz (50g) long-grain rice

1 × 7oz (200g) tin tomatoes

Freshly ground black pepper

Extract the meat from the claws and body of the crabs and set aside. Now break up the shells of the legs and claws – put them all in a small washing-up bowl, cover them with a teatowel to prevent splinters from flying around, and pound with the rounded end of a wooden rolling pin.

In a large heavy pan, soften the onion, carrot and celery in the butter or oil, then pack the pounded shell on top. Warm the brandy in a small saucepan or ladle, light it, and pour it flaming over the shell and vegetables. When the flames have subsided, add three quarters of the stock with all the wine, and leave to simmer for 20 minutes. Meanwhile, boil the rice in the remaining stock until it is soft and creamy.

Strain the soup into another saucepan, making sure that you get every drop of liquid through the sieve. (If you were using lobster or prawns, you would then further pound the shell to a fine purée to add to the soup, but crab shell is too hard for this.)

Gently re-heat the soup. Cream the brown crab meat and whisk it in. Stir in the flakes of white meat. Process or blend the cooked rice and tomatoes until smooth, or push through a wire sieve, and add these to the soup, stirring carefully all the time. Check the seasoning and add freshly ground pepper if you like. Serve straight away, or gently re-heat when you are ready to eat.

Variation: Lobster or prawn bisque can be made in exactly the same way.

To make a much quicker creamy crab soup leaving out the stock-making stages, clean, chop and gently fry 2 onions, 2 carrots, 2 trimmed leeks and 3–4 crushed garlic cloves in 3 tablespoons of olive oil until soft. Add a 14oz (397g) tin of tomatoes, 1 tablespoon tomato purée, a bouquet garni and 2 tablespoons long-grain rice. Season with black pepper, then pour in 2 pints (1.1 litres) boiling water. Simmer uncovered for 25 minutes. Purée the soup in a blender or food processor, then re-heat in a heavy pan. Stir in 1lb (500g) fresh crab meat, simmer for a few minutes, then, with the pan off the heat, stir in 4 tablespoons natural yoghurt or single cream. Garnish with chopped parsley and serve with crusty bread and Rouille (page 77).

Crab, mango and grapefruit salad with a tangy dressing

The fruit and the sharpness of the sauce is a wonderful contrast to the richness of the crab, and yet the characteristic flavour of the shellfish shines through. If mango is unobtainable, use a small melon. Serve with warm rolls or slices of fresh brown bread.

Serves 4

1–1½lb (500–750g) fresh crab meat

Dressing:

2 tablespoons lemon juice

A little grated lemon rind

Pinch of salt, freshly ground white pepper

Pinch of sugar

1 tablespoon olive oil

4 tablespoons fromage blanc

1 tablespoon tomato ketchup

Salad:

1 grapefruit

1 mango

Lettuce hearts

1 punnet cress

First make the dressing. Whisk together the lemon juice, rind, salt, pepper, sugar and oil in a bowl until the sugar has dissolved, then whisk in the fromage blanc and tomato ketchup. Put the dressing in the refrigerator while you prepare the salad.

Peel and segment the grapefruit and cut it into small chunks. Slice halfway through the mango, work your knife around the stone and pull it out, then finish cutting the fruit in half. Scoop out the flesh and cut it into chunks. Combine the two fruits and their juices with the crab meat. Arrange the lettuce heart leaves around the border of a serving dish, pile the fruit and crab into the centre and pour over some of the dressing. Scatter the cress over the salad and serve the remaining dressing separately.

Variation: This is also very good with cooked shelled lobster, crawfish or Dublin Bay prawns.

Winter days and the aroma of warm smoked or hot and spicy fish dishes: Baked spicy haddock Indian-style (page 114); Smoked haddock soufflé (page 118); Warm smoked mackerel with lemon minted potato and spring onion sauté (page 185).

(Overleaf) Tempt children away from the eternal fish fingers with Herring fillets in oatmeal (page 172), Crab-stuffed pancakes with spinach sauce (page 205), Fish and fennel risotto (page 273) and Lemony fish croquettes with hazelnut coating (page 262).

Crab-stuffed pancakes with spinach sauce

These light pancakes can be made in advance. So can the Spinach Sauce: a good tart accompaniment to the richness of the crab filling. I find that the taste of wholemeal flour competes with rather than complements the flavour of crab, so I use a good white plain flour for these pancakes. They can be served as a starter, or as a main meal with steamed broccoli and grilled tomatoes.

Makes 12 to 15 pancakes

12oz (350g) fresh crab meat (from whole crab weighing about 1½–2lb (750g–1kg))

½–1oz (15–25g) butter

2 spring onions, finely chopped, including all the good green parts

Cayenne pepper

Freshly ground black pepper

1 quantity Spinach Sauce (see page 72) to serve

Pancake batter:

8oz (250g) plain flour

2 eggs

10fl oz (300ml) skimmed or semi-skimmed milk

10fl oz (300ml) water

Sunflower oil for frying

First make the pancake batter. Put all the ingredients in the bowl of a blender or food processor and whizz for 30 seconds. Set the batter aside to rest in a cool place for 30 minutes. Next make the sauce and leave it to one side in a saucepan until you are ready to serve.

Now cook the pancakes. Using a brush or folded piece of kitchen paper, lightly oil a 8–9in (20–23cm) heavy pancake or omelette pan and heat until very hot. Pour in a large spoonful of the batter and swiftly tilt the pan so that the mixture runs to the edge of the pan to form a pancake. Let it cook for about 1 minute until lots of little bubbles appear. Flip it over with a flexible spatula and cook for a further minute. The first pancake you cook is usually too thick, uneven, and will undoubtedly stick to the pan. Carry on, as the remaining pancakes will be perfect. Just lightly brush the pan with oil between each one. As you cook the pancakes, stack them on a warmed plate and keep them warm in the oven.

Heat the butter in a small saucepan and gently soften the spring onions for about 5 minutes. Add all the crab meat and stir very gently to heat it through. Season with cayenne and freshly ground black pepper.

To fill the pancakes, spoon some of the crab mixture on to the centre of each one, roll up and tuck both ends under to form an oblong parcel. Arrange on a large warm serving platter and keep warm while you gently heat the sauce through. Trickle the sauce over and around the pancakes and serve straight away.

Crawfish

Also known as spiny lobster, there are many kinds of crawfish all over the world and they are always regarded as a delicacy. The taste of crawfish is similar to lobster, but the texture is coarser. It does not have large main claws like lobster, but the tail meat is rich and a little goes a long way. If you are trying it for the first time, eat it fresh and warm with crisp lettuce, a piquant mayonnaise and yoghurt dressing, and quarters of lemon. This is one of the most delightful ways to appreciate its superb flavour. A whole cooked crawfish makes a spectacular centrepiece in a seafood platter (see page 224), and can be used in place of lobster in any lobster recipe in this book.

Crawfish with tagliatelle

One small crawfish, mixed with lots of pasta and tomato sauce, makes a grand lunch dish: use freshly made pasta if possible. Serve with a crisp green salad and a good chilled dry white wine.

Serves 4

1 × 2lb (1kg) crawfish, cooked

1oz (25g) butter

1 tablespoon sunflower oil

1 medium onion, finely chopped

1 clove garlic, crushed

1 × 14oz (397g) tin tomatoes, rubbed through a sieve to extract the seeds

1–2 tablespoons dry white wine

1 tablespoon basil, chopped, plus a few whole leaves to garnish

Pinch of salt, freshly ground black pepper

1 tablespoon single cream (optional)

1lb (500g) tagliatelle

Extract the meat from the crawfish, dice and set aside. To make crawfish stock, break up and pound the shell, place it in a heavy saucepan, add water to half-way up the shell and boil for 20 minutes. You should then have half the original amount of liquid.

Heat the butter and oil in a heavy pan and gently fry the onion with the crushed garlic until it is soft but not brown. Add the sieved tomatoes, the wine and 4 tablespoons of the crawfish stock. Simmer for 20 minutes until the sauce is reduced to a thick creamy consistency. Add the crawfish meat to the sauce with the chopped basil and salt and pepper to taste, and heat it through gently. Add the cream, if using.

Now cook the pasta in boiling salted water. Fresh pasta takes no more than 2 minutes to cook; dried takes longer – follow the directions on the packet. Tip the hot drained pasta into a warmed serving bowl and toss in the crawfish sauce. Garnish with a few whole basil leaves.

Variation: Lobster or Dublin Bay prawns may be used instead of crawfish.

Freshwater crayfish

Crayfish is highly prized in France, but is not so widely appreciated in this country. I find the flavour rather bland. Catching crayfish, however, is a popular and unique sport in some areas of Britain. Bait, in the form of a lump of slightly high liver or a sheep's head, is put into a balloon-shaped net with a hole in the bottom, and lowered into the river. The crayfish eagerly scramble out of the mud and into the net.

Live crayfish should be cooked in a court bouillon (see page 69) for 5 to 10 minutes. Before they are cooked, the intestine can be removed by grasping the middle tail fin, twisting once to the left and once to the right, then giving a sharp pull away from the tail. I prefer to remove the intestine when shelling the crayfish after they are cooked.

Crayfish salad

One of the best ways of eating crayfish is with a good mixed salad and the following dressing. A light chilled rosé wine (served in chilled glasses) and brown bread are perfect accompaniments. Allow 8 crayfish for each person.

Serves 4

32 freshwater crayfish, cooked

4 tablespoons home-made mayonnaise

4 tablespoons fromage blanc

2 tablespoons tomato ketchup

1 tablespoon fennel or dill leaves, finely chopped, plus a few whole leaves to garnish

Mixed salad leaves: radicchio (red lettuce), spinach, sorrel, dandelion, endive,

cornsalad (lamb's lettuce), watercress, as available

1 lemon, quartered

Shell the crayfish, reserving 4 intact to use as a garnish.

Whisk together the mayonnaise, fromage blanc, tomato ketchup and herbs to make the dressing.

Wash and pat dry the salad leaves and make a pretty arrangement on each of four elegant plates. Arrange the shelled crayfish on the leaves and top with some of the dressing. Tuck one whole crayfish into the leaves on each plate as a garnish, with a sprig or two of fennel or dill and a quarter of lemon.

Lobster

Homard à l'américaine

My adaptation of this classic dish of lobster simmered with wine, tomatoes, garlic and herbs easily matches the authentic French method and does not involve cutting up the poor lobster live. If you do want to use live lobsters, kill them and cook them humanely as described on pages 27 and 28.

When cooking an expensive fish like this, it is wise to use the very best-quality additional ingredients. I suggest either plainly cooked tiny new potatoes or basmati rice as a side dish for this rich and luxurious special-occasion recipe.

Serves 4

2 × 1½lb (750g) lobsters, cooked

Stock:

Olive oil

2 onions, chopped

2 carrots, chopped

10fl oz (300ml) water

4 spring onions, finely chopped, including all the good green parts

1 clove garlic, crushed

1lb (500g) very ripe tomatoes, peeled, de-seeded, chopped, and with juice reserved

1 tablespoon tomato purée

1 tablespoon parsley or tarragon, chopped

10–15fl oz (300–450ml) dry white wine

Salt, freshly ground black pepper

1 tablespoon cognac

Boiled rice to serve

Extract the meat from the lobster shells, reserving the shells. Slice the tail meat into pieces and set aside. Usually only the tail is used in this recipe, but I dice all the main claw and leg meat and use this too. Beat well or sieve the liver (tomalley) and set this aside with the roe, if any, for the final stage.

Heat a little olive oil in a large heavy pan and sweat the onions and carrots in it for 5 minutes. Break up or pound the lobster shells, pack these on top of the vegetables, add the water, cover the pan and simmer for about 20 minutes. Strain and set aside.

Heat 2 tablespoons olive oil in a heavy frying pan and fry the spring onions and crushed garlic for 1 minute, then stir in the tomatoes and their juice, the tomato purée, chopped parsley or tarragon (reserve a little to use as a garnish), strained stock and wine. Season the sauce, simmer until it has reduced to a fairly thick consistency and stir in the lobster liver and roe. Now add the lobster meat and let it gently warm through in the sauce. Warm the cognac in a separate small pan or ladle, light it and pour it flaming over the lobster. When the flames have died away, let the lobster cook gently for a further 5 minutes. Do not allow the sauce to boil.

Arrange the lobster and sauce in a ring of boiled rice, scatter with the reserved chopped herbs and serve immediately.

Variation: Substitute crawfish or Dublin Bay prawns for the lobster meat.

Lobster salad with coriander dressing

This dish is so enthralling that it belies the effortless preparation. Lobster is expensive but worth every penny, and it is advisable to order live lobster from a good fishmonger. Ask for one from Cornwall or Scotland for the best flavour. If you cannot cope with cooking the lobster live (see page 28), your fishmonger should be happy to do this for you.

Serves 4 as a starter, or 2 as a main meal in the shell

1 × 2½lb (1.25kg) lobster, cooked

Green salad leaves – for instance, cornsalad, endive and purslane

10fl oz (300ml) natural yoghurt

10fl oz (300ml) home-made mayonnaise (see page 74)

1 bunch coriander, finely chopped

1 lemon

Extract the meat from the lobster following the method on page 28. If the dish is for 2 people, keep the 2 halves of the shell to use as containers for the lobster and dressing. Carefully wash and lightly oil the shell halves. If the body section breaks from the tail, do not worry, as this can easily be disguised in the presentation. Cut the lobster tail meat into ½in (1cm) rounds and dice the claw meat. Set aside the liver and the roe if present.

Wash the salad leaves, pat them dry with kitchen paper, place in a polythene bag and put in the refrigerator to crisp.

Now whisk together the yoghurt, mayonnaise and lobster liver and add 1 or 2 tablespoons of chopped coriander (to your taste: test as you go) plus a squeeze of lemon juice. The dressing should be pleasantly arresting, not too sharp or sour – it should complement rather than compete with the rich taste of the lobster – and it should have a creamy yet airy consistency.

To serve 2 people, cover the base of a large round or oval plate with the crisp salad leaves. Set the empty lobster shell halves on the leaves so that they nestle in attractively. Use the broken-off tail fins as decoration. Fill the shells with the coriander dressing. Along the tail section, arrange the slices of tail meat, pink side up, at ½in (1cm) intervals. The main body section can be topped with the claw meat, lemon slices and berries if you have them.

If you are serving the dish as a starter for 4, arrange the salad leaves on 4 dinner plates, top with lobster meat and garnish the legs with slices of lemon.

Prawns and Shrimps

This is rather a confusing group of crustaceans, as the names 'prawn' and 'shrimp' mean different things in different countries. In North America, for example, shrimp is the term used to describe what we would call small prawns in this country. By and large, it is reasonable to describe very small creatures, like the Pink Shrimp (common prawn), as 'shrimps', and larger creatures, like the Green Tiger Prawn or Giant Red Shrimp, as 'prawns'! Giant prawns from the Mediterranean, on the other hand, are often called 'crevettes' . . .

Having said all that, you do not need to worry too much about the scores of names for this group as the same cooking methods can be used for all of them. You will find that cold water prawns and shrimps will have a better flavour than their cousins from warmer waters – and that farmed prawns and shrimps can never compare in flavour to the bucket of shrimps that you have fished for yourself and consumed on the spot with brown bread and butter, wedges of lemon and cool wine. Tiny brown shrimps can be eaten whole.

If using frozen prawns or shrimps in recipes, it is important to thaw them correctly and pat them dry with absorbent kitchen paper before using.

King prawns in their shell with coriander and chilli

This starter has a clean decisive taste. You need uncooked prawns in their shell. The recipe gives the amount of coriander and chilli that I find successful – but consider your personal taste when wielding your chopping knife. Offer fresh bread with this dish.

Serves 4

8–16 uncooked large prawns or king prawns (depending on size)

Pinch of salt

1–2 tablespoons good-quality olive oil

1–2 tablespoons coriander leaves, chopped

2 red chilli peppers, de-seeded and very finely chopped (see page 57)

Lemon quarters to garnish (optional)

Dressing:

5fl oz (150ml) natural yoghurt

4fl oz (125ml) home-made mayonnaise (see page 74)

2 cloves garlic, crushed

Squeeze of fresh lemon juice, to taste

Marinade:

Juice of 2 lemons (about 8 tablespoons)

4 tablespoons olive oil

2 tablespoons coriander leaves, chopped

Freshly ground black pepper

First make the dressing. Combine the yoghurt, mayonnaise, crushed garlic and a squeeze of fresh lemon juice to taste. Set this aside to allow the flavours to mingle.

Combine the marinade ingredients in a shallow bowl large enough to hold all the prawns in a single layer.

Rinse the prawns and pat dry with kitchen paper. Place each one, shell side down, on a chopping board and, with a small sharp knife, cut through the centre down the flesh, from the head to the tail end. Remove the black vein – and make sure you do this thoroughly, using your fingers and the pointed tip of your knife. With scissors, snip off the little 'legs' along the edge of the shell. Now turn over the prawn, so that the edge of the shell is uppermost. Using the knife, gently cut almost through the centre of the shell from top to bottom, to flatten and 'butterfly out' the prawn. There will be a slight crunch as you use your knife and thumb to do this. Turn the flattened, cleaned prawn flesh side up again and make a few scores along the grain of the flesh. Sprinkle with a little salt: this will prevent the prawn from curling up as it is cooking. Don't worry if the flesh looks grey and translucent at this stage – it will turn white when cooked. Now place all the flattened prawns, flesh side down, in the marinade and leave them for 15 minutes.

Heat the olive oil in a large, shallow, lidded frying pan. Place the prawns *shell side down* in the hot oil, sprinkling a little chopped coriander on top of each one. At the same time, quickly spoon a little of the chopped chilli along the middle of each prawn. Let them sizzle for 1 minute, then turn down the heat a little and spoon over the remaining lemon-and-oil marinade. There will be a hiss and whoosh as you clamp down the lid and let the prawns continue to cook for a further 2 to 3 minutes.

Serve the prawns piping hot with the cold mayonnaise dressing, garnished with quarters of lemon if you wish.

Prawn tempura with nori

This beautiful and delicate Japanese dish gives the deep-fried morsels of fish and strips of vegetables a crisp snowy appearance. The nori (Japanese dried seaweed, see page 61), which you should be able to find in health food shops or oriental supermarkets, is not essential – but it does give an authentic character to the dish.

Serves 4 as a starter

12 giant prawns

2 courgettes

4oz (125g) button mushrooms

1 onion

1 sheet of nori

Sunflower or safflower oil for deep-frying

Dipping sauce:

1½in (3.5cm) piece root ginger

5fl oz (150ml) soy sauce

1 quantity Batter No. 1 (page 83)

If the prawns are whole, remove their heads. Carefully peel off the shells down to the last joint, and leave on the tail fins. De-vein them by carefully cutting or pulling out the dark vein that runs down the centre of the back. Score four small cuts across the underneath of each prawn and straighten it out. Wash the prawns and pat them dry with kitchen paper: they must be thoroughly dried. Cut the courgettes in half lengthways, and then into 2in (5cm) sticks. Wipe the mushrooms and slice them into halves or quarters, depending on their size. Slice the onion into very thin rings. Using a pair of sharp scissors, cut the sheet of nori into 1½ × 3½in (3.5 × 8.5cm) strips.

To make the dipping sauce, peel and very finely grate the ginger. Put the soy sauce into four little dipping bowls and divide the grated ginger between them.

Make the batter just before you are ready to cook and do not beat or whisk it too much.

Before you start to cook, have ready a warmed plate or dish with crumpled kitchen paper on it for draining, and a large warmed serving platter for presenting the finished dish.

Heat 2–3in (5–7.5cm.) of oil in a wok until it is hazy but not smoking. To test that it is the correct temperature, drop a cube of bread into the hot oil – it should sizzle up to the surface and brown in seconds. Dip the prawns into the batter, shake off any excess and fry in the oil for about 2 minutes in batches. They should be crisp and pale: the light batter does not give an even coating but forms a lovely white bubbly skin. Drain on the kitchen paper and keep warm. Continue in the same way with the courgettes, mushrooms and onion – all of which will need 1 minute's cooking time – and finishing with the (unbattered) nori, which will turn a golden brown. All the frying should be done as quickly as possible, bringing the oil up to the correct temperature again between each batch of cooking. If you wish, you can fry half the ingredients first and serve them, frying the remaining ingredients for a second helping.

Arrange the prawns and vegetables attractively on the large warmed serving platter, and use chopsticks or your fingers to dip the pieces in the soy and ginger sauce.

Chilled lemon and prawn soup with ginger

This summery soup, based on the Greek Avgolemono soup, has a delightful lemony taste. You need a good clear fish stock, which is given extra flavour by adding the prawn shells during the simmering stage.

Serves 6

1lb (500g) shell-on prawns

2 pints (1.1 litres) fish stock (see page 70)

1in (2.5cm) cube root ginger, peeled and cut into very thin matchsticks

2 eggs

Juice of 1 large lemon

Chopped chives and 2 tablespoons thin natural yoghurt or cream to serve

Peel the prawns and set them aside. Simmer the heads and shells in the stock for 5 minutes. Strain thoroughly through a sieve, making sure that the stock is really clear. Simmer the ginger in 1in (2.5cm) of this stock for 5 minutes, then strain, reserving the ginger. Return the ginger-flavoured stock to the main pan of stock and bring to the boil. Beat the eggs in a bowl with the lemon juice, then pour 2 tablespoons of hot stock into the mixture and beat well. Remove the stock pan from the heat, add the egg mixture and stir with a balloon whisk. Return the pan to the heat and cook very gently as the soup thickens to the consistency of thin custard. Do not let the soup boil, or it will curdle. Cool the soup, then chill thoroughly in the refrigerator.

To serve, pour the soup into shallow soup bowls and add the reserved prawns and ginger matchsticks. Garnish with chives and a swirl of yoghurt or cream.

Prawn pitta rolls

Fromage blanc, now commonly available in good grocery stores and supermarkets, is quite the best low-fat substitute for cream and mayonnaise. I say substitute, but really its light fresh taste has its own individual strength. These crunchy pitta rolls make a good snack and have a delightful taste. Very fresh pitta bread is essential for success.

Serves 4

6oz (175g) peeled prawns, de-frosted if frozen

4 *round* wholemeal pitta breads

4oz (125g) lettuce heart

2oz (50g) spring onions, finely chopped, including all the good green parts

1 tablespoon root ginger, very finely chopped

1 tablespoon mint, finely chopped

4–5oz (125–150g) fromage blanc

Freshly ground black pepper

If the prawns are at all damp, dry them on kitchen paper. Carefully slice open the pitta bread rounds, making each into two separate halves. Wash, dry and shred the lettuce.

In a mixing bowl, combine the spring onions, shredded lettuce, ginger, mint and prawns with the fromage blanc, and add a shake of freshly ground black pepper to taste. Spoon a generous amount of this mixture on to each pitta bread half and roll it up (rather like a stuffed pancake), securing it with a cocktail stick.

Mussels

Mussels are cheap and plentiful: and yet, quite rightly, they are regarded as a special seafood. The glistening blue shells yawning open with plump pinkish-orange meat make sensuous soups and seafood dishes, and their sweet flavour gives a lift to all kinds of sauces and stuffings.

It is important to clean and prepare the mussels thoroughly (see page 36). Make sure that you buy them fresh and heavy from a good fishmonger (see page 16).

Moules à la marinière

The most popular mussel dish must be Moules à la Marinière, and it is certainly the simplest to prepare. It is difficult to judge quite how many mussels to buy because you must discard any that are open or cracked, but 2 pints (1.1 litres) for each person should be fine.
Serve with hunks of fresh bread.

Serves 3 to 4

6 pints (3.4 litres) mussels, scrubbed, with beards removed (see page 36)

1oz (25g) butter

1 onion, finely chopped

1 clove garlic, finely chopped

10fl oz (300ml) dry white wine or dry cider

3 tablespoons parsley, chopped

Pinch of salt, freshly ground black pepper

In a very large pan, melt the butter and soften the onion and garlic in it. Then add the wine and 2 tablespoons of the chopped parsley, and bring up to simmering point. Now add the mussels. You may have to steam them open in two batches if the pan will not hold them all. Shake the pan around as the mussels open and cook: this will take just 1 or 2 minutes. They will be shrivelled and tough if you overcook them.

Using tongs or a perforated spoon, transfer the mussels to a large warmed serving bowl or tureen, remembering to discard any that have not opened. Reduce the cooking liquor a little by hard boiling and season to taste. Strain it through a fine sieve or muslin, and pour it over the mussels. Sprinkle with the reserved tablespoon of chopped parsley and serve immediately.

If you wish for a slightly thicker and richer sauce, whisk a little butter or cream into the liquor after straining.

Mussels served on the half-shell with special mayonnaise

Mussels look beautiful served in their shells, in simple soups and in pasta or rice dishes. This more formal presentation makes a superb centrepiece and can be served as a starter with brown bread, or as a light lunch with herbed rice and salad. I have allowed 12 mussels for each serving.

Serves 4

48 medium to large live mussels

1 shallot, peeled and finely chopped

2 cloves garlic, unpeeled

5fl oz (150ml) white wine

1 quantity mayonnaise (see page 74), made with lemon juice

1 tablespoon parsley, very finely chopped

Clean the mussels, discarding any which are open, or do not close when tapped, or are cracked.

In a large heavy pan, gently stew the shallot and garlic in the wine for 4 or 5 minutes. Turn up the heat, add the cleaned mussels and shake the pan as they steam open. If you are using a small pan, the mussels can be steamed in two or three batches – take care to reserve the juices from each batch.

When all the mussels are open (this takes just 1 or 2 minutes), remove them from the pan, discarding any that have not opened, and strain the cooking liquid through a sieve lined with muslin. Now boil the strained liquid until considerably reduced, and allow to cool.

Pull each shell apart, keeping the mussel on the half-shell. If necessary, use a small knife to release each mussel so that it is easy to eat. Arrange the mussels in concentric circles on a large round tray or platter.

Beat 2 or 3 tablespoons of the reduced mussel stock into the mayonnaise, and spoon a little into the round edge of each shell, just covering the end of each mussel. Garnish each shell with a tiny pinch of very finely chopped parsley.

Scallop fritters with sesame soy sauce

Using a light tempura batter to coat the tender sweet slices of scallop ensures they cook swiftly and cleanly in sizzling sunflower oil to produce an irresistible starter. Serve them arranged simply and elegantly on plates garnished with, for instance, 'leaves' fashioned from cucumber skin. Note that it is not feasible to cook this dish for a large number of people as the small batches of deep-frying must be served immediately.

Serves 2–3 as a starter

6 large scallops

1 large Spanish onion

1 cucumber

2 tablespoons white sesame seeds

5fl oz (150ml) soy sauce

Tempura batter (see page 83)

Sunflower oil for frying

Unless you have bought the scallops ready prepared, open and trim them as explained on page 35. Slice each white lobe into two, reserving the pink coral. Peel the onion and cut 2 or 3 thin slices from the middle to produce 10–12 large onion rings. (Keep the remaining onion for another recipe.) Prepare the cucumber garnish by peeling off large sections of skin and, using a small sharp knife, creating pretty curly leaf shapes from these. The remaining cucumber can be de-seeded and cubed as a side dish for the fritters, or reserved for a salad or soup.

Toast the sesame seeds in a dry pan over a high flame until golden, then grind them to a flaky paste with a pestle and mortar, or grinder, and combine with the soy sauce. Pour into a small serving dish.

Prepare the batter and have ready 2 or 3 plates as appropriate – just warm – and a large plate lined with crumpled kitchen paper for draining the fritters.

Heat up the oil in a wok or deep-sided pan suitable for deep-frying (see page 45). Swiftly dip the onion rings and scallops in the batter and drop them into the oil, in batches. They should take no more than a minute to cook perfectly. Drain each batch on the kitchen paper and keep warm as you continue to fry the remaining scallops and onion rings. Finally dip and fry the corals which will need only 20 seconds to cook. Serve immediately garnished with the cucumber leaves and accompanied by the dipping sauce.

Scallop kebabs with pasta and basil butter

Only a little butter is used to create this creamy sauce, served with the grilled scallops. This dish is perfect for a starter, or with green salad for a light lunch.

Serves 4 as a starter or 2 for lunch

8 scallops

8oz (250g) pasta spirals, noodles or ribbons

1 medium onion, or two shallots, peeled and finely chopped

6 tablespoons dry white wine

10fl oz (300ml) fish stock (see page 70)

1 small carrot, peeled and finely chopped

1 stick of celery, scrubbed and finely chopped

2oz (50g) chilled butter

½–1 tablespoon basil, finely chopped, to taste

Freshly ground black pepper

Unless you have bought the scallops ready prepared, open and trim them (see page 35). Slice each white lobe in half, and thread onto 4 lightly oiled skewers, interspersing occasionally with the pink corals.

Cook the pasta in lots of boiling water to which you can add a drop of oil to prevent the pasta sticking. Drain and keep warm on a large serving plate.

Now make the basil butter. Put the onion, wine, stock, carrot, and celery in a pan, bring to the boil and continue boiling until reduced by half. Strain through a sieve, then return to the pan. Bring the liquid back to the boil, drop in pieces of the chilled butter and whisk in until the sauce is creamy. Now add the basil and a sprinkling of freshly ground black pepper. Keep warm.

Light the grill and let it get hot. Grill the scallops, turning occasionally, until golden brown – about 4 or 5 minutes. Lay them on the bed of pasta, pour the sauce all over and serve immediately.

Squid and Cuttlefish

Unlike most other fish, squid and cuttlefish are not naturally tender. They seem to benefit either from very brief and brisk cooking, or from long slow cooking – anything in between results in a chewy rubbery texture. The gangly body and tentacles of these creatures can be unnerving the first time you deal with them. However, they are now also available tidily prepared and packaged at good fishmongers and supermarkets. The recipes given here are for squid as this is more easy to come by, but they are equally suitable for cuttlefish.

Stir-fried squid

The curly tentacles of the squid give an exotic appearance to this tasty stir-fry. As with any stir-frying, remember that all the ingredients must be gathered together and prepared before you start to cook. Don't attempt to cook this recipe for a large number of people as only a limited quantity can be stir-fried at one time and it must be served immediately.

Serves 2 as a main meal, or 4 as a starter

1lb (500g) whole squid

2–3 tablespoons olive or sunflower oil

2 sticks celery, finely sliced

1 red pepper, de-seeded and cut into thin strips

1 bunch spring onions, sliced diagonally, including all the good green parts

2in (5cm) piece root ginger, peeled and grated or finely chopped

2–3 tablespoons rice wine or sherry

Juice of 1 lemon

Pinch of salt, freshly ground black pepper

Deep-fried seaweed (see page 61), to garnish

First prepare the squid (see page 36). Chop the tentacles in half, slice the fins and slice the main body into ¼in (0.5cm) rings.

Heat the oil in a wok or shallow frying pan and stir-fry the squid for 2 minutes. Transfer with a slotted spoon to a warm dish. Now add the celery, pepper, spring onions and ginger and stir-fry for 1 or 2 minutes. Return the squid to the wok and re-heat, then dash in the rice wine or sherry, lemon juice, salt and pepper. Continue to stir until everything is heated through. Serve immediately, garnished with the seaweed deep-fried according to the instructions on the packet.

Baked stuffed squid in tomato sauce

There are many variations of this marvellous dish. Choose medium-sized squid – small ones are very awkward to stuff. Serve hot with plain rice to mop up the juices, or chill and slice into ½in (1cm) rings to serve with salad.

Serves 4 to 6

2lb (1kg) squid

Olive oil

2oz (50g) Parmesan cheese, finely grated

Stuffing:

Tentacles and fins of the squid

1 large onion, finely chopped

2 tomatoes, peeled and chopped

12 black olives, stoned and chopped

2 tablespoons green herbs, chopped (for instance, parsley, oregano, thyme, etc.)

4oz (125g) fresh breadcrumbs

1 egg, beaten

Sauce for baking:

1 × 14oz (397g) tin tomatoes

1 clove garlic

1 onion, roughly chopped

Pinch of salt, freshly ground black pepper

1 glass good red wine

Pre-heat the oven to gas mark 3, 325°F (170°C).

Prepare the squid. Chop the fins and tentacles for the stuffing and place in a bowl. Add all the other stuffing ingredients and combine to make a moist stuffing.

Now stuff the squid sacs. Use a trussing needle to sew up the ends with kitchen string, and place the stuffed squid in a lightly oiled casserole dish. Don't overstuff them as they will burst during baking.

Whizz the sauce ingredients together in a food processor or blender to make a smooth sauce, pour this over the squid, cover the dish and bake in the oven for about 1½ hours or until the squid is tender. Sprinkle grated Parmesan cheese over the dish and flash under a pre-heated grill until golden brown and bubbling.

To microwave
Prepare as above. Put the squid and sauce in a large bowl, cover and cook on MEDIUM (60%) for 25–30 minutes. Complete as above.

Portuguese-style barbecued squid

If you see small fresh squid, snap them up for this excellent barbecue dish – use herbed oil (see page 59) to baste them. They are fiddly to prepare but well worth the effort. Serve with a crisp salad.

Serves 4

1–1½lb (500–750g) small squid

Pinch of salt, freshly ground black pepper

½ tablespoon fennel leaves, chopped

1oz (25g) butter, softened

Herbed oil (see page 59)

Lemon wedges to garnish

First prepare the squid (see page 36). Chop the tentacles fairly finely, season and combine with the fennel leaves and softened butter. Stuff the squid sacs and secure with wooden toothpicks or cocktail sticks.

Now light the barbecue (or heat the grill). When you are ready to cook, brush the squid with herbed oil and barbecue for about 15 minutes, turning them for even cooking. Serve with wedges of lemon.

Iced seafood platter

A selection of shellfish, beautifully prepared and presented on a platter of crushed ice, makes a spectacular centrepiece for a party table. Your fishmonger or off-licence should be able to supply ice. Keep it in your freezer until you are ready to assemble the dish.

Your selection does not necessarily have to be expensive. An exotic arrangement of mussels, cockles, clams, prawns and scallops in their shells, interspersed with lemon or lime wedges and greenery, with separate dishes of dips and dressings, can be assembled at relatively low cost.

Whole split or cracked crabs, spider crabs or swimming crabs could be included (see page 27 for preparation). Two or three dressed crabs (see page 199) could be surrounded with oysters and queen scallops in their shells. Dishes of Tabasco sauce, chopped fresh root ginger, or spicy yoghurt and mayonnaise can be served alongside, with fresh warm bread and crisp salads.

My Iced Seafood Platter is a selection of my favourite shellfish which I can easily obtain where I live. It should be possible to shop around in your area to find a selection for a similar presentation. Remember that seafood is versatile, and that any combination of really fresh shellfish, carefully prepared, will be pleasing and most worthwhile.

Winkles

Winkles served with garlic butter are surprisingly good – if you have the time and patience, after cooking them, pick them out of their shells with a pin and toss them in 2oz (50g) butter sizzling with 2 crushed cloves of garlic. When they have heated through, serve immediately with crusty bread.

Alternatively, briefly cook 1 finely minced onion and 2 crushed cloves of garlic in 2 tablespoons olive oil. Add some shelled winkles and heat through and then stir into a waiting bowl of freshly cooked pasta.

Whelks

A retired Yorkshire miner who used to spend time in our local pub would suck on a whelk or two whilst watching the darts match. Whether or not he ever swallowed them I don't know, but in my opinion whelks are best used as flavouring in soups or stews – the flesh is too tough for anything else.

Freshwater Fish

The flesh of freshwater fish is usually mild and fragrant compared with that of sea fish and the acknowledged stars are salmon and trout, both of which are becoming cheaper thanks to fish farming. To taste the less familiar species, however, like perch and pike, you'll probably need to cultivate a keen angler!

Carp

Roast stuffed carp

The common and spiegel (mirror) carp are the two varieties of this fish you will usually find at a good fishmonger's. The common carp has beautiful large scales which are tough to remove (it helps to plunge the fish into boiling water for a few seconds). Carp is traditionally eaten on Christmas Eve in eastern parts of Europe but, in spite of increasing imports of farmed carp to this country, it is not as well known here as it deserves to be. Wild carp can have a muddy flavour – before cooking, soak the cleaned fish for an hour or two in 4 pints (2.3 litres) water to which you have added 6 tablespoons vinegar and a little salt.

A 4lb (2kg) fish may seem large for four people, but remember that the gut makes up a good proportion of this weight. Any roast carp left over can be diced with its well-flavoured jelly and served cold with a chicory and fresh orange salad the following day.

Serves 4

1 × 4lb (2kg) carp, scaled and gutted

A little sunflower oil for roasting

Stuffing:

2 sticks celery, thinly sliced

4 spring onions, finely sliced, including all the good green parts

1½ oz (40g) butter

½ teaspoon rosemary, finely chopped

½ teaspoon thyme, finely chopped

½ teaspoon marjoram, finely chopped

4oz (125g) prawns

Pinch of salt, freshly ground black pepper

Pre-heat the oven to gas mark 8, 450°F (230°C) – this is hotter than usual because the carp is going to be roasted rather than baked.

Wash the carp inside and out and pat dry with kitchen paper. You will find that the large belly cavity will take a copious amount of stuffing.

Now prepare the stuffing. Gently soften the celery and spring onions in the sizzling butter. Combine with the herbs and prawns and season to taste. Stuff the carp with this mixture and put it in a lightly oiled roasting tin.

Brush the carp with oil and roast in the oven for 25 to 30 minutes according to the size of the fish. Using two spatulas, carefully transfer the cooked carp to a warmed serving dish, let the stuffing spill out of and around the fish as a garnish and douse with the cooking juices.

Elvers

Elvers with chilli and garlic

Elvers (young eels) are mainly exported to Europe, but you may occasionally see them on sale here. This recipe was supplied by a friend who eats them like this in Spain. Freshly caught sand eels, gutted and heads removed, are also surprisingly good cooked in the same way – although they are more commonly used by anglers as bait!

Serves 4 as a starter

12oz–1lb (350–500g) elvers

Olive oil for frying

2 cloves garlic, very finely chopped

1 chilli pepper, de-seeded and finely chopped

Lemon wedges and brown bread to serve

Wash the elvers well in salty water to remove any slime and pat dry.

Heat ½in (1cm) olive oil in a heavy frying pan or wok, toss in the garlic and chilli pepper, sauté for 30 seconds and add the elvers. Shake them around – they will turn white in seconds – then cook for no more than a minute. Drain them quickly on kitchen paper, and serve straight away.

Salmon

The increased availability of farmed Atlantic salmon and imported frozen Pacific salmon means that this king among fish is not quite the rare and exclusive treat it once was. However, prime fresh wild Atlantic salmon is still considered to have the finest flavour of all, as its price reflects. It is best poached whole, and served with the minimum of simple accompaniments. Farmed Atlantic salmon is a good alternative: it is cheaper and the supply is more stable. Imported frozen Pacific salmon cannot compare to fresh wild prime salmon, although it is acceptable for dishes like Gravad Lax (page 234) or Kulebiaka (salmon pie, page 232). You will sometimes see sea trout on the fishmonger's slab labelled 'salmon trout' – in fact sea trout is a different species and has a more delicate flavour than true salmon. Always buy salmon from a reliable fishmonger.

Whole poached salmon

For special summer parties, a whole poached salmon makes a most beautiful table. Use only the best ingredients for a simple accompanying salad and home-made mayonnaise: the exquisite and delicate flavour should not be overwhelmed with rich fussy sauces.

The salmon may be served warm or cold. It may be skinned and covered in many appealing and decorative ways with, for instance, overlapping thinly sliced cucumber to form glistening almost transparent 'scales'. Alternatively, use thin slices of radish and lemon, or sprigs of dill, tarragon or parsley. You can hire fish kettles from some kitchen shops for poaching large fish, or you can improvise with aluminium foil (see page 40).

It is certainly worth boning the salmon after it is cooked: you then reassemble the fish to its original shape. It is an easy operation which can be performed well in advance, and it makes serving at table easier for everyone. In many ways, cold poached salmon is a dream of a dish for a host or hostess – all the preparation can be carried out well beforehand, then very little more needs to be done except to grace your table with this wonderfully handsome fish on an elegant platter with some simple salads, mayonnaise and tiny new potatoes. If you do not have a serving platter big enough to take a really large fish, you could deck out an oval tea-tray with a dense bed of watercress and spirals of thinly pared lemon rind.

The following recipe is for poaching a whole fresh salmon to be served cold. I prefer not to cover the salmon with aspic. However, I have given instructions for doing so since many people like the glistening watery effect it gives to the fish. The salmon shown on page 272 is not aspic-coated. To give a gleaming splendour to this particular presentation, brush the cucumber with a little chilled water or poaching liquid just before serving.

Serves 10

1 × 4–5lb (2–2.5kg) whole salmon, gutted

About 2½ pints (1.5 litres) court bouillon (see page 69)

2 cucumbers *or* 1 bunch shiny red radishes *or* 3 teaspoons capers and parsley, dill or tarragon to garnish

Mayonnaise (see page 74), thinned slightly with fish poaching liquid, to serve

For the aspic (optional):

1½oz (40g) powdered gelatine

2 tablespoons sherry

Snap out the gills of the salmon as these can give a bitter taste to the poaching liquid. Wash the fish inside and out, if necessary removing with your thumb any remaining blood along the inside of the backbone, and pat dry with kitchen paper. Do not de-scale the salmon as the skin and scales will help to keep its shape, and the fish will be skinned after poaching. A very large salmon should be trussed in two or three places so that it retains its shape.

If you are using a fish kettle to cook a small to medium-sized salmon, place the fish on the rack and lower it into the lukewarm court bouillon, making sure that the fish is totally covered. A very large salmon – 8lb (3.5kg) – should start off in *cold* court bouillon to ensure even cooking. Heat to simmering point and let the poaching liquid bubble, then turn the heat down until it is just shuddering. Poach, with the lid on, for 5–10 minutes. Now remove the kettle from the heat and allow the salmon to cool completely in the liquid. It will be perfectly cooked and moist. Reserve the poaching liquid.

Alternatively, if you do not have a fish kettle or large cooking vessel, cut the salmon in two across the middle. Use a large roasting tin or pan in which to poach the two pieces as described above. The two pieces can be re-united on the serving dish, and the join easily disguised with garnish.

When the salmon is cold, lift it out of the poaching liquid, using the rack, aluminium foil handles or muslin wrap, and place it on a sheet of damp greaseproof paper. (See page 40 for how to construct aluminium foil handles and how to wrap whole large fish in muslin so that they can be lifted out of their poaching liquid.) The skin will peel off easily. Carefully roll the fish over using the greaseproof paper to stop it breaking up. Skin the other side. Fresh salmon sometimes has a brown creamy curd between the skin and flesh along the middle of the fish which can be gently scraped off with a knife.

Now, using the greaseproof paper, very carefully lift and roll the salmon on to the serving dish. Using a sharp knife, cut out the fins and pull out the fine bones attached. Cut around the head to loosen the flesh, and then run the knife lengthways along the middle of the fish to divide the upper fillet in two. Very carefully, using two spatulas, lift these fillets off. Do not worry too much if they break in half, as you can disguise the join later with garnish. Using small sharp scissors, snip through the backbone at the head and tail ends and free the bone from the lower portion. Check that all the bones have been removed before putting the two top fillets back in place. If you have poached the fish in two halves, use the same method for skinning and boning, and reposition the two halves on your serving plate to form a whole salmon.

To make the aspic, boil 2 pints (1.1 litres) of the well-strained salmon poaching liquid until it is reduced by half. Soften the gelatine in 1 or 2 tablespoons of cold water for 10 minutes, then add it to the pan of stock with the sherry. Simmer for 1 to 2 minutes until the gelatine has completely dissolved.

Now decorate the fish. You could cover the entire salmon with very finely sliced cucumber halves to make a scaled effect. Another idea is to arrange sprays of parsley, dill or tarragon along the middle of the fish, interspersed with capers or very thin slices of radish.

When the fish is beautifully adorned to your liking, pour the aspic into a glass basin and set it into a larger basin filled with iced water or ice cubes. Using a metal spoon, stir it until it starts to thicken. If lumps form, you will have to re-heat the aspic gently again. When you have a pouring but gelling consistency – rather like syrup – carefully spoon the aspic over the fish to make a thin layer. It should set rapidly as you do this. I think that one layer is enough; but, if you like, you can repeat the process once more after the first layer has set. The salmon can now be left in the refrigerator or in a cool place until it is needed. Serve with the mayonnaise to which you have added 1 or 2 tablespoons of cold poaching liquid to thin it down and improve the flavour.

Poached salmon steaks with tarragon sauce

Careful poaching in a good court bouillon or stock is essential for this cold, fragrant dish.

Serves 4

4 thick salmon steaks or cutlets

1 quantity warm court bouillon (see page 69)

2 cucumbers, peeled, de-seeded and cut into matchsticks

½ teaspoon salt

1 teaspoon sugar

2 tablespoons white wine vinegar

1 × 8oz (250g) packet frozen petits pois

7oz (200g) mayonnaise (see page 74) made with tarragon vinegar

7oz (200g) natural yoghurt

1 tablespoon tarragon, chopped, plus a few sprigs to garnish

1 lettuce or endive, shredded

Wash the salmon steaks or cutlets and pat dry with kitchen paper. Place the fish in the warm court bouillon and bring gently up to simmering point. Let the liquid bubble for a few seconds, then remove the pan from the heat and allow to cool. When half-way through the cooling process, carefully turn the steaks using a slotted spoon or tongs and leave them in the liquid until they are completely cold: they will then be cooked to perfection. Transfer them to a plate and set aside. Reserve the poaching liquid.

Toss the cucumber matchsticks in a basin containing a marinade made of the salt, sugar and vinegar and leave in a cool place for 1 hour. Cook the petits pois briefly and briskly, drain them and leave them to cool. Beat together the mayonnaise and yoghurt, stir in the chopped tarragon, then carefully fold in about 4 tablespoons of the cooled poaching liquid, until the mixture is of a coating consistency.

On a large serving platter, make a bed of the shredded lettuce or endive and arrange the salmon steaks in the centre. Mix the petits pois with the drained cucumber and arrange in an attractive border around the salmon. Pour over the sauce and garnish with sprigs of fresh tarragon.

To microwave
Put the salmon in a large shallow dish with 4 tablespoons court bouillon. Cover and cook on HIGH for 6–9 minutes, depending on the thickness of the fish. Cool in the poaching liquid. Complete as above.

Terrine of salmon

Buy some soft moist scraps of smoked salmon from your fishmonger to add to left-over poached salmon, and you have the basis of this speedily prepared terrine. Serve it chilled.

Serves 4 to 6 as a starter

8oz (250g) cold poached salmon, flaked

8oz (250g) smoked salmon

1 tablespoon brandy

4oz (125g) butter, softened

Pinch of salt, freshly ground black pepper

Pound the smoked salmon scraps, brandy and butter until you have a paste, then fork in the cold poached salmon and season to taste. Chill before serving.

Kulebiaka or coulibiac

Use farmed or imported frozen salmon for this famous Russian pie: it is a substantial and filling dish for which cold left-over salmon could also be used. The absolutely authentic Kulebiaka contains viziga, *the dried spinal cord of sturgeons, and – not surprisingly – this ingredient is rather hard to come by at the average food shop!*

Serves 6

1lb (500g) salmon fillet, de-frosted if frozen

Salt, freshly ground black pepper

A little butter, melted

1 onion, finely chopped

2oz (50g) unsalted butter

16fl oz (475ml) water

4oz (125g) brown rice

6oz (175g) mushrooms, sliced

1 hard-boiled egg, roughly chopped

Grated rind and juice of ½ lemon

1 rounded tablespoon fresh dill, chopped, *or* 1 level tablespoon dried dill

1 rounded tablespoon parsley, chopped

1lb (500g) frozen puff pastry, defrosted

1 egg, beaten

10fl oz (300ml) natural yoghurt or fromage blanc to serve

Pre-heat the oven to gas mark 2, 300°F (150°C).

Check that the salmon fillet is entirely free of bones, wash or wipe the fish and pat dry with kitchen paper. Season with a pinch of salt and freshly ground black pepper. Brush a sheet of aluminium foil with a little melted butter, parcel up the salmon fillet in it and bake for 25 minutes, or until the fish is cooked. When cool enough to handle, peel away the skin and cut the flesh into fairly large cubes. Meanwhile, sweat the onion in 1oz (25g) unsalted butter in a heavy saucepan. When pale and soft, add 16fl oz (475ml) water with a pinch of salt, bring it to the boil, and add the rice. Simmer for about 20 minutes until all the liquid is absorbed, and then leave to cool.

Soften the mushrooms in the remaining unsalted butter in another saucepan – they should be *just* cooked and still firm. Leave them to cool. Now mix together the rice, onion, mushrooms, salmon, hard-boiled egg, grated lemon rind and juice, dill and parsley. Season to taste with pepper.

Pre-heat the oven to gas mark 8, 450°F (230°C). To make the pie, roll out half the pastry into a rectangle about 12 × 7in (30 × 17.5cm). Place in the centre of a lightly greased baking sheet. Lay the filling on the top, leaving a good border of pastry, and brush this edge of pastry with water. Roll out the remaining pastry to a slightly larger rectangle and lay it carefully over the filling. Press the pastry edges together. Make a couple of tiny cuts in the top of the pie to release steam during cooking, then brush all over with the beaten egg. Bake in the oven for 35 to 45 minutes, or until the pastry is a rich golden brown. Serve hot or cold with the yoghurt or fromage blanc.

To microwave
Put the salmon in a shallow dish. Brush with melted butter, cover and cook on HIGH for 4–8 minutes, depending on the thickness of the fish. Complete as above.

Baked salmon steaks with avocado sauce

This easily prepared dish is just right for a summer supper. Make the sauce immediately before it is needed, because avocado discolours if it is kept waiting. Supermarkets and fishmongers sell cutlets or steaks of imported or farmed salmon at reasonable prices, but do see page 11 for how to shop for good-quality fresh fish. Serve with a crisp green salad.

Serves 4

4 cutlets or steaks of fresh salmon

Pinch of salt, freshly ground black pepper

Sprigs of tarragon, dill, coriander or parsley (according to availability and preference)

1oz (25g) butter, melted

For the Avocado Sauce:

1 ripe avocado

5fl oz (150ml) natural yoghurt

Pinch of salt, freshly ground black pepper

Juice of ½–1 lemon (to taste)

Pre-heat the oven to gas mark 2, 300°F (150°C).

Wash or wipe the salmon cutlets or steaks and pat them dry with kitchen paper. Season lightly with a pinch of salt and pepper, place a sprig of tarragon, dill, coriander or parsley on each cutlet and parcel the fish up in a sheet of aluminium foil lightly brushed with the melted butter. Bake in the oven for about 25 minutes, according to the thickness of the cutlets.

Meanwhile, prepare the sauce. Peel and stone the avocado and cube the flesh, making sure that you scrape out every bit of brighter green flesh near the skin as this gives the sauce its delicate colour. Put the diced avocado into the bowl of a food processor or blender. Add the yoghurt, salt, pepper and lemon juice to taste. Whizz until smooth and creamy. Check the seasoning – you may need more lemon juice. Now whisk in 1 tablespoon of the cooking juices from the fish – no more, as the sauce must not become too thin.

Have warm plates ready. Pour a puddle of the avocado sauce into the middle of each plate and place a warm salmon cutlet in this. Trickle a little more sauce over each cutlet and garnish with a sprig of fresh tarragon, dill, coriander or parsley.

To microwave
Prepare as above. Put the fish in a shallow dish with the herbs and the butter. Cover and cook on HIGH for 6–9 minutes, depending on the thickness of the fish. Complete as above.

Gravad Lax

I once demonstrated how to make Gravad Lax (pickled or marinated salmon) – also called Gravlax – on a live television programme. Of course, in time-honoured tradition, I had taken along a previously prepared Gravad Lax, and after the programme it was devoured with astonishing speed by a group of South American Indians who were on a world dance tour. They yipped and yowled with pleasure at every mouthful. Although Gravad Lax is Swedish, they told me that they ate fish marinated in the same way in their country but prepared with their own regional spices and herbs. The glum producer, who had not managed to secure the tiniest bite, was told it was the best meal they had had since leaving home. It certainly is a wonderful and luxurious treat, and a particular favourite of mine. See page 179 for the same method using mackerel with pleasingly different results.

The following recipe uses a modest-sized piece of middle or tail cut. A whole salmon makes Gravad Lax an expensive dish, but this will serve a lot of people and is excellent for a party – increase the curing mixture accordingly. Home-made Gravad Lax is far, far superior to and much, much cheaper than the ready-prepared vacuum-packed variety, and your own Mustard and Dill Mayonnaise is certainly well worth making. Freeze-dried dill is an acceptable alternative to fresh, and I have tried substituting fennel with good results.

Serves 4 to 6

1½lb (750g) tail piece or middle cut salmon, de-scaled and filleted, with skin left on

1 large bunch dill

Dill sprigs or wild flowers to garnish

Curing mixture:

2 teaspoons black peppercorns, roughly crushed

2 tablespoons sea salt

1 tablespoon caster sugar or clear runny honey

1 tablespoon brandy

Mustard and Dill Mayonnaise

1 large egg yolk

5fl oz (150ml) good-quality olive oil

Lemon juice or white wine vinegar to taste

2 tablespoons Dijon or German mustard

1 tablespoon caster sugar (or less, to taste)

1 tablespoon dill, finely chopped

Wash the salmon fillets and pat dry with kitchen paper.

Combine all the ingredients for the curing mixture.

Place a few sprigs of dill in a shallow dish and put half of the fish, skin side down, on top of it. Scatter over half the curing mixture and rub this into the flesh. Top with plenty of dill sprigs. Rub the other half of the fish with the remaining curing mixture and place it, skin side up, on the first fillet, forming a sandwich of the whole fish. Cover with foil, then put a weighted plate or basin on top. Refrigerate for at least 36 hours, turning the fish every 12 hours.

During the 'curing' time, the pale pink flesh of the salmon is compressed and deepens to the colour of smoked salmon. A surprising amount of oil is released too.

Make the Mustard and Dill Mayonnaise 1 to 2 hours before you are ready to eat. Start by making a mayonnaise in the usual way (see page 74), then add the mustard, sugar and chopped dill to taste.

To serve, scrape off the curing mixture and dill off the fish and, using a very sharp knife, cut thinner-than-paper slices on the bias. Arrange these delicate slices of fish on plain elegant plates and garnish with discreet sprigs of dill or wild flowers. Serve the Mustard and Dill Mayonnaise separately.

Hot and cold smoked salmon salad

There is a surprising crunch to this salad. The secret is in the hot al dente leeks which are swiftly introduced to the waiting dressing and assembled ingredients. Serve the dish immediately with fresh bread as a starter, or stretch it out for a more substantial meal by tossing it into a dish of hot pasta. Offcuts of smoked salmon can be found at an economical price at fishmongers or supermarkets.

Serves 4 as a starter

4–6oz (125–175g) smoked salmon offcuts, cut into thin strips

1 avocado pear, ripe but firm

10oz (300g) leeks, sliced into 1in (2.5cm) rounds

2 tablespoons olive oil

2 tablespoons white wine vinegar

Freshly ground black pepper

Squeeze of lemon juice

Lemon wedges for serving

Steam the leeks over boiling water in a covered saucepan or steamer until cooked but still firm. Meanwhile slice the avocado pear lengthways around the stone, twist apart the two halves and remove the stone. Peel the skin away from each half and chop the flesh into small bite-sized pieces.

Quickly combine the oil, vinegar, pepper and a squeeze of lemon juice in a mixing bowl. When the leeks are cooked, put them straight into this dressing, then immediately add the smoked salmon and avocado pear. Use two spoons to turn all the ingredients and mingle the flavours. Serve immediately before the leeks cool. Offer wedges of lemon and more black pepper with this dish.

To microwave
Put the leeks and 2 tablespoons of water in a bowl. Cover and cook on HIGH for 4–5 minutes, stirring once. Drain and complete as above.

Choose your own selection of seasonal shellfish to compose an Iced seafood platter (page 224).

Pike

Poached pike with hollandaise and green peppercorn sauce

I have to admit that I find pike both bland and bony. It probably tastes better if you have caught it yourself! Because the flesh tends to be dry, hollandaise sauce is a good accompaniment. Pike is also the classic fish for Quenelles (see page 259).

Serves 4 to 6

1 pike, about 3lb (1.5kg), scaled and gutted

Court bouillon (see page 69)

1oz (25g) butter, melted

Chopped parsley to garnish

For the Hollandaise and Green Peppercorn Sauce:

1 quantity Hollandaise Sauce (see page 77)

1 teaspoon green peppercorns

Wash the pike and pat it dry with kitchen paper. Place it in the warm court bouillon, heat until barely simmering and poach carefully until cooked.

Meanwhile, make the Hollandaise Sauce. Soak the green peppercorns for 1 to 2 minutes in hot water. Drain them thoroughly, then pound and add to the sauce. The sauce can be kept in a warmed vacuum flask, or in a bowl over a pan of simmering water, as you transfer the pike to a warmed serving dish.

Glaze the fish with a little melted butter and scatter with chopped parsley. Serve the sauce in a separate dish.

Fresh, light and fragrant – Simple grilled trout with lemon and mint (page 243).

Trout

Farmed rainbow trout has made an enormous impact on the old luxury dinner-party image the fish used to have. It is now regarded as an every-day fish of consistent quality, available all year round.

Of course, you can still catch your own wild brown trout (*farmed* brown trout go to stock trout streams), and if you do here is the classic way to poach it.

Blue trout

This is a dish for experts. The trout should preferably be alive, or at least very fresh, just before you begin to cook, and the natural slime on the skin should not be washed away – this produces the characteristic slaty blue when it is cooked. You should have a pan of simple court bouillon made with white wine vinegar and water ready simmering before you start. Give each trout a smart thwack on the head on the edge of a worktop, snap out the gills with your fingers and swiftly gut the fish through the gills (see page 19). The trout will curl up when you drop them into the poaching pan. When they are cooked, drain and serve immediately with slices of lemon and a sauce of your choice from pages 72–83.

Simple grilled trout with lemon and mint

This delightful dish would go well with a purée of minted peas and new potatoes.

Serves 4

4 × 14oz–1lb (400–500g) rainbow trout, gutted, with heads removed if preferred

1 tablespoon mint, finely chopped

Grated rind and juice of 1 lemon

Freshly ground black pepper

A little sunflower oil

Halved lemon slices and whole mint leaves to garnish

Wash the trout thoroughly and pat dry with kitchen paper. Make two or three slashes to the bone along both sides of each fish. Season inside and out with the chopped mint, lemon rind and juice and pepper. Rub this mixture particularly well into the slashes. Leave the fish in a cool place for 1 to 2 hours for the flavours to permeate the flesh.

When you are ready to cook, heat the grill to medium heat. Lightly oil the grill rack, and give the trout a light brushing with sunflower oil. Grill for about 4 minutes on each side, according to the thickness of the fish, until the flesh is tender but still firm and the skin is brown and speckled. Serve immediately on warmed plates. Garnish each trout with very thin overlapping halved slices of lemon and whole mint leaves tucked between each slice, or with extra grated lemon rind and mint leaves.

To microwave
Remove the heads from the trout and prepare as above. Put in a large shallow dish and brush with oil. Cover and cook on HIGH for 12–14 minutes, rearranging once during cooking.

Trout fillets with almond sauce

Do you really want a recipe for trout with almonds? Probably not, but here is an interesting version of this classic partnership. Freshly ground almonds make all the difference to the success of this dish.

Serves 4

1lb (500g) rainbow trout fillets

Pinch of salt and freshly ground black pepper

Pinch of ground cumin

Grated rind and juice of 1 lemon

1 tablespoon sunflower oil

5fl oz (150ml) fruity white wine

3oz (75g) ground almonds

5fl oz (150ml) single cream or fromage blanc

Watercress and lemon wedges to garnish

Wash the fish and pat dry with kitchen paper.

Season the flesh with a little salt, a grinding of pepper and a pinch of ground cumin, then sprinkle with half the lemon rind and juice. Set aside the fillets for 1 to 2 hours for the flavours to develop.

Now heat the oil in a heavy frying pan and fry the fillets for 2 or 3 minutes on each side. Arrange them on a warm serving dish and keep them warm while you make the sauce.

Add the wine to the frying pan and heat it to simmering point. Remove from the heat and stir in the ground almonds, the remaining grated lemon rind and the cream or fromage blanc. Cook over a very gentle heat for 5 minutes, stirring all the time. Remove from the heat and whisk in the remaining lemon juice. Check the seasoning – you may need to add a little pepper – and pour the sauce over the fillets. Serve garnished with watercress and wedges of lemon.

Baked stuffed trout

This is a good way to give a boost to the delicate flavour of trout – with a simple stuffing and fresh-tasting tangy sauce. I bake this dish in a really hot oven, which gives superb results. Serve it with fresh warm bread, or new potatoes, and follow with a crisp green salad.

Serves 4

4 × 12–14oz (350–400g) fresh trout, cleaned, heads removed if preferred

Stuffing:

1 bunch spring onions, trimmed and very finely chopped, including all the good green parts

4oz (100g) button mushrooms, wiped and very finely sliced

Grated rind and juice of 1 orange

1in (2.5cm) cube of fresh ginger, peeled and grated

Dash of soy sauce

Juice of 2 oranges

Juice of 2 limes

1 bunch spring onions, finely chopped, including all the good green parts

2oz (50g) butter (optional)

Freshly ground black pepper

Pre-heat the oven to gas mark 8, 450°F (230°C).

Wash the fish and pat dry. Fill the bellies with the combined stuffing ingredients and place the fish side by side in a shallow baking dish. Pour over the juice of the oranges and limes, scatter over the chopped spring onions, dot the fish with tiny scraps of butter, if using, and grind some black pepper over each fish.

Cover the fish with aluminium foil and bake in the very hot oven for about 8–10 minutes, depending on the thickness of the fish. Use two spatulas to transfer the fish to warmed plates, letting the stuffing spill out a little to form an attractive garnish. Spoon over a little of the bubbling cooking juices and chopped spring onions, and serve straight away.

Variation: Try this method with steaks of salmon or sea trout.

To microwave
Remove the heads from the fish and prepare as above. Cover and cook on HIGH for 12–14 minutes, rearranging halfway through. Complete the recipe.

Baked trout with oranges and thyme

This dish can be served warm with steamed potatoes and spinach, or cold with a green salad and fresh brown bread.

Serves 4

4 × 12–14oz (350–400g) trout, gutted and boned but left whole

1 small onion, very finely chopped

Grated rind and juice of 1 orange

4 tablespoons white wine vinegar

4 sprigs fresh thyme or ½ tablespoon dried thyme

2 sprigs parsley

Pinch of salt, crushed black peppercorns

Orange slices to garnish

Wash the fish and pat it dry with kitchen paper. Slash twice on each side. Mix the onion with the orange rind and juice, the vinegar, herbs and seasoning. Place the fish in a shallow dish, pour over the marinade and leave in a cool place for 4 to 6 hours, turning occasionally.

When you are ready to cook, pre-heat the oven to gas mark 4, 350°F (180°C). Bake the trout in the marinade for 20 to 25 minutes, according to the size and thickness of the fish.

To serve, lift the fish out carefully with two spatulas so that they do not break up, place them on warmed plates and garnish with thin slices of orange.

To microwave
Slash the fish twice on each side and remove the heads. Prepare as above, then cover and cook on HIGH for 12 minutes, rearranging once during cooking.

Marinated trout with chervil and green peppercorn dressing

Slices of raw marinated pink trout make a special starter served with a delicate, creamy, whipped dressing. Start the preparation a day ahead – the trout needs to marinate in the walnut oil and dill for 12 hours.

Serves 4

1lb (500g) plump fillets very fresh rainbow trout

1 bunch dill, chopped

6–8 tablespoons walnut oil

Juice of 1 lemon

1 tablespoon coarse sea salt

Fresh coarsely ground black pepper

Dressing:
4 tablespoons fromage blanc

1 tablespoon single cream

1 tablespoon chervil, finely chopped

1 teaspoon green peppercorns soaked for 1 minute in boiling water

To serve:
Reserved sprigs of dill, endive leaves and thinly sliced wholemeal bread

Wash the fillets and pat them dry. Place them in a shallow glass or china dish and cover with the dill (remember to reserve four sprigs for garnish) and walnut oil, 2 tablespoons lemon juice, sea salt and shake of coarsely ground black pepper. Cover and leave in a cool place for at least 12 hours, turning the fillets occasionally.

To prepare the dressing, use a balloon whisk to whip together the fromage blanc and single cream, then fork in the chervil and drained green peppercorns.

Lift the trout fillets from the marinade and scrape off all the salt and ground black peppercorns. Use a very sharp knife to slice paper-thin slices of fillet on the bias, and arrange these on 4 plates with a spoonful of dressing placed to the side of the fish. Sprinkle the fish with the remaining lemon juice, garnish with the reserved dill and 1 or 2 leaves of endive and serve with the dressing and slices of wholemeal bread.

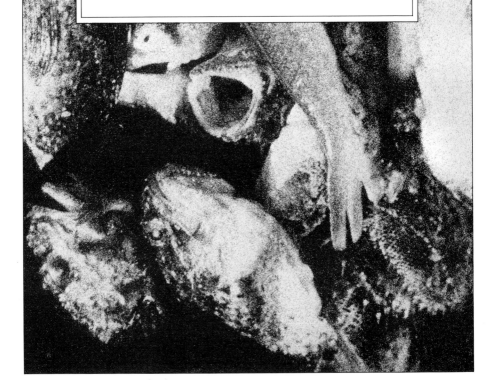

Mixed Fish Dishes

This chapter includes many of the classic mixed fish dishes, soups and stews. Other recipes give a blueprint for dishes where the ingredients may be varied according to seasonal availability and these offer great scope to the imaginative fish cook.

Bouillabaisse

This classic dish, for which there are countless different recipes, offers great scope to the adventurous fish cook. It is a one-pot soup or stew, originating in the French Mediterranean where many otherwise ignored species of fish are used with flair and imagination. The sequence of cooking should be carefully timed and planned so that all the prepared ingredients are cooked to perfection. To give flavour, use inexpensive fish like fillets of coley or whiting which will disintegrate and add body to the soup. Add small whole gurnard or red mullet for their flamboyant appearance, and finer firm-fleshed fish like monkfish, bass or John Dory. Shellfish can be added too. To serve, the fish is lifted from the stew and put into shallow soup bowls and the soup or broth is poured around it. The essential saffron, olive oil and rouille provide the classic basis of the dish, but the taste and appearance of every bouillabaisse depends upon the choice of available fish. You will need a very large heavy saucepan for this dish.

Serves 8 to 10

2½lb (1.25kg) assorted fish (e.g. cod, haddock, hake, ling, catfish, dogfish or whiting; then gurnard, redfish or red mullet; and John Dory, bass or monkfish)

8oz (250g) shellfish (Dublin Bay prawns, whole shrimps or mussels)

3–4 tablespoons olive oil

3 fat cloves garlic, crushed

2 large onions, chopped

2 sticks celery, roughly chopped

1lb (500g) tomatoes, peeled and coarsely chopped

Bouquet garni

2 pieces orange peel

4 pints (2.3 litres) boiling water

Pinch of salt, freshly ground black pepper

1 sachet saffron powder

2 potatoes, peeled and sliced

1–2 tablespoons chopped parsley to garnish

1 quantity Rouille (see page 77) and French or garlic bread to serve

First clean and prepare the fish. Cut the larger fish like cod or John Dory into steaks, cutlets or fillets; gut, scale if necessary and leave whole the small gurnards, red mullet or redfish; wash all the fish and pat dry. Rinse the prawns or shrimps, scrub the mussels if using, and set aside.

Heat the oil in a large heavy saucepan and gently fry the garlic, onions and celery until pale and soft. Add the tomatoes, bouquet garni and orange peel, pour in the boiling water, bring back to the boil and stir whilst boiling hard for 3 or 4 minutes until the resulting basic soup has slightly thickened.

Now turn down the heat and add the softer fillets of inexpensive fish, like coley, whiting or dogfish. Add a pinch of salt, a good shake of pepper and the saffron powder. Top with the potato slices and simmer for 10 to 15 minutes. Now add the small whole fish, and the pieces of cod, hake, monkfish or John Dory. Continue to simmer for a further 10 minutes, then add the mussels, prawns or shrimps and cook for a further 5 minutes or until the fish is cooked and the mussels (if using) have opened.

Using a perforated spoon, transfer the fish, shellfish and potatoes to a large warmed serving dish, or divide among eight to ten shallow soup bowls. Strain the remaining soup through a colander or sieve and pour it over and around the fish. Sprinkle with chopped parsley and serve straight away with the Rouille and warmed French or garlic bread. Provide knives, forks and soup spoons, and a dish for discarded mussel shells and fish bones.

A warm salad of smoked salmon and langoustines with walnut oil dressing

This is a rather expensive but spectacular starter or light lunch. If your fishmonger cannot provide you with langoustines (Dublin Bay prawns), you could substitute scallops – but in any case you should talk to him or her and order only the very best ingredients. You could use hazelnut oil instead of walnut oil. If neither of these oils is available in local shops, use a good-quality olive oil. Hunt around in your garden, or find an enterprising greengrocer, for a pretty selection of salad leaves. If you cannot find the more unusual leaves suggested below, a crispy Webbs Wonderful lettuce shredded into ribbons takes a lot of beating, and a few dandelion leaves will give a good bitter bite to it. Serve with fresh bread.

Serves 4

8oz (250g) smoked salmon, sliced

1oz (25g) butter

16 langoustines (Dublin Bay prawns), cooked and shelled

Lemon wedges to garnish

For the dressing:

4fl oz (125ml) walnut oil

4fl oz (125ml) sunflower oil

2 spring onions, finely chopped, including all the good green parts

1 teaspoon Dijon mustard

1 fat clove garlic, finely chopped

Juice of 1 lemon

3 tablespoons white wine vinegar

Pinch of sugar, salt, freshly ground black pepper

For the salad:

Handful of nasturtium leaves

1 curly endive

Dandelion leaves, wild sorrel leaves, cornsalad (lamb's lettuce), radicchio (red lettuce)

1 tablespoon chopped parsley, chervil or tarragon (to taste or as available)

First make the dressing at least several hours in advance to allow the flavours to mingle and develop. Simply whisk together all the ingredients in a basin, or place them in a screw-top jar and shake until blended.

Wash and pat dry the salad leaves. Toss the salad in the dressing, reserving 2 tablespoons. Divide the salad between four plates and arrange rolled slices of smoked salmon among the leaves. Fluff up the leaves to make the salad look lively.

Now melt the butter in a heavy frying pan and sauté the langoustines briskly for 2 or 3 minutes. Transfer 4 to each plate alongside the smoked salmon rolls. Quickly add the 2 reserved tablespoons of dressing to the pan, stir briefly, then pour these hot juices over the salad. Sprinkle over the chopped herbs and serve at once garnished with lemon wedges.

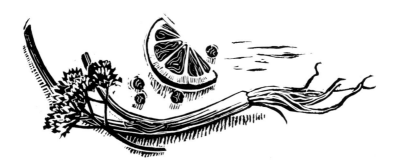

La bourride

A well made Aïoli (strong garlic mayonnaise) and good fish stock are the essential basis for this famous French soup. Any firm white fish can be used.

Serves 4 to 6

2lb (1kg) firm white fish (cod, brill, turbot or monkfish, etc., or a combination of these), filleted and skinned

2 leeks, sliced into thin rounds

1 onion, finely sliced

1lb (500g) potatoes, peeled and sliced

2–3 cloves garlic, crushed (optional)

1½ pints (900ml) fish stock (see page 70)

5fl oz (150ml) dry white wine

15fl oz (450ml) Aïoli (see page 76)

Freshly ground black pepper

4–6 slices French bread, toasted or fried in olive oil with garlic

1–2 tablespoons chopped parsley to garnish

Wash the fish fillets, pat them dry with kitchen paper and cut them into large pieces.

Put the leeks, onion and potatoes into a large shallow poaching pan with the garlic (if using), arrange the pieces of fish on top and pour in the fish stock and wine. Poach gently (do not boil: see page 40) until the fish is just cooked. Using a perforated spoon, transfer the pieces of fish to a warmed serving dish and keep warm.

Bring the remaining stock up to boiling point and boil hard to reduce it to half of its original volume. During this time, remove the potatoes when they are tender and keep warm with the fish.

Put 10fl oz (300ml) of the Aïoli into a saucepan and warm over a gentle heat. Strain the reduced stock, then slowly pour it into the Aïoli, whisking or beating all the time. Gently bring the soup up to just under simmering point: do not boil. It should be thick, pale and creamy. Check the seasoning and add a little pepper if necessary.

Now put a slice of toasted or fried bread into each large shallow soup bowl and arrange the pieces of fish and slices of potato on top. Pour the soup all around the fish. Dollop a teaspoon of the remaining Aïoli on top of the fish and sprinkle with chopped parsley. Serve straight away, with the rest of the Aïoli in a separate dish.

Chinese seafood omelette

This brisk action-packed omelette needs no salt or pepper, for the Chinese five-spice powder, or 'Chinese seasoning' as it is sometimes labelled, gives it a good pep. If you use soy sauce, remember that this contains plenty of salt. The resulting 'broken' omelette is slightly scrambled, and a sprinkling of sautéed seaweed makes an attractive dish, suitable for a starter or light lunch.

Serves 3 to 4

8oz (250g) shelled prawns, Dublin Bay prawns or crab meat

4oz (125g) bean sprouts

4 eggs

2 tablespoons water

2 tablespoons skimmed milk

2–3 tablespoons sunflower oil

3oz (75g) spring onions, sliced diagonally, including all the good green parts

Good pinch of five-spice powder

Nori (see page 61) or soy sauce to serve

As usual with stir-frying, make sure you assemble all your prepared ingredients before you start to cook. If you are using cooked peeled prawns, pat them dry so that they do not add moisture to the hot oil; if you are using Dublin Bay prawns, shell them and slice them in half; if you are using a fresh crab, see page 29 for preparation. Rinse the bean sprouts and pat them dry. Crack the eggs into a jug, but *do not* beat them. Add the water and milk to the eggs and gently stir in, breaking the yolks up slightly as you do so.

Heat the oil in a wok and throw in the prawns, spring onions and five-spice powder. Stir-fry for not more than 1 minute. Pour in the egg mixture and bean sprouts and move all the ingredients around the wok until they are evenly distributed. Spread the omelette well up the sides of the wok and let it cook through for about 45 seconds. Break it up and turn it all over with a stir-frying action until all the egg is set. Divide straight on to warmed plates and garnish with the nori – or offer soy sauce when serving.

Sweet and sour stir-fry

This tingling stir-fry is an excellent way to cook firm white fish like dogfish (also called huss, flake or rigg) or catfish (often sold as rockfish). Thin slices or strips of monkfish, skate nobs or scallops are also ideal. Serve on a bed of hot noodles.

Serves 3 to 4

8oz (250g) firm white fish fillets, skinned and trimmed

4oz (125g) peeled prawns

1 tablespoon tomato purée

1 tablespoon soy sauce

1 tablespoon white wine vinegar

Juice of ½ orange

Juice of ½ lime or lemon

1lb (500g) thick noodles

1 tablespoon sunflower oil

8 spring onions, trimmed and sliced diagonally, including all the good green parts

8oz (250g) baby corn

Freshly ground black pepper

Frilled spring onions to garnish (see page 84) – optional

When stir-frying it is particularly important to prepare all the ingredients before you start to cook.

Wash the fish fillets and pat dry with kitchen paper. Slice into 2 × 1in (5 × 2.5cm) strips.

To make the sweet and sour sauce, whisk together the tomato purée, soy sauce, wine vinegar, orange and lime (or lemon) juice. Cook the noodles in boiling water, strain and keep warm in a serving dish in a low oven.

Now heat the oil in a wok and briskly stir-fry the spring onions and baby corn for 45 seconds. Keep stirring as you add the fish and prawns and continue to cook for a further 45 seconds to 1 minute, then add the sweet and sour sauce. As soon as it bubbles, let it cook through for a further 30 seconds. Tip the mixture over the noodles and serve straight away sprinkled with freshly ground black pepper and garnished with frilled spring onions if you like.

Sashimi

Sliced raw seafood, lovingly prepared and elegantly presented, is the soul of Japanese cuisine. All kinds of fish can be used for a mixed sashimi – cod, monkfish, fresh tuna, scallops, carp or mackerel; the most important thing is that it must be very very fresh. Frozen fish is not suitable. You can buy seaweed specially for sashimi in oriental supermarkets.

In Japan sashimi is served before a main meal as a communal dish. Artistic presentation is important. You use chopsticks to lift mouthfuls of fish and vegetables, dunking them into the tangy dipping sauces as you go.

Serves 4 to 6

1½lb (750g) fillets of very fresh firm-fleshed pink fish (salmon, tuna or prawns – try for contrast in colour) combined with white fish (monkfish, cod or scallops)

1 cucumber

Dried green seaweed, prepared according to the packet instructions

1 daikon (long white radish), shredded into long fine strips

1 large carrot, shredded into long fine strips

1 onion, sliced into very thin rings

1 lemon or lime, quartered

Dipping sauce 1:

1 tablespoon root ginger, peeled and very finely grated

3 tablespoons light soy sauce

Dipping sauce 2:

1 tablespoon horseradish powder (from an oriental supermarket)

4 tablespoons dark soy sauce

Skin the fish and remove any remaining bones. Wash and pat dry with kitchen paper. Remove the shells from the shellfish. Now, using a *very* sharp knife or cleaver, slice the fish and shellfish into thin rounds, or strips on the bias, according to the nature and shape of the fillets. You will find it easier to cut really fine slices if the flesh of the fish is first firmed by chilling just before you begin.

Cut the cucumber in half. Cut one half in half lengthways, scoop out the seeds and slice the flesh into matchsticks, leaving on the skin. Cut the other half in half lengthways and scoop out the seeds, then peel off strips of skin as large as you can manage and finely dice the peeled flesh. Cut flower or leaf shapes from the pieces of skin.

Make the dipping sauces. Combine the soy sauce and root ginger and pour into two or three little dipping bowls. Mix the horseradish powder to a paste with the dark soy sauce and place on small saucers or dipping bowls.

Assemble the dish on a beautiful large plain serving platter (not patterned as this will detract from the fish) or a scrubbed wooden board. Fashion the rounds of fish into various flower shapes and curls, interlaced with flourishes of seaweed and mounds of daikon, scrolls of carrot and hoops of onion – with discreetly placed cucumber 'leaves' or 'flowers'. Serve with the dipping sauces and quarters of lemon or lime.

Monkfish and salmon terrine

Here is one those recipes with an off-putting list of expensive ingredients, and a presentation which makes you think: 'I can't do that.' But you can, and easily. This terrine (or fish loaf) is ideal for special parties or picnics. You need to make it a day in advance to allow for chilling overnight.

Serves 6 to 8

1lb (500g) spinach

1lb (500g) whiting fillets, skinned and chopped

1lb (500g) salmon fillets, skinned and cut into strips

1lb (500g) monkfish, skinned and cut into strips

3 eggs

4oz (125g) fresh breadcrumbs

10fl oz (300ml) crème fraîche or fromage blanc

Pinch of salt, freshly ground black pepper

Freshly grated nutmeg

12 shell-on prawns and sprigs of dill, fennel or tarragon to garnish

Pre-heat the oven to gas mark 3, 325°F (170°C).

Wash the spinach well, remove the stalks and ribs and cook the leaves briskly – there is no need to add water as there will be enough left on them after washing. Drain the spinach thoroughly and squeeze out excess moisture with your hands. Place the whiting fillets in a food processor with the eggs, breadcrumbs, spinach, crème fraîche or fromage blanc, salt, pepper and nutmeg and process until smooth. Alternatively, chop the whiting and spinach very finely, place in a large bowl and mix in the eggs, breadcrumbs, crème fraîche or fromage blanc and seasoning. This rougher-textured mixture will also produce excellent results.

Mix together the strips of salmon and monkfish and season lightly with salt and pepper. Line a 2lb (900g) loaf tin or terrine with lightly oiled aluminium foil and layer it alternately with the spinach mixture and strips of salmon and monkfish, finishing with a layer of the spinach mixture. Press everything carefully but firmly into the tin and cover with lightly greased greaseproof paper, pricked with a few holes.

Place the terrine in a roasting tin and pour enough boiling water around it to come two thirds of the way up the loaf tin. Bake in the oven for 1 to 1½ hours, or until the loaf is set and firm. Let it cool, then chill it overnight.

When ready to serve, remove the greaseproof paper and invert the loaf on to a flat dish. Carefully cut into slices and garnish with prawns and sprigs of dill, fennel or tarragon.

To microwave
Prepare as above. Stand the terrine on a microware roasting rack or an upturned soup plate. Cover with greaseproof paper and cook on MEDIUM (60%) for 20–25 minutes until slightly risen in the centre and firm to the touch. Complete as above.

Fish chowder

Like many other fish soups, this chowder can be partly prepared in advance, then re-heated when you are ready to eat, at which stage you add the fish for its brief cooking time. Chowders are homely and comforting – this is my own favourite. It is plain and simple: a good fish stock is essential for its characteristic hearty flavour: use the shells from the prawns to give it a little more body. Serve with fresh bread.

Serves 4 generously

1lb (500g) cod fillet, skinned

8oz (250g) smoked haddock, skinned and boned

1oz (25g) butter

1 medium onion, finely chopped

1 pint (600ml) fish stock (see page 70)

1 pint (600ml) semi-skimmed milk

2–3 potatoes, peeled and finely diced

4oz (125g) cooked peeled prawns

Squeeze of lemon juice (to taste)

Freshly ground black pepper

Wash the cod fillet, pat dry with kitchen paper and cut it into bite-sized pieces. Cut the smoked haddock also into bite-sized pieces.

Melt the butter in a large heavy pan over a low heat and sweat the onion in it until it is pale and soft. Now add the stock and milk, bringing it gently up to simmering point and then adding the diced potatoes. Simmer (but do not boil or the milk will curdle) for 6 to 8 minutes, when the potato is two-thirds cooked. At this stage you can turn off the heat and continue cooking later if you wish.

Add the cod and haddock to the simmering chowder and cook very gently for 2 or 3 minutes, adding the prawns, a squeeze of lemon juice to taste and a good shake of pepper for the last minute of cooking. Do not let the fish overcook – it will disintegrate and spoil the chowder.

Spicy fish balls in sweet red pepper sauce

I use monkfish for these easy fish balls, but any firm white fish would be suitable. I love the coriander flavour, but you could substitute a tablespoon of chopped fennel leaves if you prefer. The sauce can be made a day or two in advance if you wish. Serve with plain boiled rice and a crisp side salad.

Serves 4

1lb (500g) monkfish, skinned and boned

2 teaspoons coriander leaves, finely chopped

Pinch of salt, freshly ground black pepper

2 eggs

5fl oz (150ml) single cream or natural yoghurt

4oz (125g) fresh breadcrumbs

Juice of ½ lemon

Sunflower oil for frying

Sweet Red Pepper Sauce (see page 152) to serve

Wash the fish, pat dry with kitchen paper and cut into small pieces. Place it in the bowl of a food processor with the coriander, salt, pepper, eggs, cream or yoghurt, 2oz (50g) of the breadcrumbs and the lemon juice and process for 45 seconds until the mixture is smooth and creamy. Alternatively, chop the fish very finely, add the well-beaten eggs and cream or yoghurt, coriander, seasoning and lemon juice and mix thoroughly. Chill the mixture for 1 hour.

When you are ready to cook, pre-heat the oven to gas mark 6, 400°F (200°C).

Then heat a little oil in a heavy frying pan. Using your hands, form the fish mixture into snooker-ball-sized balls, roll them in the remaining breadcrumbs and fry them gently, turning them occasionally, until they are all an even golden brown. Place the cooked fish balls in a shallow baking dish and pour over the sauce. Bake in the oven for 20 minutes until bubbling.

To microwave
Prepare as above. Place the cooked fish balls in a shallow dish and pour over the sauce. Cover and cook on HIGH for 3–5 minutes until bubbling.

Terrine of fresh and smoked trout

This pleasingly simple recipe, given to me by the British Trout Association, can be served warm – in which case it will need slicing fairly thickly and very carefully. However, it is probably better made the day before for a lunch or supper party, when it can be chilled and sliced thinly. Serve with a light dressing of yoghurt and mayonnaise or a chilled fresh tomato sauce.

Serves 6–8

2 × 1½lb (750g) fresh trout, filleted and skinned

2 × 8–10oz (250–300g) smoked trout, filleted and skinned

2oz (50g) white bread

2½fl oz (60ml) dry sherry

2 large eggs, separated

5fl oz (150ml) natural yoghurt or cream

Freshly ground black pepper

2–3 tablespoons parsley, chopped

Grated zest and juice of ½ lemon

12oz (350g) spinach or cabbage leaves

Pre-heat the oven to gas mark 4, 350°F (180°C).

Wash the fresh trout, pat dry with kitchen paper and cut into pieces. Flake the smoked trout.

Soak the bread in the sherry for a few minutes, then place in the bowl of a food processor or liquidiser with the flesh of the fresh trout, egg yolks, yoghurt or cream and pepper. Process until smooth, check the seasoning and add the egg whites. Process again until the mixture is very thick.

Alternatively, chop the fresh trout very finely and beat in the soaked bread, egg yolks, yoghurt or cream and pepper. Beat the egg whites until stiff and fold into the fresh trout mixture.

Now mix the flaked smoked trout with the chopped parsley and the lemon rind and juice. Blanch the spinach or cabbage leaves in boiling water for 1 minute, drain, refresh in cold water, drain again and pat dry with kitchen paper, making sure that the leaves are really dry, then remove any large veins or coarse bits of stalk. Use three-quarters of the leaves to line the base and sides of an oiled 2lb (1kg) loaf tin, letting the leaves overlap the edges of the tin by a few inches. Spread half the fresh trout mixture into the tin. Top with the smoked trout, smoothing it carefully in to make an even layer. Now add the final layer of fresh trout. Each layer should be gently smoothed down as you go to remove air pockets. Fold in the overlapping leaves and cover the terrine with the remaining spinach or cabbage leaves. Cover again with a double layer of aluminium foil and prick a few holes in it. Stand the loaf tin in a roasting tin and pour enough boiling water around it to come half-way up the loaf tin. Bake in the oven for 1 hour or until the loaf is just firm to the touch. Allow it to cool and set for half an hour if you are serving it warm. Invert the tin and carefully let the loaf slide out on to a serving dish. Alternatively, chill in the refrigerator for at least 12 hours and serve cold.

To microwave
Prepare as above. Stand the terrine on a microware roasting rack or upturned soup plate. Cover with greaseproof paper and cook on MEDIUM (60%) for 20 minutes until firm to the touch. Complete as above.

Quenelles

Essentially, quenelles are rather special dumplings. Even though there seem to be so many things that can go wrong when you are making them, quenelles can always be rescued if they disintegrate: simply call them a mousse or a pâté.

There are two kinds of fish quenelles: one is a mousseline, made with a purée of cream, egg whites, fish and seasoning; and the other is combined with a panada or choux paste to produce the characteristic velvety dumpling – Quenelles Lyonnaise – for which pike is usually used. Pike is a bony fish, and I find it rather bland. Any firm-textured fish such as conger eel, whiting, halibut, monkfish or cod can be substituted: use salmon for very special quenelles. Nutmeg is a traditional flavouring, but other herbs or spices may also be used. Other additions may include finely chopped mushrooms, nuts or pimentoes.

The mousseline (that is, without the choux paste) is the easier mixture for successful quenelles. Once poached, it can be kept refrigerated and re-heated with a variety of sauces. This mousseline may also be used in other ways: as a stuffing for a whole fish, as part of a layered terrine, or in paupiettes (rolled fillets).

Very easy quenelles

Use any good white fish for these basic quenelles. The mixture can be prepared a day or two in advance and kept in the refrigerator. Once cooked, the quenelles can be frozen and whipped out for supper at a moment's notice.

Serves 6

1lb (500g) fillets cod, monkfish, hake, pike or conger eel, skinned and trimmed

6fl oz (175ml) double cream

2 egg whites

Pinch of salt, freshly ground black pepper

Freshly grated nutmeg

Fresh Tomato Sauce (see page 81) to serve

Check that the fish is entirely free of bones, wash it and pat dry with kitchen paper. Cut into small pieces, place these in the bowl of a blender or food processor and whizz for 20 seconds. Add the cream, egg whites and seasoning and whizz for a further 30 to 40 seconds until the mixture is completely smooth. Chill in the refrigerator for at least 30 minutes.

Heat a large shallow pan of water to just below simmering point. Have ready a small basin of chilled water and two dessertspoons. Use the two spoons to shape a spoonful of the mixture into an oval before carefully sliding it into the simmering water. Dip the spoons in the chilled water and continue the process until you have poached about 6 quenelles (according to the size of the pan). When they have flipped over (they will do this of their own accord), let them cook for a further 2 minutes, then use a perforated spoon to lift them out. Drain them on kitchen paper and keep them on a warm serving plate. Continue until all the quenelles are cooked. Pour over the hot sauce and serve straight away.

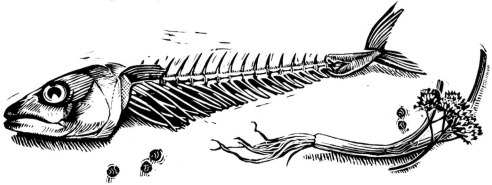

Fish cakes

Good fish cakes are universally popular (especially with children). The time-honoured combination of fish and potatoes can be the basis for an infinite combination of ingredients. Home-made fish cakes are also much better than the frozen or shop-bought variety. Perhaps the most popular are the simplest: a mixture of plain mashed potatoes, coarsely chopped parsley and really fresh cooked white fish such as cod, haddock or whiting. Shaped into cakes or croquettes, and rolled in lightly seasoned flour, dipped in beaten egg and breadcrumbs, or coated with sesame seeds or oatmeal, they should be shallow-fried or baked in the oven and served immediately – with tomato sauce, tartare sauce, mayonnaise or just a squeeze of citrus juice (lemon, lime or orange). Use a good tasty variety of potato and do not be tempted to add too much butter, cream or milk when you mash them, or soggy fish cakes will result. Here is a basic recipe and some useful variations.

Favourite fish cakes

Although these are best made with freshly cooked fish, they are still very good if left-over cooked fish is used. A green salad is an excellent accompaniment.

Makes 8 to 10 fish cakes

1–1½lb (500–750g) white fish fillets (cod, haddock, ling, whiting, pollack, coley, etc.), skinned

1½lb (750g) potatoes

1–2oz (25–50g) butter

Pinch of salt, freshly ground black pepper

2 good tablespoons parsley, coarsely chopped

1 teaspoon cayenne pepper (optional)

1 egg

4oz (125g) breadcrumbs

Sunflower oil for frying

Fresh Tomato Sauce (see page 81) or tomato ketchup to serve

Scrub the potatoes (do not peel), cut into even-sized chunks and cook in a large covered pan of boiling salted water until just soft.

Heat the grill and oil the grill rack. Dot the fish fillets with a few scraps of butter, season lightly with salt and black pepper and grill them for 2 to 4 minutes, according to their thickness. Let them cool, then flake them and remove any stray bones.

Drain the cooked potatoes, peel off their skins and mash them with the butter if you wish. Beat with a wooden spoon for a smooth texture. Fork in the parsley, then the flakes of cooked fish and check the seasoning, adding cayenne pepper if you wish. Chill the mixture for a few hours, or overnight.

When you are ready to cook, beat the egg, and place the breadcrumbs on a dinner plate. Shape a handful of the fish mixture into a ball in your hands, then flatten it into a cake. Dip it in the egg, then turn it on the plate of breadcrumbs so that it is well coated. You should get 8 to 10 fish cakes from this quantity of mixture.

When you are ready to eat, heat up a little oil in a heavy frying pan and fry the fish cakes for 2 or 3 minutes on each side until they are crisp and hot right through. Serve straight away with Fresh Tomato Sauce or tomato ketchup. Variations on this basic recipe follow.

Smoked salmon fish cakes with dill and soured cream dressing

Using the same basic ingredients as for Favourite Fish Cakes (see page 261), add 2–3oz (50–75g) finely chopped smoked salmon (you can buy cheap offcuts from your fishmonger) and substitute finely chopped fresh dill for the parsley. When serving, pour a spoonful of soured cream over each fish cake and garnish with a sprig of dill.

Lemony fish croquettes with hazelnut coating

Add the very finely grated rind of 1 lemon to the basic Favourite Fish Cakes mixture (see page 261), sprinkle with a little lemon juice and substitute 1 tablespoon finely chopped coriander leaves for the 2 tablespoons chopped parsley. Grind 4oz (125g) hazelnuts in a food processor or coffee grinder fairly finely. Shape the chilled mixture into croquettes, brush with beaten egg, coat with hazelnuts and shallow-fry in sunflower oil (see page 45), turning all the time for even cooking. Serve on nests of salad leaves with a yoghurt and mayonnaise dressing.

Boursin fish cakes with sesame seed coating

These fish cakes have a wonderful crisp crunchy coating and a meltingly creamy centre. Use the same basic ingredients as for Favourite Fish Cakes (see page 261). When you are rolling a ball of the mixture in your hands, push a teaspoon of Boursin or a similar garlic- and herb-flavoured soft cheese into the centre of the ball. Alternatively, mix a crushed clove of garlic into a teaspoon of plain soft cheese and push it into the centre of the ball. Shape the mixture all around the cheese, then flatten it into a fish cake, dip in beaten egg and coat well with sesame seeds. Shallow-fry in the usual way (see page 45).

Father's fish cakes

My father was the fish expert in our home. He remembers that when he was a child in Yorkshire, his local fish shop sold the most marvellous little fish cakes for a halfpenny (½d) for two (fine fast food!) – and these you ate from your hand as you walked home from school.

12oz (350g) white fish fillets (for instance, cod, hake, brill or whiting), skinned

6 large potatoes

Pinch of salt, freshly ground black pepper

Sunflower oil for deep-frying

1 quantity Batter No. 2 or 3 (see pages 83–84)

First scrub the potatoes and cook in a covered pan of boiling salted water until they are *half*-cooked. You can peel them before or after cooking, as you prefer. Allow to cool enough to handle and slice into ¼in (0.5cm) rounds.

Check that no bones remain in the fish fillets, wash them, and pat dry with kitchen paper. Mince the fish by chopping thoroughly on a board with a very sharp knife. Season with salt and pepper.

When you are ready to cook, heat the oil in a wok or deep-fryer. Sandwich 1–2 tablespoons minced fish between 2 slices of potato, and carry on in this way until you have used all the fish and potatoes. Coat each fish cake in batter, drop into the hot oil and cook for 2 or 3 minutes or until golden brown. Serve straight away.

Seviche

Although this is a raw fish dish, you could say that the fish is 'cooked' in citrus juices. In any case it makes a most refreshing and attractive starter or lunch.

Pieces of white fish should be marinated in this way for no more than 4 hours, but pieces of mackerel can be left in the refrigerator for up to 5 days as they slowly 'pickle', and this also makes an excellent appetiser.

Serves 4 to 6 as a starter

1–1½lb (500–750g) monkfish, bass, salmon or scallops, or a mixture, skinned and boned

Salad leaves and lemon or lime wedges to serve

Marinade:

Juice of 2–3 limes

Juice of 2–3 lemons

1 tablespoon coriander seeds, crushed

1 tablespoon parsley, finely chopped

1 red chilli pepper, de-seeded and finely chopped

1 onion, sliced

4 tablespoons olive oil

Cut the fish into small pieces and place them in a glass bowl. Combine the marinade ingredients and pour over the fish. Leave in a cool place for 4 hours, turning the fish occasionally. Serve on elegant plates, garnished with salad leaves and wedges of lime or lemon – a little of the marinade will also serve as a dressing for the leaves.

Fish couscous

Couscous is a kind of hard wheat semolina which has been ground and rolled in flour. It is as common to North Africans as the potato is to us and is simple to cook even if you do not have a couscousier (a purpose-made cooking vessel). You can improvise with an ordinary colander or large metal sieve, lined with muslin or a teatowel. The couscous then steams over a pan of simmering vegetables, with meat or fish. The 'hot' sauce is harissa, made from chillies and spices, available from delicatessens or good food stores: use this with caution, for it is very hot.

This recipe is an adaptation of a typical Tunisian fish couscous. Any left-over stew can be turned into a soup or frozen and kept for another day.

Serves 6

2½–3lb (1.25–1.5kg) fish fillets (cod, hake, ling, gurnard, or a mixture), skinned

1 small aubergine

1 teaspoon salt

2 tablespoons olive oil

2 medium onions, chopped

4 fat cloves garlic

½–1 teaspoon cumin seeds (to taste)

½–1 teaspoon harissa (to taste, see above)

Freshly ground black pepper

1 pint (600ml) fish stock (see page 70)

1 × 14oz (397g) tin tomatoes

1 bay leaf

1lb (500g) couscous

2 carrots, sliced into ½in (1cm) rounds

1 small turnip or swede, sliced into ½in (1cm) rounds

4 medium potatoes, sliced into ½in (1cm) rounds

1oz (25g) butter

Slice the aubergine in half, sprinkle the cut sides with salt and set it aside for 20 minutes so that excess moisture and the bitter juices can drain off. Then rinse and pat dry. Cut the two halves into ½in (1cm) slices.

Heat the oil in a large heavy pan, first making sure that the colander or sieve for the couscous will fit tightly on top. Gently cook the chopped onions and 1 crushed clove of garlic until they are pale and transparent. Then add the cumin and fry for 30 seconds. Add the harissa (diluted with 1 or 2 teaspoons of cold water) and a shake of pepper and cook for a further 30 seconds. Add the stock, the tomatoes and their juice and the bay leaf and bring up to simmering point. Put the couscous into the colander or sieve. To prevent the grains falling through the holes of the colander, line it with clean muslin or a boiled teatowel. Place the colander or sieve over the gently simmering sauce, cover tightly and leave the couscous to steam for 15 minutes.

Meanwhile, prepare the fish fillets. Check that no bones remain and cut the fish into large pieces.

Fluff up the couscous with a fork and remove the sieve or colander for a moment or two while you stir all the prepared vegetables into the sauce. Re-heat to simmering point, place the couscous over the pan once more, cover and continue to simmer and steam for a further 15 minutes. While this is happening, slice the remaining 3 cloves of garlic very thinly and push them at random into the couscous grains.

After 15 minutes, the vegetables should be about two thirds cooked. Remove the couscous sieve or colander again for a moment and put the pieces of fish into the stew. Replace the couscous over the pan, scatter scraps of the butter over the couscous, fork up as it melts in and leave the stew and couscous to cook for a final 10 to 15 minutes. By this time, the fish and vegetables in their thick sauce will be tender and the couscous perfectly cooked.

Spoon the couscous grains around the edge of a large shallow serving plate. Use a perforated spoon to place the fish and vegetables in the centre, and spoon over the remaining sauce. Serve immediately.

Paella

All Spanish cooks have their individual paella and all will claim theirs to be the definitive version. A paella can include all kinds of shellfish, chicken, rabbit, red and green peppers, garlic, herbs, peas and saffron. With such a widely adapted dish, it is not worth arguing about the correct ingredients or method of cooking. The most important ingredient is your enthusiasm and flair, combined with good-quality ingredients (cheap and humble or exotic), and a fair degree of organisation.

It is a glorious feast and only worth cooking for a special supper or party. A paella (the cooking pan that gives the dish its name) should be used, from which guests help themselves – and it is eaten from simple plates or bowls with spoons. Vary the choice of shellfish according to seasonal availability and price. Serve with a crisp green salad.

Serves 8 to 10

1 small chicken, quartered

Pinch of salt, freshly ground black pepper

Bouquet garni

1 glass dry white wine

2 pints (1.1 litres) mussels, scrubbed and with beards removed (see page 36)

12 Dublin Bay prawns *or* 1 small lobster or crawfish, cooked (see page 28)

1 medium squid

Olive oil for frying

1 red pepper, de-seeded and chopped

1 large onion, finely chopped

2 cloves garlic, finely chopped

1lb (500g) long-grain rice

1 sachet saffron powder

8oz (250g) frozen petits pois or peas

First poach the chicken with a little seasoning and the bouquet garni in the wine, and added water if necessary, for 20 to 30 minutes. Skin the chicken and cut it into small pieces. Strain and reserve the stock.

Steam the mussels open in a large pan containing ¼in (0.5cm) boiling water. Drain them and set them aside, reserving their juicy stock. Discard any mussels that have not opened.

If using Dublin Bay prawns, shell 8 of them, and reserve 4 in their shells for garnishing the finished dish. If using lobster or crawfish, extract the meat (see page 28), cut into bite-sized pieces and set aside.

Prepare the squid (see page 36) and slice the body and tentacles. Fry the squid rings briefly in a little olive oil, drain and set aside.

Heat 2 tablespoons olive oil in the paella (or a large heavy frying pan) and gently soften the red pepper, onion and garlic. Add the rice and turn it in the hot oil until it is glistening and golden. Pour in the reserved chicken and wine stock, the mussel stock and enough water to make up the liquid to twice the volume of the rice. Heat to simmering point and stir in the saffron powder. Cover the paella with aluminium foil and leave it to cook for 10 minutes without even peeping at it. Then remove the cover: by now the rice should have taken on a golden saffron hue and absorbed most of the stock. Add all the other ingredients, cover again and continue to cook gently for a further 10 minutes, adding the petits pois for the last 5 minutes. Garnish with the reserved prawns and take the dish straight to the table for serving.

Fish and cockle pie

Here is a variation of the ever-popular fish pie with potato topping. The preliminary poaching of the fish in milk provides the basis for a well-flavoured, light, creamy sauce. Fresh cockles are essential; preserved ones simply will not do. Try to make the parsleyed potatoes into a not-too-thick topping to ensure that it becomes crunchy when baked and serve the dish with steamed Cornish greens if you can get them.

Serves 4 to 6

1½lb (750g) white fish fillets (e.g. hake, haddock, cod, ling, huss), skinned

8oz (250g) fillets smoked cod, whiting or haddock, skinned

8–12oz (250–350g) fresh cockles, cooked and shelled

2lb (1kg) good mashing potatoes (for instance, King Edward)

2oz (50g) butter

10–13fl oz (300–375ml) plus 2 tablespoons skimmed milk

1 bunch parsley, including stalks

2 sticks celery, finely diced

½ lemon, sliced

Sprig of thyme

1 bay leaf, broken in half

Freshly ground black pepper

2–3 tablespoons white wine

2 teaspoons cornflour

1–2 teaspoons English made mustard, to taste

2 tablespoons fromage blanc or single cream

Scrub the potatoes, cut them into even-sized chunks and boil in salted water until they are tender. Allow to cool, then peel them and mash thoroughly with 1oz (25g) of the butter and 2 tablespoons milk, forking in 2 handfuls of chopped parsley from the bunch in the final stages. Set aside.

Pre-heat the oven to gas mark 6, 400°F (200°C).

While the potatoes are cooking, prepare all the white and smoked fish. Cut into large pieces, check that no bones remain, wash and pat dry with kitchen paper. Rinse the cockles quickly and ensure that they are free of sand and grit.

In a shallow poaching pan, warm 10–13fl oz (300–375ml) milk gently to just under simmering point. Add the celery, the lemon slices, the sprig of thyme, the broken bay leaf and a bouquet of parsley from the bunch with stalks broken or bruised. Let these ingredients infuse in the nearly simmering milk for a few minutes, before adding the white and smoked fish with a shake of pepper and the white wine. Re-heat the milk to just under simmering and continue to poach for about 4 or 5 minutes, or until the fish is just cooked, taking care not to let the liquid boil. Remove and discard the lemon slices and herbs. Use a slotted spoon to transfer the fish carefully to the base of a lightly oiled pie or baking dish. Reserve the liquid. Top the fish mixture with the cockles.

Cream the cornflour in a little cold water, then add this to the poaching liquid with the mustard. Bring to a simmer and whisk, using a balloon whisk, until the liquid thickens to a creamy sauce. Check the seasoning at this stage – remember that as you are using smoked fish you do not need to add salt. Now stir in the fromage blanc. Pour this sauce over the fish, allow to cool and settle, then spoon over the mashed potatoes to form the topping, dotting it with scraps of the remaining butter. Bake the pie in the oven for 30 to 40 minutes until it is golden brown on top. When serving, scatter it with more chopped parsley from the bunch.

Smoked fish pie

This is a filling pie – just right for a winter's night. It goes well with grilled tomatoes or steamed greens.

Serves 6

1½lb (750g) undyed smoked haddock

1lb (500g) potatoes

10fl oz (300ml) semi-skimmed milk

½ lemon, sliced

2oz (50g) butter

2 large onions, chopped

1oz (25g) flour

Freshly ground black pepper

2 hard-boiled eggs, roughly chopped

2oz (50g) cheese, grated

2oz (50g) fresh breadcrumbs

Scrub the potatoes, cut into even-sized chunks and cook in boiling salted water until nearly tender. Allow to cool enough to handle, then peel and slice them.

Now poach the fish in the milk with a few slices of lemon for about 4 minutes until just cooked. Lift it out with a slotted spoon, remove the skin and bones and flake it. Reserve the poaching liquid for the sauce.

Melt 1oz (25g) of the butter in a saucepan and gently cook the chopped onions until soft and transparent, then lift them out with the slotted spoon and add to the fish. Add the rest of the butter to the pan, stir in the flour over a gentle heat and slowly add the fish poaching liquid, stirring all the time to make a smooth creamy sauce. Season to taste with pepper.

When you are ready to cook the pie, pre-heat the oven to gas mark 5, 375°F (190°C). Lightly grease a pie or baking dish and put in the flaked fish, onions and chopped hard-boiled eggs. Pour over half the sauce, top with the sliced potatoes and cover with the remaining sauce. Combine the grated cheese with the breadcrumbs, scatter over the pie and bake for 20 to 30 minutes until the topping is golden brown.

To microwave
Prepare as above. Put the haddock and milk in a shallow dish, cover and cook on HIGH for 4 minutes. Complete as above.

Inviting hot stews and pies for wintry days: Bouillabaise (page 247); Fish and cockle pie (page 268); Star-gazey pie (page 190).

(Overleaf) The classic elegance of Whole poached salmon (page 228) with home-made mayonnaise (page 74) and Chilled lemon and prawn soup with ginger (page 215).

Fish and fennel risotto

Quick and simple to prepare, the ingredients for this popular family supper dish can usually be found in the average supermarket. The risotto is a filling meal in itself, but you may wish to serve steamed courgettes or grilled mushrooms with it.

Serves 4

1lb (500g) fillets cod, haddock, ling or hake, skinned

8oz (250g) peeled prawns

1 onion, finely chopped

2 teaspoons sunflower oil

12oz (350g) Florentine fennel bulb

Grated rind and juice of 1 lemon

8oz (250g) long-grain brown rice

1 pint (600ml) boiling water

4oz (125g) spinach or watercress, shredded

Pinch of salt (optional)

8oz (250g) tomatoes, chopped

2oz (50g) slivered almonds

Gently soften the onion in the hot oil in a large pan until it is pale but not brown.

Remove the tough outer skin of the fennel, trim the base and stalks, and slice the bulb into chunky strips; reserve the feathery fronds to use as a garnish. Add the fennel and grated lemon rind to the onion and cook for a further 2 or 3 minutes. Add the rice, mix in well, then pour in the boiling water. Return to the boil, cover and cook on the lowest possible heat for 30 minutes until nearly all the water is absorbed.

While the rice is cooking, cut the fish fillets into bite-sized pieces. If using frozen prawns, make sure that they are completely de-frosted and patted dry. Add the fish and prawns to the rice, stirring carefully. Continue to cook for a further 5 minutes. Now add all the other ingredients to the risotto. Stir carefully and cook for 2 or 3 more minutes. Season to taste with a pinch of salt if you like, and add the lemon juice. Serve immediately, garnished with the feathery fennel fronds.

Stuffed jacket potatoes

This is the sort of nourishing snack that children love. It is a simple way of using up left-over fish of any kind. You could use day-old jacket potatoes, or quickly cook 4 potatoes in the microwave. Fresh coriander gives a spicy taste, but you could use parsley if you prefer. A mixed green salad or home-made coleslaw is a perfect accompaniment.

Serves 4

12oz (350g) cooked fish

4 large baked jacket potatoes

6oz (175g) Cheddar cheese, grated

2 tablespoons parsley or coriander, finely chopped

1–2 tablespoons milk

Freshly ground black pepper

1 tablespoon sesame seeds (optional)

Pre-heat the oven to gas mark 6, 400°F (200°C).

Remove all skin and bones from the fish and flake the flesh.

Cut the potatoes in half lengthways and scoop out the flesh. Mash it finely, forking in 4oz (125g) of the grated cheese, the chopped parsley or coriander and the milk, until the mixture is smooth. Now carefully fork in the flaked fish and season to taste with pepper. Pile the mixture back into the potato shells, scatter with the remaining 2oz (50g) grated cheese, and sesame seeds if using, and bake in the oven for about 20 minutes until the topping is bubbling and golden.

To microwave

Prick the potatoes all over with a fork and cook on HIGH for 15 minutes or until tender, turning over halfway through cooking. Stuff the potatoes as above, then cook on HIGH for 3–5 minutes.

Glossary

There are hundreds of species of fish and shellfish in our seas and rivers. This section is a guide to most of the common and not-so-common fish to be found at fishmongers, quaysides or markets.

Bear in mind when consulting this section that seasons vary according to weather conditions and the movement of fish; quality will not be so good when fish are spawning.

Many fish have more than one common or scientific name, leading to confusion in regional and international translations. This guide gives the accepted British common names of fish, with some reference to local variations.

The fish industry usually divide fish into the following categories:

Pelagic: fish which live in large groups or shoals, and frequent the middle and surface layers of the sea, such as mackerel, herring, pilchard and salmon.

Demersal: fish which live on or near the sea-bed, such as flat fish, cod, monkfish and mullet.

Shellfish: which are further divided into molluscs, crustaceans and bivalves.

Scientific classification groups fish in families and their relations. For example, the Shark family, or the Order of Cod. However, for the purpose of cooking fish, the groups of fish in this guide have been simplified:

1 Round white fish

2 Flat fish

3 Oily fish

4 Freshwater fish

5 Shellfish

6 Smoked fish

Round white fish

The cod and its relations dominate this group of seafish. Cod has a less than glamorous image, but with its sweet lean flesh it is a star-quality fish. Hake, haddock and whiting also have firm, tasty flesh; the blander coley (saithe) is a reasonable option for soups or mixed seafood stews.

Enterprising fishmongers will have less familiar round white fish. John Dory, for example, with its extraordinary large bony head and telescopic jaws, has superb succulent flesh. Grey mullet has a good flavour and is less expensive than bream and the impressive bass. The exotic appearance of the little red gurnard gives character and colour to any dish that calls for a flourish in presentation, such as Bouillabaisse or Paella (pages 247 and 266).

Bass   *(sea bass, salmon bass)*

Description: grey on back and white on belly: smaller bass may have black spots. Up to 2 feet (60cm).

Season: all year except April and May.

Cooking: excellent flavour with firm flesh and almost bone-free. All methods suitable except deep-frying: best baked and stuffed or steamed. Scale unless poaching.

Red sea bream

Description: silver skin with rosy tinting, red fins and dark blotch above pectoral fin, large eyes.
Oval body, 11–16in (27.5–40cm). Avoid confusing with 'redfish'.

Season: fresh British June to December; imported all year but check with your fishmonger.

Cooking: delicate fine flavour. Any method but best poached or stuffed and baked in herb oil; if *very* fresh use for *sashimi*. Scale; easy to fillet or cook whole.

Catfish *(wolf fish, rock turbot)*

Description: long blue-grey or green body with extremely fierce jaws; usually sold beheaded and skinned. Up to 4 feet (1.2m).

Season: February to July.

Cooking: good flavour with firm pink-white flesh; usually sold in fillets. All methods suitable; can be cooked like veal.

Cod *(smaller fish, codling)*

Description: colour varies, but usually sandy with brown mottling on back and white belly. Up to 3 feet (90cm).

Season: all year, not so good in spring; fresh roe available January to February.

Cooking: excellent flavour with firm sweet flesh when really fresh, easily flaked. Sold whole or in fillets, steaks and cutlets. All methods suitable. Cheeks and throat are a delicacy; roe is available fresh and smoked; liver rich in polyunsaturated oil. Head and trimmings excellent for stocks.

Salt cod

Description: sold in flat rigid pieces, usually white-yellowish in colour.

Season: all year from specialists or to order from fishmongers.

Cooking: soak overnight in several changes of fresh water, then poach. Use regional European or West Indian methods; make beignets or gratins.

Coley *(saithe, coalfish, blackjack)*

Description: dark green-brown or black. Up to 3 feet (90cm) though usually smaller. Often skinned on landing.

Season: all year.

Cooking: coarse texture with undistinguished flavour; dark-coloured flesh turns white when cooked. All methods suitable, but best in stews, soups or pies.

Conger eel

Description: powerful body grows up to 10 feet (3m). Colour varies, but usually uniform grey-brown; fierce jaws.

Season: March to October.

Cooking: strong distinctive flavour; firm flesh that can be dry; tail end is bony. Best braised and steamed; cutlets can be cooked by all methods except deep-frying.

Dogfish *(huss, flake, rigg)*

Description: slender, long small shark. Back brown or yellow-grey with many small spots; usually skinned on landing. About 25in (62.5cm).

Season: all year; best autumn.

Cooking: versatile non-bony white-pink flesh. Usually shallow or deep-fried, but all methods suitable.

Gurnard *(red, grey and yellow)*

Description: large tapering body with large scales and very spiky fins. Usually 8–12in (20–30cm).

Season: all year; best July to April.

Cooking: good-quality flesh, though slightly dry. Braising, baking, shallow-frying and grilling are best, or use in mixed seafood stews.

Haddock

Description: back dark green-brown or charcoal; belly pale, easily distinguished by 'thumbprint' (supposedly thumbprint of St Peter). Up to 2 feet (60cm).

Season: all year round, best autumn and winter.

Cooking: good flavour; roe is a delicacy and liver is good. All methods suitable for fillets and cutlets, or can be baked or steamed whole.

Hake

Description: long pointed head with streamlined body, slate grey or blue-black and silvery-white belly. Usually 1–2 feet (30–60cm).

Season: all year except March, April and May.

Cooking: good, fairly soft flesh and flavour. Easily boned or filleted; all methods suitable. Good served hot or cold.

John Dory

Description: thin body, flattened from side to side. Sandy beige colour tinged with yellow and silvery blue. Round dark mark on each side referred to as 'thumbprint'. Very tough sharp spikes. Usually 15in (40cm).

Season: all year; not so good June to August.

Cooking: excellent flavour. Easy to fillet. All methods except deep-frying recommended; best poached or baked. Large bony head excellent for stock. Some cooks say taste is better if kept two or three days before cooking.

Ling

Description: long fish with mottled brown or green skin; bronze marbled sheen; fins have white edges. Up to 3 feet (90cm).

Season: all year except August.

Cooking: good flavour and texture. Fillets and cutlets respond well to all methods. Prepare salt or dried ling as salt cod. Liver rich in poly-unsaturated oil.

Monkfish   (angler fish)

Description: head large, strange and flattened; tail normal fish shape. Brown to green-brown skin with dark blotches. Up to 6 feet (1.8m) but usually smaller.

Season: all year; best in winter.

Cooking: superb flavour and firm bone-free flesh; only tail meat is used. Often sold skinned: larger tails have best flavour. All methods suitable but poaching, steaming, baking and shallow-frying best; ideal for cubing and grilling on skewers.

Grey mullet   (common grey mullet)

Description: streamlined grey-silver or blue-green body covered with scales. Herbivore; mullet from estuaries can be muddy. Up to 2½ feet (75cm).

Season: all year except March or April; best in autumn and winter.

Cooking: moist, firm flesh with good flavour. Baking whole fish or grilling cutlets best; steaming and deep-frying not suitable. Some say taste is better if kept for two or three days with guts intact. Smoked roe is occasionally obtainable. Muddy or oily fish should be soaked in several changes of a salt water and vinegar solution; fresh mint in belly while baking gives a fragrant flavour.

Red mullet

Description: long body. When alive, colour varies with depth, emotion and time of day; usually rosy and may have horizontal yellow stripes. Up to 16in (40cm), but most about 8in (16cm).

Season: best in summer.

Cooking: excellent and unique flavour. Always cook it with liver intact which is the main source of flavour. Deep-frying and steaming not recommended.

Pollack

Description: similar shape to cod; variable colours from brown to dark green with yellow spots. Usually 18in (45cm) but occasionally up to 3 feet (90cm).

Season: May to December.

Cooking: flesh is inferior to cod but satisfactory for padding out pies, stews and soups.

Ray thornback *(skate or roker)*

Description: Grey or brown with mottling, coarse prickles and very rough skin. Up to 34in (85cm).

Season: May to February.

Cooking: good flavour. Cook as for skate.

Redfish *(ocean perch)*

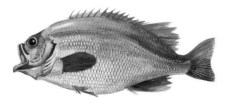

Description: Bright orange or orange-red with rosy belly and dusky gills. Sharp spines.

Season: all year.

Cooking: Scale. All methods, but best poached; good in soups.

Shark *(porbeagle)*

Description: blue-grey above and white belly. Usually 9–12 feet (2.7–3.6m).

Season: All year imported, but check with supplier.

Cooking: steaks are firm and meaty, best shallow-fried or brushed with oil and grilled.

Angel shark

Description: large fins resembling angel's wings, hence the name. Grey-brown or green tinge with dark mottlings. Up to 6 feet (1.8m).

Season: All year, but rarely available in the UK.

Cooking: good flavour with firm bone-free flesh. Only tail meat is used: all methods are suitable. Rarely available.

Skate *(blue skate)*

Description: grey or olive-brown upper skin with blotches, blue or pale grey belly. Distinctive huge wings and exceptionally long nose. Width from wing tips varies from 20–60in (50cm–1.5m).

Season: all year; best in winter.

Cooking: good flavour, firm texture. Usually only wings available, often skinned. Pink and moist flesh. Skate nobs are sometimes available and are good. Best two days after being caught; characteristic ammonia smell disappears when cooked. All methods suitable, but especially good poached or shallow-fried.

Whiting

Description: olive, sandy or blue upper body with silver mottled belly. Up to 1 foot (30cm).

Season: all year; best in winter.

Cooking: firm white flesh with delicate flavour; flakes easily. All methods suitable; poaching, shallow-frying and light steaming best.

Blue whiting *(couch's whiting)*

Description: blue-black with silvery sides and belly. Up to 16in (40cm).

Season: all year; best in winter.

Cooking: good firm flavour. Cook as for whiting; too small to fillet.

Flat fish

Turbot and Dover sole shine out as the flat fish of exquisite flavour and texture. Others, like megrim, for instance, are dull and bland compared to the good meaty taste of brill and halibut, but almost all flat fish are quick, simple and a joy to cook. Their uncomplicated bone structure also makes it easy to fillet them.

Flat fish have a doleful appearance. I sometimes fancy that this must be because they lead such dark, contemplative lives on the sea-bed. Only the halibut ventures into the middle waters of the sea to feed, and if encountered by fishermen, puts up a spirited fight.

All flat fish begin their lives as round fish. Hatched near the surface of the sea, they undergo a metamorphosis in their young form, as one eye migrates over the top of the head to join its companion, and the roundness of the body shape is compressed from side to side to form the familiar flat fish shape. Soles, flounders and halibut have their two eyes on the head on the right side of the body, and turbot, brill and megrim on the left side.

Brill

Description: colours of upper skin range from sandy, grey-brown to dark brown with darker flecks and lighter spots; underside creamy white. Up to 2 feet (60cm).

Season: available all year except March, April and May; best in summer.

Cooking: excellent flavour, firm meaty flesh with yellow tinge. Recipes for turbot can be used. Remember to scale. All methods suitable, but best poached, steamed or grilled. Serve hot or cold. Bones and trimmings make excellent gelatinous stock.

Dab

Description: oval body; upper skin sandy brown with green freckles. Up to 10in (25cm).

Season: all year except January and February.

Cooking: pleasant sweet flavour. Very bony. All methods suitable (cook as sole), but best poached, grilled or fried; also good in pies and stews. Thin fillets, so allow 4 per serving.

Flounder

Description: dull brown or green upper skin, sometimes with orange speckles. Usually 1 foot (30cm). Tolerates fresh water and is commonly found in estuaries. Flounder is generic name for other flat fish, including the excellent American witch and summer flounder.

Season: all year except March and April; best in winter.

Cooking: requires enthusiastic approach because of inferior flavour. All methods suitable but as flesh is rather watery, a highly flavoured stuffing is recommended.

Halibut

Description: the longest flat fish – can be up to 13 feet (4m). Grey to olive-grey skin with pearly white blind side. Large jaws.

Season: all year except April and May.

Cooking: excellent flavour with thick firm flesh but inclined to dryness. All methods suitable except deep-frying. 'Chicken' halibut, about 2lb (1kg), can be cooked whole, but fillets or cutlets only are available from large halibut.

Megrim *(sail fluke or whiff)*

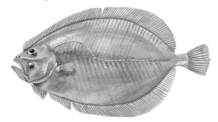

Description: sandy brown with dark blotches. Usually 8–14in (20–35cm) but up to 2 feet (60cm).

Season: all year except March.

Cooking: Soft flesh with bland flavour. All methods suitable; use plenty of flavourings.

Plaice

Description: warm brown with orange or red spots; coloration varies with habitat. Can be to 2 feet (60cm) but usually 8–14in (20–35cm).

Season: all year except March and April.

Cooking: good flavour. All methods suitable, but best grilled, poached, steamed or shallow-fried.

Dover sole

Description: Varies from brownish or greyish-brown with creamy white underside. Head very small in proportion to body. Maximum length is 20in (50cm).

Season: all year except April.

Cooking: excellent taste and texture. All methods suitable but grilling is best. Cook simply – whole on the bone, skinned on the bone or filleted. No elaborate sauces necessary. Flavour is best when 2–3 days old.

Lemon sole

Description: not a true sole and not related to Dover sole. Colour from warm brown to yellow brown, mottled with darker brown, dull yellow or orange. Up to 26in (65cm).

Season: all year; best in spring.

Cooking: good flavour. All methods suitable; good steamed, grilled or shallow-fried.

Turbot

Description: colours range from light grey-brown to dark chocolate-brown depending on habitat. Non-scaly skin has bony nodules. Small bony 'nail head' with eyes above head when facing left. Usually 32in (80cm); occasionally 39in (1m).

Season: all year; best in summer.

Cooking: superb flesh is firm, meaty and succulent. Avoid blue-tinged fish. All methods suitable except deep-frying; poaching specially recommended. Small (chicken) turbot can be cooked whole but fillets or steaks are only available from larger turbot.

Witch *(Torbay sole)*

Description: pale or grey-brown. Usually 14in (35cm) but occasionally up to 2 feet (60cm).

Season: all year except June and July.

Cooking: slender fish with good flavour. All methods suitable, but best poached, grilled, steamed or shallow-fried.

Oily fish

Unlike white fish which store their richly nutritious oil in their livers, the oil of these fish is throughout their bodies.

The streamlined powerful bodies, built for speed, streak through the middle and surface areas of the sea in huge shoals. The most familiar are herring, which feed in vast shoals on plankton and mackerel. The popularity of the pilchard and sprat has declined in this country. Most of our pilchards now are exported to Italy.

Oily fish lend themselves well to grilling and barbecueing; their skins give natural lubrication and protection. Sharp fruity sauces help to counteract their richness. Marinated in wine or vinegar, they are a classic starter and an excellent part of a cold table. It is important that these fish are very fresh, as they deteriorate quickly.

Anchovy

Description: clear green back when fresh that turns black as the fish spoils.

Season: occasionally June to December from British waters; year round if imported.

Cooking: good distinctive flavour. Avoid any hardened backs. Scale and gut. Bake and grill.

Herring

Description: streamlined, torpedo-shaped silvery fish with steely blue back, white belly and forked tail. Up to 8in (20cm).

Season: all year except spring.

Cooking: good flavour, easy to bone. Grilling or marinating is best, also shallow-fry or bake. Roes may be cooked separately or incorporated in stuffing or sauce.

Mackerel

Description: blue-green back with black tabby markings and silvery-white belly. Streamlined, slender body. Usually 9–12in (22.5–30cm).

Season: all year, best February to June.

Cooking: very good flavour, easy to bone or fillet. All methods suitable except deep-frying.

Pilchard

Description: herring shape with blue-green back, golden sides and silver belly. Up to 10in (25cm).

Season: April to November.

Cooking: distinctive flavour. All methods suitable but best grilled. Easy to bone out for well flavoured stuffing.

Sardine

Young pilchard; same as above.

Shad

Description: known as the king of the herring family with deep blue back and silvery sides. Up to 2 feet (60cm).

Season: all year except spring.

Cooking: treat as a fine fat herring. The large roe is a delicacy.

Smelt *(rainbow smelt, sparling)*

Description: light olive green with creamy white belly. Usually 6in (15cm.)

Season: Best January to March.

Cooking: good flavour. Best fried or barbecued on skewers; smells like cucumber when very fresh.

Sprat

Description: blue-green back with silvery sides and belly. Up to 6in (15cm).

Season: September to March.

Cooking: tasty. Best grilled after cleaning through the gills (see page 19).

Tuna

Description: Usually sold in steaks recognisable by the deep red colour of the flesh. Best species are blue fin and yellow fin.

Season: all year but check with your fishmonger.

Cooking: good, fine flavour with firm meaty flesh. Blue fin is the richest; available whole from 14lb (6.2kg).

Yellow fin available whole or frozen in steaks. Best meat cut from the belly; remove mid lateral strips of dark flesh with bitter taste. Slice thinly for serving raw, or lard steaks with anchovy strips and shallow-fry until centre is pink; grill steaks or pieces and cook in foil parcels; disappointing if braised.

Whitebait

Description: transparent or with silvery white tinge; the fry of a mixture of various fish, mainly herring, sprats and sardines.

Season: February to July.

Cooking: excellent flavour. Best lightly coated in flour and briskly deep-fried, or spiced and stir-fried.

Freshwater fish

Salmon and trout are the best known fish caught or farmed in British fresh water but there is increasing interest in the supply of imported freshwater fish. Angling is also hugely popular, so this guide includes a selection of some of the less familiar fish. Some, like elvers (young eels), are caught mainly for export; others, like farmed carp, are often imported from Israel.

The taste and texture vary; many freshwater fish are mild and fragrant in comparison to sea fish, and many, like perch and pike, are bony.

Bream

Description: body silver to golden-olive with dark brown fins and slimy skin. Average size 10–16in (25–40cm).

Season: fresh British June to December; imported all year.

Cooking: good eating, but bony. All methods suitable.

Carp *(mirror, common, etc.)*

Description: Some have beautiful large scales, colours vary. Mostly farmed. Usually 15–20in (37.5–50cm).

Season: all year except April and May.

Cooking: flesh white with good flavour. All methods suitable, but best baked or poached. Wild carp needs good cleaning and soaking in several changes of salt water and vinegar. Plunge in boiling acidulated water for several seconds if scales are difficult to remove.

Eel

Description: dark green back with silver belly. Males usually 18in (45cm); females about 36in (90cm).

Season: all year, best in autumn.

Cooking: best bought alive; hit head smartly against table, bleed, skin, bone and chop. Eel blood is painful in an open cut and can irritate eyes. Grill, fry, bake or braise. Good in pies and soups.

Elvers

Description: young, threadlike, silver eels only 3in (7.5cm) long.

Season: March and April.

Cooking: deep-fry whole like whitebait, or steam or stew. First wash in salt water to remove slime.

Grayling

Description: large brown- or red-edged dorsal fin on dark silver body. Usually 12in (30cm).

Season: best September or December.

Cooking: fragrant flesh, similar in texture to trout; use same methods.

Perch

Description: Similar to pike perch but with startling orange or red fins. Usually 6–12in (15–30cm).

Season: all year except March and April; best in summer.

Cooking: scale as soon as possible; excellent flavour, but very bony. All methods except deep-frying.

Pike

Description: greeny-brown and flecked with lighter green. Long toothy jaws and long body. Usually 2 feet (40cm).

Season: all year, fresh or chilled imported.

Cooking: bland flavour and bony. Best used for quenelles, or poached with sauce for flavouring.

Pike perch *(zander)*

Description: silver-brown body with distinctive dark vertical bars. Up to 2 feet (60cm).

Season: all year, fresh or chilled imported.

Cooking: good flavour. All methods except deep-frying.

Salmon

Description: plump silvery body, occasionally black spots above lateral line. Usually 30–48in (75cm–1.2 metres).

Season: farmed available fresh all year; Irish, Scottish and English wild February through August. (Grilse is a young salmon, returning to spawn for the first time, considered by some to be more succulent. Available fresh or frozen, it looks the same as salmon but is smaller.)

Cooking: superb flavour; hard to distinguish difference between good-quality and wild. Firm pink flesh tends to dryness, so poaching usually favoured, but can be baked in foil or pastry or grilled. Can be cooked whole or in cutlets or steaks.

Brown trout *(wild)*

Description: colour varies from silver with small black spots to brown, gold or green with large pink and black spots. Weight usually 1–3lb (500g–1.5kg).

Season: February to September; seldom caught commercially.

Cooking: exquisite flavour. Cook simply, best briefly poached in court bouillon (see page 69). If cooked *au bleu* do not wash off slime which turns characteristic blue.

Rainbow trout *(farmed and wild)*

Description: silvery green back with tiny black spots and white belly. Farmed or wild, popular size is 12oz–1lb (350–500g).

Season: all year.

Cooking: delicate flavour. Versatile and easy to bone or fillet. Best baked, grilled, shallow-fried or steamed. Treat smoked as smoked mackerel.

Salmon trout *(sewin)*

Description: related to brown trout, it is smaller than Atlantic salmon. Resembles young salmon but blunter head, with dark spots above and below lateral line. Up to 3 feet (90cm).

Season: February to August.

Cooking: excellent flavour; poach, grill, marinate or bake, whole or in fillets or steaks. Treat as salmon.

Shellfish

Crustaceans and molluscs hold a fascination for all who love shellfish – from the rustic charm of cockles and mussels and the romance of the oyster to the luxury of lobster. Naturalists have occasionally re-classified certain species and the regional variations of shellfish names can be confusing too, particularly in the shrimp and prawn families. Generally speaking, a crustacean has a shell and also a form or limb, e.g. shrimps, crabs, lobsters. Molluscs are either single-shelled, like winkles, or bivalves, like mussels, oysters and scallops. A lay person might be surprised to learn that squid, cuttlefish and octopus (cephalopods) are classified as molluscs, even though they have no visible shell. The 'shells' of squid are internal and, in fact, the octopus does not have a shell at all!

Many of us are conservative and ultra-cautious about eating shellfish. This means that the wide range available is mostly sold to restaurants.

Crustaceans

Crab *(common edible)*

Description: brick-coloured shell. Cocks have longer main claws; tail flap on the underside is pointed on cock and round on hen. Flesh is coarser in larger sizes. A 2lb (900g) crab will yield approximately 12oz (350g) meat.

Season: all year, best April to December.

Cooking: see page 29. Eat the rich and filling meat cold with salads, hot devilled or in chowder and soups. Can also be used as a stuffing.

Spider crab

Description: large, bright orange to red-brown shell with long spider-like legs. Small main claw has sharp nip. Maximum length 8in (20cm). Meat is mainly in legs; best buy is female when carrying eggs under tail flaps.

Season: all year.

Cooking: as for common crab (see page 29). Sweeter flesh than common crab but fiddly to extract. Take off upper shell, then chop all meat and coral.

Swimming crab

Description: back swimming legs are paddle-shaped; has 'evil' red eyes. Usually 3–4½in (7.5–11.25cm) across shell.

Season: all year.

Cooking: as for common crab (see page 29). Claw meat is sweet and tender; brown meat and coral also good. Called soft-shelled crab between moults and can then be deep-fried whole.

Crawfish　*(spiny lobster)*

Description: red or brown prickly shell with yellow markings. Similar to lobster but without main claws. Look for ones 3–4lb (1.3–1.7kg) in weight.

Season: April to October.

Cooking: see page 28. Similar in taste and texture to lobster, but with coarser meat.

Freshwater crayfish

Description: brown or grey-green shells which turn pink when cooked. About 3in (7.5cm).

Season: all year.

Cooking: see page 28. Firm white meat, but flavour not as pronounced as sea crustaceans.

Lobster

Description: blue-tinged shell turns pink when cooked. Sizes range from 2lb (900g) to 6lb (2.6kg). Amount of meat varies.

Season: April to November.

Cooking: see page 28. Claw and white body meat has firm, superb flavour. Larger lobsters have slightly coarser meat. Shells make excellent stock.

Prawn

Description: a range, farmed and wild, various sizes. Colourless shells turn pink when cooked.

Season: all year.

Cooking: Flavour varies with species; avoid those treated with chemical additives. Remove intestinal vein before or after boiling, steaming, grilling or frying.

Dublin Bay prawn

(langoustine, Norway lobster, scampi, etc)

Description: pink with red claws, maximum length 10in (25cm).

Season: all year.

Cooking: as for prawns. Tail meat is firm and white with excellent flavour. Fiddly but possible to extract scraps of meat from claws.

Shrimp *(brown shrimp)*

Description: translucent shell which turns brown when cooked. About 2½in (6cm).

Season: February to October.

Cooking: Boil, steam or stir-fry. Eaten whole in France. Good flavour.

Molluscs *(cephalopods)*

Cuttlefish

Description: usually dark with beautiful pale stripes. Internal shell sold for pet birds. Up to 10in (25cm).

Season: all year.

Cooking: as for squid.

Octopus

Description: blue-grey skin with round suckers on the tentacles. Usually about 2 feet (60cm) but can be as large as 9¾ feet (3m).

Season: all year.

Cooking: as for squid. Traditionally 'beaten' at least 99 times prior to cooking to tenderise, or if not, preliminary slow stewing recommended.

Squid *(calamari)*

Description: from tiny to giants up to 2 feet (60cm) long. Common squid has mottled skin, white flesh, two tentacles, eight arms and flap-like fins.

Season: May to October; frozen year round.

Cooking: pouch-like body and tentacles are used (see page 36); texture can be rubbery. Slice and stir-fry or stuff and bake whole.

Molluscs *(Bivalves)*

Clam

Description: bi-valves of various sizes and colours.

Season: varies with species but usually all year; frequently available species are Quahog, Venus, Carpet shell and razor.

Cooking: see page 35. Can be steamed and eaten whole or used in soups and stews.

Cockle

Description: cream-coloured shells with many ridges. Usually 1–1½in (2cm).

Season: best in summer.

Cooking: see page 35. Distinctive taste; often served drowned in brown vinegar; good with salad or hot with pasta.

Bi-valves

Mussels

Description: slate-blue shell; Farmed ones are usually brownish with thinner shells. Sage pale orange flesh. Up to 3in (7.5cm).

Season: September to March.

Cooking: see pages 216–18. Good flavour; use in soups, Paella (see page 269), salads, etc. British stock are good but vary in quality from season to season. Belgian and Dutch mussels are also plump and good, and French ones are usually smaller and sweeter.

Oysters *(European flat or native oyster, Portuguese, and Pacific or Japanese oyster)*

Description: varies according to species from round fairly smooth shape to irregular shape with highly serrated surface.

Season: some varieties available all year – others according to traditional season; available fresh, sometimes shucked, and frozen.

Cooking: see page 32 for opening.

Scallops

Description: double-shelled with flat bottom. Usually 4–6in (10–15cm.)

Season: best December to March.

Cooking: see page 35. Tender white flesh and pink coral are ideal for poaching, grilling, shallow- or stir-frying or raw if very fresh. Do not overcook. Available intact, whole on the shell, or shelled, chilled and frozen.

Queen scallops

Description: smaller than a scallop with both shells rounded. About 3½in (8.75cm).

Season: best December to March.

Cooking: as for scallops.

Single shells

Whelks

Description: Spiral shell, usually 2in (5cm).

Season: best in summer.

Cooking: see page 224; tough and rubbery flesh.

Winkles

Description: small dark grey or brown sea snails. Usually 1in (2.5cm).

Season: all year.

Cooking: see page 224; fiddly to extract meat, but have good taste.

Smoked fish

In theory, any fish can be smoked. Traditionally, oily fish were smoked after brining to preserve them further. Now all kinds of fish are smoked. Any fish from the most humble and coarse, to the finest quality salmon are transformed by time-honoured methods of light brining and smoking. (See page 13 for shopping and page 48 for home smoking.)

Arbroath smokies

Small herring that are beheaded and gutted but left whole, then tied in pairs and hot smoked.

Bloaters

Whole herring, lightly salted and cold smoked. Plump, mild and piquant, the best ones come from Great Yarmouth.

Buckling

Herring, beheaded, gutted and hot smoked until golden; regarded by many as the best smoked herring.

Smoked eel

Rich meaty flesh in cutlets or long fillets.

Finnan haddock

Headless split haddock, lightly brined and cold smoked; straw-coloured.

Glasgow pale

Small haddock, more highly smoked than Finnan haddock.

Smoked halibut

Not widely available; should be thinly sliced.

Kipper

Fine fat herring in mildest cure and brine, split and beheaded.

Smoked mackerel

Available hot and cold smoked, whole or in fillets, moist flesh.

Red herring

Left whole, ungutted, heavily brined and smoked for two or three weeks until very firm. Soak before use.

Smoked salmon

Available thinly sliced, or as a whole side, loose or vacuum packed, various colours from pale oily glossy pink flesh to bright drier red flesh. Pale (Irish) slightly deeper (Scottish) is best quality.

Miscellaneous

Several 'exotic' species of fish are beginning to make an appearance at fishmongers and in restaurants. You may find the brilliantly coloured parrot fish on display alongside bourgeois and a whole variety of groupers and snappers. Occasionally to be found are farmed tilapia (sometimes sold as St Peter fish), pompano, crevalle and trigger fish – all of these may, in general, be treated like round white fish.

Swordfish steaks have a dense meaty texture and excellent flavour, and may be marinated and grilled or barbecued, or shallow-fried. The dark firm flesh of bonito steaks may be cooked in the same way or – if it is extremely fresh – it is suitable for slicing raw for Seviche (page 264).

Index

Italic page numbers indicate a colour illustration

Useful Addresses

Please remember that all plants are now protected by law and it is illegal to uproot plants without the permission of the landowner. There is a list of over 50 plants that may not be picked under any circumstances – for this and further information on the conservation of wild plants send a large S.A.E. to:

The Nature Conservancy Council,
The Library,
Northminster House,
Peterborough
PE1 1UA

For fact sheets, recipe leaflets and information write to:
The Sea Fish Industry Authority
144 Cromwell Road
London SW7 4EF

The British Trout Association
PO Box 189
London SW6 5LY

Scottish Salmon Information Service
26 Fitzroy Square
London W1P 6BT

Further reading: There are many excellent fish books available but two of my favourites are Alan Davidson's comprehensive *North Atlantic Seafood* (Penguin 1980) and *Mediterranean Seafood* (Penguin 1972).